PAN-AFRICANISM

The Idea and Movement
1776-1963

PAN-AFRICANISM

The Idea and Movement
1776-1963

P. Olisanwuche Esedebe

HOWARD UNIVERSITY PRESS
Washington, D.C.   1982

Copyright © 1982 by P. Olisanwuche Esedebe. First published in the United States in 1982 by Howard University Press. Published in 1980 by Fourth Dimension Press.

Printed in the United States of America.

Library of Congress Cataloging in Publication Data

Esedebe, P. Olisanwuche.
  Pan-Africanism: the idea and movement, 1776–1963.

  Bibliography: p.
  Includes index.
  1. Pan-Africanism—History.   2. Nationalism—Africa
—History.   3. Blacks—Race identity—History.
4. Organization of African Unity.   I. Title.
DT30.E77 1982   320.5'4   82-18692
ISBN 0–88258–124–4
ISBN 0–88258–125–2 (pbk.)

CONTENTS

PREFACE

In spite of the fast growing literature on Pan-Africanism not much that is really new has emerged in the preceding decade. Most of the published works seem to repeat or confirm, albeit in greater detail, what had been said before. Quite often attention is focussed on personalities and organizations whose commitment to Pan-Africanism is doubtful. Closely connected with this misplaced emphasis is the tendency to rely heavily on the records of the European colonial regimes and to list the publications of pan-African leaders and pressure groups instead of integrating the substances of the material in the text itself. Is it still necessary to point out that all the colonial powers were hostile to the movement and did their utmost to discredit and even suppress it? Unless we pay more attention to the documents, utterances and exertions of the Pan-Africanists themselves, ask new questions or provide more satisfactory answers to old ones, we cannot make meaningful contributions. A new question that may be asked — in fact it is just beginning to be asked — is the attitude of African descendants in Asia and the Middle East to the phenomenon. Latin American aspects have hardly been investigated. Until such significant gaps are filled any dogmatic generalizations must be suspect.

Another reason why interpretations of the phenomenon cannot be conclusive at present is to be found in the handicaps imposed by the nature of contemporary history. No historian writes with complete detachment. But there is a kind of detachment possible for the historian of a past of which he is not a participator which the contemporary historian can hardly attain. As the narrative approaches the present day, the contemporary historian's temptation to take sides becomes increasingly uncontrollable although he may not be aware of it or admit it. Few, if any, contemporary writers can discuss the Nigerian civil war, for example, without being unduly influenced by national, party or personal self-interest.

A further difficulty facing the contemporary historian is that he is denied the advantage of hindsight. Only developments which he expects to have a long-term impact will appear to him to be significant and this on the basis of mere assumptions of the future course of events.

The interpretations offered in this book are therefore tentative. The study itself grew out of my doctoral thesis, "A History of the Pan-African Movement in Britain, 1900-1948," presented to the University of London in 1968. In 1972 I was fortunate to win a Senior Fulbright Fellowship enabling me to do further research in the United States having already used sources in England. As a result of my post-doctoral research in American and African archives, I have broadened the scope of the dissertation to include major developments outside of Britain from 1750 to 1900 and between 1948 and 1963.

Those who helped me in one way or another during my research are so many that it is impossible to name all of them. I would like to thank, in particular, the staff of the following institutions: King's College Library, Library of the London School of Economics and Political Sciences, Institute of Commonwealth Studies, Senate House Library — all of London University; British Museum; Public Record Office (London); Ethiopian Embassy, London (Information Section); Rhodes House Library (Oxford); National Library of Scotland; New York City Public Library; Columbia University (New York); Howard University Library (Washington D.C.); Library of Congress (Washington D.C.); Fourah Bay College (University of Sierra Leone) Library; Ghana National Archives (Accra and Cape Coast); George Padmore Research Library (Accra) and 'Institute of African Studies (Legon, Ghana).

I am indebted to the late Mr. George Bennett of the Institute of Commonwealth Studies, Oxford for suggesting the theme of my doctoral dissertation as well as Dr. Christine Moody and the late Mr. Reginald Bridgeman, both of whom allowed me the use of documents in their possession. To Mrs. Violet Creech-Jones, Lord Brockway, Dr. Malcolm Joseph-Mitchell, Professor Kenneth Little, Dr. Hugh W. Springer and Dr. Richard Pankhurst, I am grateful for the readiness with which they answered my queries. My gratitude also goes to Professor J. E. Flint who supervised the greater part of my thesis at King's College, London before going to Dalhousie University (Canada); Professor Gerald S. Graham, Professor George Shepperson and Mr. Douglas H. Jones for their kindness and guidance during the absence of my supervisor.

My research was made possible by grants from three major sources: Commonwealth Scholarship Commission in the United Kingdom who sponsored my doctoral research in England; the Nigerian Federal Government who sponsored my field work in West Africa and the United States Government who awarded me a Fulbright Fellowship enabling me to consult some important documents in America.

I greatly appreciate the comments and criticism of those friends who read my thesis or the draft of this book in whole or in part: Mazi Ray Ofoegbu, Dr. Sunday O. Anozie, Dr. N. M. B. Bhebe and Mr. John Conteh-Morgan.

Finally, I owe a special debt to Mr. Harry Caulker for typing the manuscript and my wife for her unflinching support and assistance in checking the typescript.

ABBREVIATIONS

A.A.P.C.	All African Peoples' Conference
A.C.S.	American Colonization Society
A.P.U.	African Progress Union
C.A.O.	Committee of African Organizations
C.O.	Colonial Office, London
F.O.	Foreign Office, London
G.C.A.R.P.S.	Gold Coast Aborigines' Rights Protection Society
I.A.F.A.	International African Friends of Abyssinia
I.A.S.B.	International African Service Bureau
L.C.P.	League of Coloured People
L.D.R.N.	*Ligue de la defence de la Race Negre*
M.N.C.	*Movement National Congolais*
N.A.A.C.P.	National Association for the Advancement of Coloured People
N.C.B.W.A.	National Congress of British West Africa
N.C.N.C.	National Council of Nigeria and the Cameroons
O.A.U.	Organization of African Unity
P.A.F.	Pan-African Federation
PAFMECA	Pan-African Freedom Movement for East and Central Africa
PAFMECSA	Pan-African Freedom Movement for East, Central and South Africa
R.D.A.	*Rassemblement Democratique Africain*
W.A.N.S.	West African National Secretariat
W.A.S.U.	West African Students Union

U.P.C.	Union of the Peoples of the Cameroons
U.A.P.A.D.	United Aid for Peoples of African Descent
U.N.I.A.	Universal Negro Improvement Association
African	In this book, the term is used in two senses:
	(1) indigenous Africans only
	(2) all persons of African descent including indigenous Africans.
Exile	The term applies to all men of African blood or origin living permanently or temporarily outside Africa.

CHAPTER 1

ORIGINS OF PAN-AFRICAN IDEAS

Despite the flood of books and articles on Pan-Africanism in recent years the study of the phenomenon is still in its infancy. Writers tend to bury its aspirations and dynamics in a minutiae of fascinating but largely irrelevant details. Not surprisingly there is still no agreement on what it is all about. Explanations that some African scholars and politicians give often differ from those suggested by African descendants abroad. Sometimes the continental Africans themselves advance conflicting interpretations.

In the 1930s the veteran Afro-American scholar and agitator, W. E. B. DuBois, stated that the Pan-African movement aimed at an intellectual understanding and co-operation among all groups of African descent in order to bring about "the industrial and spiritual emancipation of the Negro people."[1] At the third annual conference of the American Society of African Culture held in 1960 at the University of Pennsylvania (U.S.A.), several speakers expressed conflicting opinions.[2] Rayford Logan, a black American historian, saw the phenomenon in terms of self-government by African countries south of the Sahara. Disagreeing, the Nigerian journalist and politician, Chief Anthony Enahoro, insisted that it included the economic, social and cultural development of the continent, the avoidance of conflict among African states, the

---

[1] *The Crisis* (November, 1933), p. 247.

[2] The proceedings of the conference have been published under the title *Pan-Africanism Reconsidered*, ed. by the American Society of African Culture (Berkeley and Los Angeles: University of California Press, 1962).

promotion of African unity and influence in world affairs. The Senegalese publicist Alioune Diop felt that it was more or less synonymous with the concept of "African Personality" or "Negritude." In the opinion of the well-known British journalist, Colin Legum, Pan-Africanism "is essentially a movement of ideas and emotions; at times it achieves a synthesis: at times it remains at the level of antithesis."[3]

For the more recent writers Pan-Africanism seems to mean anything. This was probably why Adekunle Ajala[4] failed to define it in his four-hundred-and-forty-odd page book. Accepting Shepperson's dichotomy, Robert G. Weisbord[5] used Pan-Africanism when referring to "this twentieth-century movement" and Pan-Africanism to describe "a general movement of international kinship and numerous short-lived movements with a predominant cultural element." Kenneth King[6] extends the term to include the appeal for Africans of educational institutions run by black Americans in the United States as well as the exertions of white missionaries, philanthropists and even politicians like ex-president Theodore Roosevelt of America who believed that the education of Africans and that of Afro-Americans constituted a single interdependent problem. While J. Ayodele Langley[7] thinks that Pan-Africanism is a protest, a refusal, a demand and a utopia born of centuries of contact with Europe, the German historian Imanuel Geiss[8] believes that it is an irrational concept, a matter of vague emotions. The historian's cynical assertion appears to be borne out by the several definitions

[3] Colin Legum, *Pan-Africanism: A Short Political Guide* (New York: Frederick A. Praeger, 1962), p. 14.

[4] Adekunle Ajala, *Pan-Africanism: Evolution, Progress and Prospects* (London: Andre Deutsche, 1973).

[5] R. G. Weisbord, *Ebony Kinship: Africa, Africans and the Afro-American* (London: Greenwood Press, 1973).

[6] Kenneth King, *Pan-Africanism and Education* (London: Oxford University Press, 1971).

[7] J. A. Langley, *Pan-Africanism and Nationalism in West Africa, 1900-1945* (London: Oxford University Press, 1973).

[8] I. Geiss, *The Pan-Africanism Movement* (London: Methuen, 1974).

suggested by V. Bakpetu Thompson in his book.[9] Thompson sees Pan-Africanism as a struggle in which Africans and men of African blood have been engaged since their contact with modern Europe. Elsewhere in the same study he declares that Pan-Africanism and the concept of "African Personality" are interchangeable, that Pan-Africanism is a campaign to rehabilitate the valuable aspects of African culture and that the phenomenon means the political unification of the continent.

None of these explanations seems adequate. Some of them are actually misleading. A more accurate definition is by no means easy to formulate. It cannot be given in a neat and short sentence. Before offering a working definition it will be helpful to list the major component ideas, namely: Africa as the homeland of Africans and persons of African origin, solidarity among men of African descent, belief in a distinct African personality, rehabilitation of Africa's past, pride in African culture, Africa for Africans in church and state, the hope for a united and glorious future Africa. All these elements or combinations of them form the principal aims of twentieth-century pan-African associations; they pervade the resolutions of pan-African meetings held outside and inside the continent since 1900; they permeate the utterances and publications of men like W. E. B. DuBois, Marcus Garvey, George Padmore, Kwame Nkrumah, Julius Nyerere and Stokeley Carmichael. With some simplification we can say that Pan-Africanism is a political and cultural phenomenon which regards Africa, Africans and African descendants abroad as a unit. It seeks to regenerate and unify Africa and promote a feeling of oneness among the people of the African world. It glorifies the African past and inculcates pride in African values. Any adequate definition of the phenomenon must include the political and cultural aspects. How can a phenomenon which has been institutionalized in the O.A.U. still remain a utopia? And what

[9] V. B. Thompson, *Africa and Unity: The Evolution of Pan-Africanism* (London: Longmans, 1969).

is irrational about seeking the solidarity of the African world and inculcating pride in Africa's past and culture?

The present debate on the nature of Pan-Africanism stems largely from three unfortunate tendencies. There is the tendency to overplay one aspect of the phenomenon at the expense of the other. A second source of confusion is the rather heavy reliance on the records of the European colonial administrations, all of which were hostile to the movement and did their utmost to suppress or even destroy it. Linked with this tendency is the practice of enumerating the publications of pan-African leaders and organizations instead of integrating the material in the text itself. Thus in his book, Geiss speculates on the originator of the term "pan-African" and the identity of Benito Sylvain. Yet the answers are contained in the *Schomburg Collection* listed in the author's bibliography. The careful reader will also notice that the text of Geiss' study does not show any substantial use of the works of, for example, Edward W. Blyden. Geiss' preference of the compilations of European liberals and their societies may have misled him into thinking that Pan-Africanism is an irrational concept; all the same, it serves the useful purpose of revealing sources in German, Portuguese and even English unknown to many a previous writer.

Like Geiss, Langley is open to the charge of excessive reliance on non-pan-African documents, in this case, the despatches and minutes of British colonial officers in West Africa and London. If he had as much as glanced through Akweke Nwafor Orizu's *Without Bitterness*,[10] Mazi Mbonu Ojike's *My Africa*[11] and S. D. Cudjoe's *Aids to African Autonomy*[12] and paid attention to the exertions of Dr. R. N. Duchein, founder and president of the Pan-African Unifi-

---

[10] A. N. Orizu, *Without Bitterness: Western Nations in Post-War Africa* (New York: Creative Age Press, 1944).

[11] M. Ojike, *My Africa* (New York: John Day, 1946).

[12] S. D. Cudjoe, *Aids to African Autonomy* (London: the College Press, 1949).

cation Organization, he would probably not have made the sweeping statement that the West African nationalist elite "reinterpreted Pan-Africanism to suit their economic and political interest, particularly when ideology and interest clashed."

This brings us to a third cause of the disagreement on what Pan-Africanism is all about: the failure to distinguish between what is pan-African and what is not. In their eagerness to demonstrate that Pan-Africanism is not synonymous with the activities of DuBois, Padmore and so on, many recent commentators have gone to the extreme of raking up obscure figures of doubtful pan-African stature. It is a mistake to suppose that every anti-colonial activity is a manifestation of Pan-Africanism. Thus, Ato Kifle Wodajo, an Ethiopian writer, thinks that "in Africa itself the seeds of Pan-Africanism were implanted the moment the first alien coloniser set foot on her soil."[13]

A similar opinion was expressed by the Afro-American, John H. Clarke, at the Second World Black and African Festival of Arts and Culture held in Lagos from 15 January to 12 February, 1977. In his words:

> for a period of more than a hundred years, African warrior nationalists, mostly kings ... out-manouvered and out-generaled some of the best military minds of Europe. They planted the seeds of African independence for another generation to harvest. Their Pan-Africanism was more military than intellectual, but it was Pan-Africanism.[14]

On this view every African agitator would be a pan-Africanist; the 1896 House Tax uprising in Sierra Leone led by Bai Bureh as well as the Aba Women's Riot of 1928 would qualify as

---

[13] Ato K. Wodajo, "Pan-Africanism: The Evolution of an Idea," *Ethiopia Observer*, Vol. VIII, No. 2 (1964), p. 166.

[14] John H. Clarke, "The Development of Pan-Africanist Ideas in the Americas and in Africa Before 1900." Text No. Col. 5/03/USA. 12, pp. 6-7.

pan-African episodes. But the evidence suggests that Bureh and the Aba women were solely concerned with the narrow interests of their localities, not with the wider pan-African world.

It is the view of the present writer that only persons committed to the ideals of Pan-Africanism and activities clearly linked with the pan-African movement deserve notice. A good example of this kind of link is Nkrumah's famous statement that the independence of Ghana would be meaningless unless it was linked with the total liberation of the continent.

Just as writers quarrel over what Pan-Africanism stands for, so too they clash on its periodization. Geiss feels that Pan-Africanism, in its strictest sense, started in 1958 when Nkrumah summoned two pan-African meetings in Accra, the first to be held on African soil. On the other hand, Langley has warned us against "the tyranny of dates and labels" and that "Pan-Africanism is not a movement that should be boxed and frozen into epochs and categories." Disregarding his own prescriptions he goes on to suggest in the same study that "the small gathering at Kumasi in 1953 can be seen as a new phase in the evolution of an idea and as the real beginning of the Pan-African movement in Africa."[15] Langley's inability to live up to his own declarations emphasises the necessity for periodisation however tentative.

If we accept the need to periodize, what features of the phenomenon shall we consider to be of decisive importance? Should we ignore pan-African sentiments or notions and concentrate on such concrete aspects as pan-African conferences and pressure groups? By rebuking those who "in the absence of concrete evidence, assemble any number of incidents and ideas and call it Pan-Africanism,"[16] Langley

---

[15] J. A. Langley, *Pan Africanism and Nationalism in West Africa, 1900-1945* (London: Oxford University Press, 1973), p. 368.

[16] *ibid.*, p. viii.

appears to be advocating the elimination of pan-African sentiments. If so, is it still necessary to state that every concrete thing, concrete evidence included, begins as an idea. Not only do pan-African sentiments and notions constitute an integral part of Pan-Africanism, they also help us to date the inception of the phenomenon. The question of date is important because the essential features of any phenomenon will be judged differently if it is differently delimited. Our opinions on the nature of Pan-Africanism will vary according to whether we assume that it came into existence in the eighteenth, nineteenth or twentieth century.

What year, then, did Pan-Africanism begin and who launched it? The man who first expressed pan-African sentiments will never be known. Hence it is futile to try, as some writers have attempted, to ascribe the phenomenon to any one man or trace its origin to a particular year. Of course the term "pan-African" and its derivative "Pan-Africanism" were not coined at the time the phenomenon which they describe emerged. This is hardly surprising for labels are sometimes invented after a movement has had time to establish itself. Just as a baby does not need baptism to exist, so too a creed does not require a label to be a fact of life. Though the words "pan-African" and "Pan-Africanism" became popular after the 1900 London congress, their substance had been thought out long before. In discussing the origin of Pan-Africanism, what one should look for is the period when the sentiments or concepts underlying it first attracted attention.

Pan-African thinking originally began in the so-called New World becoming articulate during the century starting from the declaration of American independence (1776). It represented a reaction against the oppression of the black man and the racial doctrines that marked the era of abolitionism. It also found expression in the independent church movement in the New World and Africa as well as in resistance to European colonial ambitions in Africa.

Although the principles of the American Revolution implied civil rights for all men, black Americans continued to suffer disabilities because of their race and complexion.[17] Alexis de Tocqueville's description of the predicament of the blacks in the United States will probably never be bettered. An extensive tour of America enabled the French lawyer to observe first hand the plight of African descendants there. What he saw drove him to remark that the black American made a thousand fruitless attempts to ingratiate himself with men who despised him. He adopted his oppressors' values, echoed their opinions and hoped by imitating them to form a part of their society.

Having been indoctrinated from infancy into believing that black men were naturally inferior to the whites, he accepted the myth and became ashamed of his personality. He saw evidence of inferiority in each of his features and if it were in his power he would gladly rid himself of everything that distinguished him from a white man.

Despairing of ever attaining equal status with the other racial groups, the Afro-American began to think seriously of returning to the fatherland. In 1787 a committee of the African Lodge, whose Grand Master was Prince Hall, sent a petition to the Legislative Assembly of Massachusetts. Despite the egalitarian principles enshrined in the national constitution hammered out in Philadelphia that year, men of African blood continued to suffer discrimination which they feared would remain the case so long as they and their children lived in America. Since they were poor and therefore in no position to return to Africa without help, the petitioners urged the Legislature to assist them and other blacks who wished to emigrate. The petition was ignored and Prince Hall was obliged to fight for civil liberties on American soil itself.

With the adoption of the Philadelphia Constitution which

---

[17] For details of some of the disabilities see P. O. Esedebe, "Pan-Africanism: Origins and Meaning," *Tarikh*, Vol. 6, No. 3 (1979), pp. 13-17.

among other things regarded a black slave as being equal to three-fifths of a person, Afro-Americans reopened the issue of emigration. In 1789 the Union Society of Africans in Newport lamented the fact that Americans of African descent were treated as strangers and outcasts. The society also drew attention to the "heathenish darkness and barbarity" engulfing the ancestral continent.

As a young man, Paul Cuffee, a half-Indian, half-black African Boston merchant and devout Quaker, had compaigned for the rights of black Americans in his native state of Massachusetts. When this met with little or no success, he switched his efforts to Sierra Leone in particular and Africa in general. His aims were to promote selective emigration to Sierra Leone and to save Africa from the scourge of the slave trade by helping Africans to develop a viable economy based on local products. Once Christianity and commerce had taken root in Sierra Leone it would become the task of blacks there to spread these blessings to other parts of the continent.

In 1808 Cuffee obtained the support of the African Institution, a British humanitarian organisation dominated by former directors of the Sierra Leone Company and still influential in the running of the affairs of the colony. Three years later, Cuffee visited Sierra Leone where he made careful plans for emigration. He also seized the opportunity to establish the Friendly Society of Sierra Leone "to open a channel of intercourse" between Negro America and Sierra Leone; as an example of his good faith, he bought a house in Freetown.[18] When he returned to America, he urged African descendants in Baltimore, Boston, New York, Philadelphia and Westport to support colonization in Africa. In 1815 he made another trip to Sierra Leone taking, largely at his own expense, about forty blacks in family groups. In the letters they

[18] Hollis R. Lynch, "Pan-Negro Nationalism in the New World Before 1862," in August Meier and Elliott Rudwick, eds, *The Making of Black Americans,* Vol. I (New York: Atheneum, 1969), p. 46.

wrote back to America, these repatriates advised other exiles to follow their example.

On his return, Cuffee gave the benefit of his experience to the founders of the American Colonization Society. Founded in December, 1816 by white American liberals and designed to finance the deportation of free blacks, the ACS received funds from private individuals, church groups, state legislatures, and a donation of $100,000 from the United States Congress.[19] Cuffee was chosen to lead emigrants to be sent by the society but he died before the first expedition left for West Africa.

Among the second batch of emigrants was Reverend Lott Cary (1780-1828), an ex-slave in Richmond, Virginia, who ransomed himself and two children for $ 850.[20] To found a "colony which might prove a blessed asylum to his degraded brethren in America, and enlighten and regenerate Africa" became Lott Cary's burning ambition. Between 1817 and 1857, the first forty years of its existence, the ACS sponsored the resettlement in Liberia alone of about 13,000 Afro-Americans, "the pioneers of African Redemption."

As citizens in a prosperous country with enormous mineral and agricultural resources, many black Americans lived in the hope that tomorrow would be a better day. Sustained by this optimism, many free black Americans hesitated or even refused to support schemes seeking to remove them from the country. They proclaimed the United States as their home and land which their fathers had built and defended against invaders.

One of the expressions of opposition to the ACS came from the Annual Convention of the Free Colored People, first held in Philadelphia in 1830 and afterward in that and other cities annually until the Civil War (1861-65). The anti-colonization case found a classic expression in an oration delivered in July,

---

[19] Leslie H. Fishel, Jr. and Benjamin Quarles, *The Negro American. A Documentary History* (Illinois: Scott, Foresman and Co. and William Morrow and Co., 1967), p. 145.

[20] *African Repository* (March, 1829), p. 11.

1830 by Peter Williams, pastor of St. Phillips Episcopal Church, New York.[21] His argument may be summarised as follows.

No people in the world possessed so high a respect for liberty and equality as the citizens of the United States. Yet no people held so many slaves or made such fine distinctions between man and man. Thus, the freedom Americans had fought for was illusory. The rights of men now depended on the colour of their skins. Though officially delivered from the letters of slavery, black Americans "are oppressed by an unreasonable, unrighteous, and cruel prejudice, which aims at nothing less than the forcing away of all the free coloured people of the United States to the distant shores of Africa." Admittedly some supporters of the American colonization society were genuinely interested in the regeneration of Africa through evangelisation and the suppression of slavery and the slave trade. All the same many leaders of the Society, "those who are most active and most influential in its cause," had openly declared the removal of the free coloured population of the country as the actual objective.

Surely Africa could be uplifted without sending all the free people of colour in the United States there. Was it not both illogical and hypocritical to state that Africa would benefit from the return of her children in exile and with the same breath denounce the same exiles as the most "vile and degraded people in the world?" How could vile and degraded men build a virtuous and progressive Africa?

Equally ridiculous and inconsistent was the suggestion of "colonizationists about improving the character and condition of the people of colour in this country by sending them to Africa." The "barbarous" environment of Africa was deemed more suitable for improvement than American society

[21] For a text of the discourse *see* Carter G. Woodson, *Negro Orators and Their Orations* (Washington D.C.: Associated Publishers, Inc., 1925). See also Leslie H. Fishel, Jr. and Benjamin Quarles, *The Negro American. A Documentary History,* pp. 145-147.

where schools and colleges abound,
where the gospel is preached at
every corner, and where all the
arts and sciences are verging
fast to perfection...
We are NATIVES of this
country, we ask only to be treated
as well as FOREIGNERS.
Not a few of our fathers suffered
and bled to purchase its independence;
we ask only to be treated as
well as those who fought against
it. We have toiled to cultivate it,
and to raise it to its present
prosperous condition; we ask only
to share equal privileges with
those who come from distant lands,
to enjoy the fruits of our labour.
Let these moderate requests be granted
and we need not go to Africa nor
anywhere else to be improved and happy.
We cannot but doubt the purity of
the motives of those persons who
deny us these requests, and would
send us to Africa to gain what
they might give us at home.

In maintaining that many a white American liberal was not really concerned about the relative backwardness of the African continent, Peter Williams was quite right. But he missed the point when he demanded the "improvement" of blacks in the United States rather than in the jungles and disease-ridden villages of Africa. The point was that most white Americans, the males in particular, saw in the growing free black American population a threat to their sexual security. For them the black man was at bottom a rapist, forever lusting after white women. This libel is adequately documented in a recent study, *Slavery, Race and the American*

Revolution, written by Duncan J. McLeod (Cambridge University Press, 1974).

The migration of free blacks to the middle and northern states after the Revolution was largely prompted by legislation in the south which made emigration a condition of emancipation. Virginia passed such a law in 1806 thereby precipitating much of the fear in other population. Within a year of Virginia's action, Delaware, Kentucky and Maryland all introduced measures denying permanent residence to free blacks from other states.

At the same time congressional debates on the abolition of the slave-trade in 1806-07 were marked by vehement opposition to the increasing free black population. And in 1809, during a debate on the enforcement of the Act, Representative Taylor of South Carolina contended that it was not the intention of the law of 1807 "to increase our population in free blacks. It was not to set free the people of this description that the law had to be passed, but to prevent them from being brought here at all."[22] Is it not significant that the Act abolishing the slave trade failed to provide for the liberation of those illegally imported? In the words of Duncan J. McLeod, "The formation of the American Colonization Society was a direct response to the urge to limit free black numbers."

However, hopes of better conditions for the blacks held out by the outbreak of the American Civil War together with Abraham Lincoln's Emancipation Proclamation (1863) seemed to prove the opponents of emigration right. As a result, the enthusiasm to return to Africa flagged. By the end of the Reconstruction Period (1877) these hopes were totally shattered. The yearning for the fatherland once more rose to the surface. This desperate craving, which is abundantly documented in the *African Repository*,[23] found expression in the

---

[22] *ibid.*, pp. 163-164.
[23] See for example *African Repository* (October, 1877), pp. 114-116.

Liberia Exodus organisations that emerged in South Carolina and the utterances of Bishop Henry M. Turner.

The back-to-Africa idea also appealed to African descendants in the West Indies. Slave escapes and disturbances used to lead to uproars in which free blacks were obliged to show documentary evidence in support of their status, for every person of that complexion was described a slave, as the Antiguan Legislature ruled in 1783, until legal proofs to the contrary were produced.

In his autobiography published towards the end of the eighteenth century, Olaudah Equiano, otherwise known as Gustavus Vasa the African, complains bitterly about the perpetual fear of re-enslavement and the impunity with which the supposedly emancipated blacks were universally insulted and robbed "for such is the equity of the West Indian laws, that no free negro's evidence will be admitted in their courts of justice."[24] At about the age of ten Equiano had been taken from his native Igboland in Nigeria by slave traders to the Southern States of America. He was then sold to a planter in the West Indies. He worked there and aboard ships operating between the Caribbean and England before he saved enough money to buy his freedom in 1776. As a free black he found the West Indies so disgusting and unsafe that he concluded that unless he left the region he would not be actually free. He eventually made his way to England where he married Susan Cullen of Ely (near Cambridge) on 7 April, 1792. Before his marriage Equiano had helped in organising the repatriation of some liberated African slaves to Sierra Leone. But an indiscreet letter attacking some of the white organisers of the expedition robbed him of the chance of returning to Africa.

When the British Emancipation Act became effective in 1838, the desire to quit the scene of humiliation and the zeal to regenerate the African race through missionary work seized

[24] *Equiano's Travels,* abridged ed. (London and Ibadan: Heinemann, 1967), p. 84.

many an African descendant. The following year, one Thomas
Keith set out from Jamaica with only a letter of recommendation from his pastor to be a missionary to his brethren.[25]
Four years later several families sailed from the same territory
with one Alfred Saker and landed in the Cameroon some
going as evangelists and teachers, others as settlers.[26] By 1858
they had become so numerous as to constitute a distinct
colony, Victoria.

In Barbados a West Indian Church Association was
launched under whose auspices persons of African origin
returned to the parent continent. Among them was John
Duport, a young man from St. Kitts, who in 1855 went to West
Africa to do missionary work in the Rio Pongas area of what is
now Guinea Republic. With the help of local chiefs and
traders, Duport was able to start a school at Falangia. "A
stream of others followed; some stayed, others were forced by
ill-health to return, and others died."[27]

Liberia also attracted the attention of Afro-West Indians.
Among them may be mentioned the Jamaican journalist, John
B. Russwurm. At first, in common with the well-known black
Americans, William Lloyd Garrison and Frederick Douglass,
he opposed emigration to Africa in general and the American
Colonization Society in particular. But unlike Garrison and
Douglas he changed his mind subscribing to the view that the
African in exile can help himself and his race best by giving
strong support to Liberia. Not surprisingly he went to Liberia
and founded a newspaper, *Liberia Herald*, in 1830.

In Latin America, the urge to emigrate to the fatherland
was not as compelling as in the United States and the Antilles.
Here the situation differed. The treatment of slaves might have

---

[25] C. P. Groves, *The Planting of Christianity in Africa,* Vol. II (London,
1954), p. 28; E. B. Underhill, *Alfred Saker* (London, 1884), pp. 169-171.

[26] C. P. Groves, *op. cit.,* p. 30.

[27] Abioseh Nicol, "West Indians in West Africa," *Sierra Leone Studies,*
New Series, Vol. LV, No. 13 (June, 1960), p. 18.

been more brutal in the Portuguese and Spanish colonies than in the Dutch, English and French Caribbean islands and possibly the North American settlements. Nevertheless in Latin America the slave had a greater chance of securing his liberty.[28] There was no doubt about the slave's fitness for freedom. Thus, in colonial Brazil, notorious for her barbarous treatment of slaves, the blacks performed nearly all the menial tasks but with manumission they filled openings in private and public employment. Racial relations were free of prejudice to such an extent that a French diplomat remarked in a despatch of 1835 that Brazil was a mulatto monarchy with nothing pure except the royal blood.[29]

If miscegenation made for integration, it was by no means the decisive factor. The crucial factor is to be found in the relatively open nature of Latin American society. Here the emancipated Negro was really a free man being by law the equal of all other free citizens. It is important to note that when slavery was ended in Brazil (1888), the crowd in the gallery showered flowers on the members of the legislature and throughout the night the masses danced in the streets of the capital city, Rio de Janeiro.[30]

All the same it will be mistaken to suppose that the African exiles in Latin America completely escaped the back-to-Africa fever. Throughout the nineteenth century, pockets of Afro-Brazilians now and again crossed the Atlantic to settle in Whydah (Dahomey) and Lagos (Nigeria). Equally significant

[28] In Cuba alone in 1827, there were some 20,000 more free persons of colour than in the whole of the British West Indies. W. L. Mathieson, *British Slavery and its Abolition* (London, 1926), p. 40. See also Frank Tannenbaum, *Slave and citizen* (New York, 1947) and C. R. Boxer, *Race Relations in the Portuguese Colonial Empire* (London: Oxford University Press, 1963).

[29] Jose Honorio Rodrigues, *Brazil and Africa,* translated by Richard A. Mazzara and Sam Hileman (Berkeley and Los Angeles: University of California Press, 1965), pp. 80; 101, fn. 118.

[30] F. Tannenbaum, *Ten Keys to Latin America* (New York: Vintage Books, 1962), p. 49.

was a remark made in 1891 by an English clergyman. Reverend Francis P. Flemynge:

> That over a million Negroes were eager to go back to Africa: He was so moved by compassion that he decided to form an " 'African Repatriation Relief Society' for the purpose of collecting funds to give free and assisted passages to these poor creatures from Brazils [*sic*] and Havana to Africa."[31]

A detailed and documented study of the activities of African descendants scattered all over Asia still needs to be done. But judging from the scanty evidence now at our disposal, it seems that though Afro-Asians still cherish memories of the fatherland, they have remained unaffected by the Pan-African movement. This apparent indifference has been attributed partly to the comparatively humane treatment meted to the them, partly to their conversion to Islam and assimilation to the local culture and partly to ignorance of pan-African developments.[32]

A second factor behind the emergence of pan-African consciousness was the racial doctrine associated with the long debate on the Atlantic slave trade. With the colonisation of the American hemisphere, the Aristotelian hypothesis that some humans are by nature slaves and others free was used to justify the enslavement of the aboriginal Amerindians and later Africans. Thus, in the sixteenth century, the Spanish propagandist Juan Gines de Sepulveda claimed that the Amerindians' inability to resist the Spanish adventures proved not only their natural inferiority but also their need of a strong and wise

---

[31] Quoted in Edward W. Blyden, "The Return of the Exiles," *African Repository* (January 1892), p. 17.

[32] Joseph E. Harris, *The African Presence in Asia: Consequences of the East African Slave Trade* (Evanston, Ill.: Northwestern University Press, 1971). See also a review of Harris' book by Vaşant D. Rao in *The Journal of Modern African Studies* Vol. 13, No. 2 (1975), pp. 356-358.

government to be provided presumably by the Spaniards. The myth of natural servitude obtained a new lease of life from the closing decades of the eighteenth century down to the entire nineteenth.

Two main currents of racial theory may be distinguished: the evolutionary and the teleological. An example of the evolutionary argument was Dr. Thomas Arnold's view of history advanced in 1841. In his inaugural lecture as Regius Professor of History at Oxford, Arnold saw history as a kind of relay race among a small team of gifted peoples each of whom produced their best, passing on their achievements to greater successors. Thus, what the ancient Greeks handed to the Romans the Romans in turn passed on to the Northern Europeans. To him modern history appeared to be not only a step in advance of ancient history but the last step. Since no gifted race remained to receive the seed of modern European civilisation, the uncreative mass of mankind must either assimilate the elements of European culture "so completely that their individual character is absorbed, and they take their whole being from without; or, being incapable of taking in higher elements they dwindle away when brought into the presence of a more powerful life and become at last extinct altogether."[33] It struck the professor's reviewer that three centuries of close contact with the powerful Europeans had failed to exterminate the Africans in exile; on the contrary, "they have actually advanced under circumstances the most hostile to advancement."[34] If the test of history was the capacity to survive, continued the reviewer, the Africans at home had shown themselves quite capable of survival in the tropics where Europeans could not live. Was it not possible

---

[33] Thomas Arnold, *Introductory Lectures on Modern History* (Oxford: Clarendon Press, 1842), p. 37.

[34] W. R. Greg, "Dr Arnold," *The Westminister Review* Vol. XXXIX, No. 1 (January, 1843), p. 6.

then that Europeans might one day pass on the products of their work to a superior race of Negroes?[35]

According to the teleological school, the Creator deliberately made men unequal. The whites, He gave intelligence to enable them to direct wisely the activities of the others. The non-whites, these usually meant blacks, He gave strong backs fortified with a weak mind and an obedient temper so that they might labour effectively under the supervision of the white masters. This interpretation proved extremely popular in the United States where it served as a principal defence of Negro slavery. Although physical anthropologists and other pseudoscientific racists were soon to vie with one another in the minute measurement of skulls and facial angles, they never abandoned the old use of skin colour as a guide to the degree of superiority or nearness to the apes. Because Europeans erected the hierarchy of races, they naturally placed whites on the top. The darker races were ranked below in order of darkness.

The middle of the nineteenth century witnessed a revival of the teleological argument. This event was marked by the appearance of virulent racist publications notably by the Englishman Thomas Carlyle, the Edinburgh anatomist Robert Knox, the French sociologist Arthur de Gobineau and the American naval officer Commander A. H. Foote. While Knox held that "the true black or negro race" reached the zenith of its ability centuries ago and had become stagnant,[36] Foote denied them any achievement worth mentioning. If everything Africans and their descendants had accomplished from time immemorial, he wrote contemptuously, were to be destroyed or forgotten, the world would lose no great truth, no profitable art, no exemplary form of life.[37] Civilisation and culture, Gobineau maintained, were the exclusive creation of the

---

[35] *ibid.*, pp. 6033, *passim.*
[36] *The Races of Men* (London, 1850), Ch. 6: "The Darker Races of Men."
[37] A. H. Foote, *Africa and the American Flag* (New York, 1854), p. 207.

superior races arguing that superiority and inferiority were not due to environment but innate.[38]

In his infamous *Occasional Discourses on the Nigger Question* written in 1849, Carlyle asserted: "That, you may depend on it, my obscure Black friends, is and was always the Law of the World, for you and for all men: To be servants, the more foolish of us to the more wise; and only sorrow, futility and disappointment will betide both, till both in some approximate degree get to conform to the same."[39]

Insinuations about the alleged permanent inferiority of the black man and assertations that he had contributed little or nothing for the comfort of humanity posed a challenge which educated elements of the African diaspora picked up. Olaudah Equiano reminded the conceited and polished European that his ancestors were once, like the Africans, uncivilised and barbarous. Pride in his African origins moved Equiano to praise his people, the Igbos, for their resourcefulness, integrity and intelligence. He went so far as to claim that deformity was almost unknown among them. Equiano blamed the European adventures for much of the inter-communal conflict among Africans and by drawing attention to conditions in eighteenth-century Europe he drove home the point that violence is not peculiar to black men.

Some Afro-Americans like the astronomer Benjamin Banneker pointed to their contemporary achievements to show that the popular notions about the African were false. The West African scientist, James Africanus Beale Horton, provided evidence from his own medical and educational career to refute the allegation of Negro inferiority showing by the experience of his own people, the Sierra Leone Creoles, that there could be a swift change from apparent barbarity to a civilised condition in a single generation.

[38] Arthur de Gobineau, *Essai sur l'inegalité des races humaines*, (4 vols) (Paris, 1853, 1855).

[39] Quoted in Phillip D. Curtin, *The Image of Africa: British Ideas and Action, 1780-1850* (London: Macmillan, 1965), pp. 380-381.

Equiano, Banneker and Horton wanted to demonstrate that African backwardness was neither inherent nor permanent but that it was due to adverse circumstances and lack of opportunity. Delving into the African past itself, David Walker, another Afro-American, not only affirmed the potential equality of the races but cited the glories of ancient Egypt as examples of the Africans' contributions to civilisation.

Following the example of his fellow American, David Walker, Reverend James Theodore Holly produced in 1857 a forty-six page booklet with the title: *A Vindication of the Capacity of the Negro Race for Self-Government and Civilized Progress, As Demonstrated by Historical Events of the Haytian Revolution and the Subsequent Acts of that People Since Their National Independence.*[40] Though marred by emotional language, which can be excused by the nature of his subject, the pamphlet is analytical, coherent and persuasive, based firmly on history not myth. Its object is threefold. One, as the title implies, is to refute "the vile aspersions and foul calumnies that have been heaped upon my race for the last four centuries, by our unprincipled oppressors; whose base interest, at the expense of our blood and our bones, have made them reiterate, from generation to generation, during the long march of ages, everything that would prop up the impious dogma of our [supposed] natural and inherent inferiority.[41] A second purpose was to convert those philanthropists who secretly doubted the equality of the races and often betrayed themselves when pressed to accept the logical consequences of their avowed beliefs. The third aim must be quoted *in extenso* if we are not to miss its Pan-African dimension:

> to inflame the latent embers of self-respect that the cruelty and injustice of our oppressors, have nearly

---

40 New Haven, Connecticut.
41 *ibid.*, p. 5.

extinguished in our bosoms, during the midnight chill of
centuries, that we have clanked the galling chains of
slavery. To this end, I wish to remind my oppressed
brethren, that dark and dismal as this horrid night has been
and sorrowful as the general reflections are, in regard to
our race; yet, notwithstanding these discouraging con-
siderations, there are still some proud historic recollec-
tions, linked indissolubly with the most important events
of the past and present century, which break the general
monotony, and remove some of the gloom that hang
over the dark historic period of African slavery, and the
accursed traffic in which it was cradled.[42]

At the end of his exposition Holly proudly announced, with
much justification then, that the African exiles in Hayti "have
already made a name, and a fame for us, that is imperishable
as the world's history."[43] The more blacks searched their past the
greater their admiration of African culture tended to grow.

Several works written by European abolitionists helped to
promote the cause of the Negro history movement. One, which
immediately became a standard source of pro-Negro arguments, was penned by the Englishman Wilson Armistead and
published in 1848 in Manchester under the title: *A Tribute for
the Negro: being a vindication of the Moral, Intellectual and
Religious Capabilities of the Coloured Portion of Mankind; with
particular reference to the African Race*. Another was contributed by H. G. Adams. Published in London in 1852 it was
entitled *God's Image in Ebony: Being a Series of Biographical
Sketches, Anecdotes, etc. Demonstrative of the Mental Powers
and Intellectual Capacities of the Negro Race*. The use of
biographical sketches to answer racists remained fashionable
for a long time as can be seen from *Memoirs of West African
Celebrities and African Leaders, Past and Present* both of which
appeared at the beginning of the present century and were
written by the Gold Coast clergyman S. R. B. Attoh Ahuma

---

42 *ibid.*, p. 6.
43 *ibid.*, p. 44.

and the neglected Nigerian pamphleteer, Adeoye Deniga, respectively.[44]

Racial antagonism was also aroused in the process of the evangelisation of Africa where it strained relations between the local clerics and their European counterparts. It culminated in a movement that sought to Africanise Christianity and tended toward the formation of independent African churches on the model of the African Methodist Episcopal churches in America already noted. "Ethiopianism" is the term usually employed to describe this phenomenon that emerged in Africa in the last third of the nineteenth century. There is no agreement as to whether the term should apply to the South and Central African separatist churches[45] or only to a type of the South African variety[46] or be used in a Pan-African sense.[47] If secession was not everywhere a feature of Ethiopianism, at least two factors were. One was the determination to save cherished indigenous values from the destructive influences of the foreign missions. The other was the principle of "Africa for the Africans" in opposition to European interference. For these reasons it seems justifiable to use the term in the wider Pan-African sense.

Influenced by the racists of the day, many a nineteenth-century European missionary behaved as if conversion and general acceptance of the African way of life were mutually exclusive. Hence most of the correspondence they sent home bristled with accounts of what they described as the wicked-

[44] See Hollis R. Lynch, "West African Biography: A Historiographical Study." Paper given at the African Historical Association meeting in New York, December 1971.

[45] George Shepperson, " 'Pan-Africanism' and 'pan-Africanism': Some Historical Notes," pp. 4-5. Seminar paper given at the Institute of Commonwealth Studies, London University, April, 1961; J. B. Webster, *The African Churches Among the Yoruba 1888-1922* (London: Oxford University Press, 1964), pp. xiv-xv.

[46] B. Sundkler, *Bantu Prophets in South Africa* (London: Oxford University Press, 1964), p. 53.

[47] Jomo Kenyatta, *Facing Mount Kenya* (London: Mercury Books, 1962), p. 269.

ness and abominable customs of pagan society. Though some of their letters were published in reputable journals mainly to stimulate missionary subscription, they became an unwitting source of racism.

Separation began to manifest itself in West and South Africa as from the 1870s. As early as 1872 a minor secession from the Hermon Congregation of the Paris Mission occurred in Basutoland. Twelve years later Nehemiah Tile broke away from the Wesleyan Mission to form the Tembu Church with Ngangelizwe, the Chief of the Tembu, as its visible head. "The cause of this important secession was not only opposition to European control, but also a positive desire to adapt the message of the Church to the heritage of the Tembu tribe. As the Queen of England was the head of the English Church, so the Paramount Chief of the Tembu should be the *summus episcopus* of the new religious organization."[48]

One of the oldest Nigerian independent churches, the United Native African Church, was established on a resolution "that a pure Native African Church be founded for the evangelization and amelioration of the race, to be governed by Africans."[49] The U.N.A. Church was not the product of a schism from a particular denomination. It was set up by men of several denominations as a purely African missionary effort.

Another secession occurred in the German Cameroon where the Native Baptist Church broke away from the Basle Mission in 1888-89.[50] This religious phenomenon appeared late in East and Central Africa becoming active during the period 1900-30 when the European colonialists had already begun to entrench their positions. In both regions the movement tended not only to centre around prophets but also to be the focus of political agitation. Thus, under the leadership of John Chilembwe in Nyasaland it culminated in an uprising

---

[48] B. Sundkler, *op. cit.*, p. 38.

[49] Quoted in J. B. Webster, *op. cit.*, p. 68.

[50] H. Rudin, *Germans in the Cameroon* (London, 1938), pp. 340, 356.

there;[51] in the Belgian Congo (Zaire) its leader Simon Kinbangu was imprisoned while the Ugandan Malaki Musaj-jakawa (whose disciples were called *Bamalaki* or Malakites) was deported. The Portuguese consistently restricted the entry of Protestant missions into their territories on the ground that they were the advance-guard of African nationalism.[52]

Thus the humiliating and discriminatory experiences of the African diaspora, the racism that accompanied the campaign for the suppression of the Atlantic slave trade, the independent African church movement as well as European imperialism, all represent the main sources of and conditions giving rise to Pan-African consciousness and ideas. If the ideas seemed vague at first, they received a more articulate expression at the hands of the West Africans J. A. B. Horton, Reverend James Johnson and Edward W. Blyden, an Afro-West Indian who later adopted Liberian nationality. Lesser pioneer Pan-African theorists include the Afro-American Anglican divine Reverend Alexander Crummell, the Haytian diplomat and publicist Benito Sylvain as well as the Nigerian clergyman Orishatukeh Faduma and Dr. Mojola Agbebi.

Born in June, 1835 in Gloucester village (Sierra Leone) to an Igbo recaptive, James Africanus Beale Horton was educat-ed partly in Sierra Leone and partly in England where he adopted the name "Africanus" to show his African identity. After studying medicine at King's College, London and the University of Edinburgh he was commissioned in the British Army where he served for twenty years in West Africa. But his interests were not confined to military and medical matters. Indeed, his knowledge of the classics, history and anthropo-logy was remarkable for a man of any race. His best known work is *West African Countries and Peoples, British and Native.*

[51] For details see G. Shepperson and T. Price, *Independent African John Chilembwe and the Origins, Setting and Significance of the Nyasaland Native Rising of 1915* (Edinburgh: Edinburgh University Press, 1958).

[52] T. Hodgkin, *Nationalism in Colonial Africa* (London: Frederick Muller, 1956), p. 98.

With the Requirements Necessary for Establishing that Self-Government Recommended by the Committee of the House of Commons, 1865; And a Vindication of the African Race published in London in 1868.[53] Several of his ideas which are Pan-African in scope can be found in this book. One is the notion of a great African past. Africa in ages past, he proudly recalls:

> was the nursery of science and literature; from thence they were taught in Greece and Rome so that it was said that the ancient Greeks represented their favourite goddess of Wisdom — Minerva — as an African princess. Pilgrimages were made to Africa in search of knowledge by such eminent men as Solon, Plato, Pythagoras; and several came to listen to the African Euclid, who was at the head of the most celebrated mathematical school in the world and who flourished 300 years before the birth of Christ. The conqueror of the great African Hannibal made his associate and confidant the African poet Terence.[54]

Africa, Horton goes on, produced many of the famous theologians of the early Christian Church notably Origen, Tertullian, Augustin, Clemens Alexandrinus and Cyril. Horton's reasoned re-assessment of the ancient history of Africa exposed the profound ignorance of Foote in particular and racists in general. Thus, Horton helped in no small measure to restore the self-confidence of the blackman which was necessary for the further progress of the cause of Pan-Africanism. Wherever Africans found themselves, he emphasised, they tended to flourish even in the face of unspeakable odds. From this he inferred that they were "a permanent and enduring people" contrary to the vapourings of Arnold. The refutation of Foote and Arnold, though Horton fails to name

[53] The book has been reprinted under the African Heritage Books Series by the Edinburgh University Press, 1969. Page references are to the reprint edition.
[54] *West African Countries and Peoples,* p. 59.

them, rendered the highway of Pan-Africanism much clearer, firmer and safer.

The rejection of the theses of Foote and Arnold also enabled Horton to hope for a grand African future, another key Pan-African concept. A careful analysis of world history revealed to Horton the long-established fact that change was an ordiance of nature. No condition was permanent. There existed a natural law of evolution and dissolution. Under this law "Nations rise and fall; the once flourishing and civilized degenerates into a semibarbarous state; and those who have lived in utter barbarism, after a lapse of time become the standing nation."[55]

Despite the speculations of Robert Knox, Africans "must live in the hope, that in process of time, their turn will come, when they will [again] occupy a prominent position in the world's history, and when they will command a voice in the council of nations."[56] There was no reason why the same race who had her churches and repositories of learning and science, who governed ancient Egypt and was the terror of no less a city than ancient Rome should not once more stand on her legs.[57] It was in recognition of the permanent and enduring character of the African race, he thought, that the Committee of the House of Commons had come to embrace "that great principle of establishing independent African nationalities as independent as the present Liberian Government."[58] The African nationalities Horton had in mind were such West African ethnic groups and communities as the Fantis and Gas in the Gold Coast, the Igbo and Yoruba of present-day Nigeria as well as the Sierra Leone Creoles. African states as we now know them had not yet emerged. All the same he would still have welcomed them for he looked beyond autonomous ethnic communities, however viable, to a united West Africa.

[55] *ibid.*, p. 60.
[56] *ibid.*, p. 61.
[57] *ibid.*, p. 60.
[58] *ibid.*, p. 69.

Horton's idea of a university was also West African in scope. Such an institution he hoped would serve not only to cure Africans of the poison of innate inferiority but also to exploit the unused human and economic resources of the region. He was far-sighted and broadminded enough not to exclude foreign agencies completely from his programme for African regeneration arguing that "It is impossible for a nation to civilize itself; civilization must come from abroad. As was the case with the civilized continents of Europe and America, so it must be with Africa; which cannot be an exception to the rule."[59]

Another significant Pan-African theorist was James Johnson, a school-mate of Africanus Horton at Fourah Bay College, Freetown. Like Horton he was a Sierra Leonean of Nigerian extraction. Unlike Horton he couched his ideas in religious language. Also a contemporary of Edward Blyden, James Johnson was a highly respected cleric of the C.M.S. Though his radicalism often embarrassed that church, his obsession with the parochial interests of Sierra Leone and Nigeria makes him a lesser African leader than Dr. E. A. Ayandele, his biographer, claims.[60] To say this is not to deny the Pan-African dimension of some of the clergyman's statements.

James Johnson subscribed to the belief in a glorious African past which he traced back to the time when the Christian Church held sway in North Africa and when such indigenous divines as Tertullian, Augustine and Cyprian lent colour and dignity to the crown of Christendom. His religious training led him to attribute the decline of this golden age to the failure of North Africans to spread Christianity throughout the continent. In spite of this set-back he looked forward to a grand future. "Africa is to rise once more," he declared in 1867

[59] *ibid.,* p. 175.
[60] *Holy Johnson: Pioneer of African Nationalism, 1836-1917* (London: Frank Cass and Co., 1970). See P. O. Esedebe, "Holy Johnson," *The Journal of African History* Vol. XIII No. 1 (1972), pp. 165-168.

and "she will take her place with the most Christian, civilized and intelligent nations of the Earth."[61] The Native Pastorate created by the C.M.S. in Sierra Leone in 1861 was for him an agency "for the development of a future African Existence" and the nucleus of a continental African church uniting the various Christian sects. In his view such a church would pave the way to a monolithic African society and foster the growth of African solidarity.

James Johnson justified the campaign for an independent church on the ground that Africans were a distinct people with peculiar traits. It was no surprise that they should condemn the habit of uprooting the African convert from his cultural milieu and treating him as a *tabula rasa* on which foreign material must be written. No consideration, he bitterly complained, was given to the African way of life. Convinced that the Creator did not wish to confound the races, he demanded the "African must be raised upon his own idiosyncrasies."[62] James Johnson is here arguing a case for the preservation of the "African Personality" but he does not use the phrase itself for it had not yet been coined by Edward Blyden who is probably the greatest exponent of Pan-African concepts.

It must not be supposed that Blyden was the originator of Pan-African ideas. The man who first advanced such notions may never be discovered. Nor can we say with certainty that he was the most original. But to suggest as Professor J. D. Hargreaves has done that "His numerous essays and orations do not really cohere into an intellectual whole"[63] is to betray one's superficial acquaintance with their contents. Of course it is possible to point to one or two inconsistencies but they do not affect the essence of his Pan-African aspirations.

The real point about the Pan-African ideas of Edward Blyden is not their logical consistency or inconsistency but

---

[61] E. A. Ayandele, *Holy Johnson: Pioneer of African Nationalism,* p. 45.
[62] *ibid.*
[63] "Blyden of Liberia," *History Today* Vol. XIX, No. 8 (August, 1969), p. 568.

their questionable originality. So striking is the similarity between his arguments and those of Africanus Horton and Alexander Crummell that one is tempted to ask: who copied from the other? If it is hard to determine how much Blyden owes to these two distinguished contemporaries of his, there is no doubt that his writings are the most elegant, articulate and forceful, reaching a wider audience. According to the Englishman Bosworth Smith, hitherto no voice had come "audible at all events to the outer world, from Africa itself."[64] It was in the pages of Blyden's tracts, he goes on, that the great dumb, dark continent had begun to speak at last.[65] A contemporary African newspaper, the *Lagos Weekly Record*, described Blyden as an oracle on both sides of the Atlantic, "the highest intellectual representative and the greatest defender of the African race."[66] The well-known Gold Coast lawyer and nationalist, J. E. Casely Hayford, who as a school boy in Sierra Leone knew Blyden, was making the same point when he said that the claim of Blyden to the esteem of all thinking Africans rested not so much upon the special work he did for any particular section of the African world as upon the general service he rendered to the race as a whole. For more than a quarter of a century Blyden sought to reveal everywhere the African unto himself and, most important of all, to lead him back unto self-respect and confidence.[67]

Edward Wilmot Blyden was born of "pure Negro descent from the Eboe [Igbo] tribe"[68] in August, 1832 on the Danish

---

[64] *The Nineteenth Century* (December, 1887), pp. 793-94.

[65] *ibid.*

[66] (November 27, 1890).

[67] *Ethiopia Unbound: Studies in Race Emancipation* (London, 1911), Ch. XVI, *passim.*

[68] *Sierra Leone Weekly News* (February 10, 1912), p. 6; Edith Holden, *Blyden of Liberia: An Account of the Life and Labours of Edward Wilmot Blyden, LL.D. As Recorded in Letters and in Print* (New York, 1966), p. 19. Several important works still contain erroneous information as to the nationality of Blyden's parents. George Padmore, *Pan-Africanism or Communism? The Coming Struggle for Africa* (London: Dennis Dobson, 1956), p. 54 claims they were from the Gold Coast probably because of the

West Indian island of St. Thomas. His parents were Romeo and Judith Blyden believed to have been born about 1794 and 1795 respectively on St. Eustatius, another Danish Caribbean island. It was the father of Romeo and grandfather of Edward Blyden who came to the West Indies from Igboland. Because of the poor circumstances of his parents Edward Blyden was at first meant for the tailoring profession. But consumed with love for the ancestral continent and a desire to contribute towards her advancement, he sailed to the United States in search of education that would equip him to work in Africa. Since he was black, American institutions of higher learning refused to admit him. Turning his mind to the budding Republic of Liberia he emigrated there in January, 1851 with the aid of the New York Colonization Society to become a journalist, a presbyterian minister of religion, diplomat, scholar and above all a Pan-African propagandist.

Blyden served as editor of *Liberia Herald* for one year before he attained the age of twenty and later of *The Negro* launched in Freetown in 1872. A correspondent to the *Lagos Weekly Record*, he was at the time of his death in Sierra Leone (1912) a resident editor of *The African World*, an English periodical. On various occasions he held the office of Commissioner to the Descendants of Africa in the United States and the West Indies, Ministry of the Interior, Secretary of State and Ambassador to London and Paris. As a scholar, Blyden excelled in classics and mathematics. He taught himself Hebrew for he was anxious to read the earliest versions of the Bible especially passages containing references to the African people.

In 1861 he became Professor of Greek and Latin at Liberia College, Monrovia and President of the College twenty years later. He first attracted public attention in England through a

author's friendship with Kwame Nkrumah; Colin Legum, *Pan-Africanism: A Short Political Guide* (New York: Frederick A. Praeger, 1962), p. 20 suggests Togoland; Claude Wauthier, *The Literature and Thought of Modern Africa* (London: Pall Mall Press, 1966), p. 307 prefers Sierra Leone.

letter he wrote to Mr. William E. Gladstone, British Chancellor of Exchequer, in appreciation of his Budget of 1860. Gladstone used to carry this letter in his pocket in order to show it to his friends. It was eventually read in the House of Lords by Lord Brougham with the following comment: "The writer of this letter was engaged in the honourable office of teaching, and his quotations from Latin and Greek showed that he had, as he represented, devoted himself to the study of the ancient as well as the modern languages... A better composed or better reasoned letter was never written."[69]

In recognition of his erudition, social and academic honours flowed to him from all corners of the globe. He was made Fellow of the American Philological Association (1880), Corresponding and Honorary Member of the Society of Sciences and Letters of Bengal (1882), Vice-President of the American Colonization Society (1884), Vice-President of the Africa Society of England as well as an Honorary Member of the highly exclusive Athenaeum Club of London. He was decorated with the Coronation Medal of King Edward VII and Queen Alexandra of Great Britain as well as by the Government of France and Turkey.[70]

More than in scholarship Blyden's fame lies in the sophisticated but articulate manner he presented Pan-African concepts. Himself a victim of colour prejudice, Blyden naturally challenged the racial doctrines about the Negro. Many of his tracts, notably *Hope for Africa*,[71] *The Negro in Ancient History*,[72] *Africa's Service to the World*[73] as well as his address "Study and Race"[74] are brilliant repudiations of

[69] Quoted in Edward W. Blyden, *The African Society and Miss Mary H. Kingsley* (Articles reprinted from the *Sierra Leone Weekly News*, March, April, May and June 1901) introduction by Alice Stopford Green (London, 1901).

[70] L. C. Gwam, "Dr. Edward Wilmot Blyden, M.A., D.D., LL.D., (1832-1912)," Ibadan, Number Fifteen.

[71] *African Repository* (September, 1861), pp. 258-271.

[72] *African Repository* (June, 1869), pp. 161-172; (July, 1869), pp. 193-201.

[73] *African Repository* (October, 1881), pp. 109-125.

[74] *Sierra Leone Weekly News* (27 May, 1893), pp. 2-4.

nineteenth-century racism. He observed that all peoples who had risen from obscurity had had the same opposition of contempt to contend against. And "when our adversaries... pour their indignities, and fasten their disgraceful epithets upon us, let us take comfort in the thought," he urged, "that we are now beginning to enjoy the means which their ancestors were obliged to possess before they could rise from their obscure, ignoble and ignorant condition."[75]

No one in the days of Caesar or Tacitus could have predicted that the savage wildness of the German would give place to the learning and culture the people subsequently exhibited. When Cicero dismissed the Britons as unfit to serve as slaves, who would have dared to suggest, without appearing to insult the intelligence of decent men, that that people would be among the leading powers of the earth? If it was true that there was innate ability in certain races to rise in the scale of civilization, why did the Britons, when Greece and Rome flourished in all their grandeur, remain insignificant and unknown? There abounded tribes in whose veins coursed "the renowned Caucasian blood, sunk to-day in a degradation as deep, and in an ignorance as profound as any tribe in Africa."[76] If civilization was inborn in the Caucasian, every land inhabited by him ought to be in a high state of civilization. Why then were the peasantry of all the European countries so far down in the scale of civilization? Why did Greece, Italy, Portugal, Spain and Turkey which once flourished sadly degenerate? "Why did not their Caucasian nature, if it did not urge them onward to higher attainments, keep them in the same leading position among the nations?"[77]

Demosthenes and Cicero, Caesar and Alexander, saw no serener sky and felt no more genial breeze than their degenerate posterity. The stars remained as beautiful and bright as when Homer and Virgil felt their inspiration. What

[75] *African Repository* (November, 1862), p. 348.
[76] *African Repository* (September, 1861), p. 261.
[77] *ibid.,* p. 263.

then caused the difference? To a large extent, Blyden explained, men were the creatures of the circumstances in which they lived. Very often what they achieved depended more on the surrounding influences than on their personal qualities. The African formed no exception to this universal rule. Between him and the other men, there was not that difference which racists laboured to established. The African was in the rear of the European "not because of any essential difference existing in their nature, but only on account of differing circumstances."[78] The wonder, Blyden contended, was that despite the numerous obstacles being continually thrown on the path of his advancement, the African was not more backward.[79]

Appealing to the Bible and classical writers including Homer, Herodotus, Pindar, and Aeschylus, Blyden endeavoured to show that ancient Africans were held in higher esteem than their contemporaries. Homer who like Herodotus travelled in Egypt made frequent mention of them. So fascinated was he by the fantastic achievements of these people that Homer raised their authors above mortals making them associates of the gods.[80] Jupiter, and sometimes the entire Olympian family, was often made to betake himself to Ethiopia (ile. Africa) to converse with and partake of the hospitality of the "blameless Ethiopians."[81]

To Africa the kings and philosophers of antiquity also resorted either to gaze upon her wonders or gather inspiration from her arts and sciences or to consult the Oracle of Jupiter Ammon. From time immemorial the Ethiopians had been generous helpers. Out of her abundance, ancient Egypt furnished grains to the starving population of Europe. In modern times the "discovery" of the New World without Africa would have been useless for neither the aboriginal

[78] *ibid.*, p. 264.
[79] *ibid.*
[80] *African Repository* (June, 1869), p. 165.
[81] *Iliad*, i, 423; xxiii, 206.

Amerindian nor the European adventurers possessed the physical labour power to exploit the dazzling wealth before them. No history of modern civilization would be complete without a reference to the "black stream of humanity, which has poured into America from the heart of the Soudan."[82]

Nor could it be denied that the material development of England was aided beyond measure by the same black stream. "By means of Negro labor sugar and tobacco were produced; by means of sugar and tobacco British commerce was increased; by means of increased commerce the arts of culture and refinement were developed. The rapid growth and unparalleled prosperity of Lancashire are partly owing to the cotton supply of the Southern States, which could not have arisen to such importance without the labour of the Africans."[83] Contrary to the fulminations of the racists, then, Africans possessed not only an enviable past, though slightly marred by aberrations of barbarism; they had also made immense contributions to the general progress and happiness of mankind. Blyden expressed the hope that European writers would drop their discredited speculations and ridiculous assertions at least now that the Atlantic slave trade had been suppressed and the necessity to deny the humanity as well as the attainments of the Africans no longer existed.[84] Misled by the false theories of racists "superficial teachers in Africa" were trying to Europeanize the African that he might by losing, if possible, his identity "escape the doom which according to their amiable theology hangs over him — a curse which so far as he is concerned never had any existence — a miserable fiction, a wild phantasy of exploded commentators."[85] When "God lets men suffer and gives them to pain and death, it is not the abandoned, it is not the worst or the guiltiest, but the best

82 *African Repository* (October, 1881), p. 114.
83 *ibid.,* pp. 114-115.
84 *From West Africa to Palestine* (Freetown, 1873), p. 106.
85 *Sierra Leone Weekly News* (9 April, 1892), p. 3.

and the purest, whom He often chooses for His work, for they will do it best."[86]

Blyden's admiration of the African past partly led him to take enormous pride in African culture. The phase "African Personality" was first used not by Kwame Nkrumah but by him in a lecture "Study and Race" read before the Young Men's Literary Association of Sierra Leone.[87] Among other things he regretted that there were Africans, especially those trained abroad, who were so unpatriotic as to advise:

> ..."Let us do away with the sentiment of Race. Let us do away with our African personality and be lost, if possible, in another Race." This is as wise or as philosophical as to say, let us do away with gravitation, with heat and cold and sunshine and rain. Of course the Race in which these persons would be absorbed is the dominant race, before which, in cringing self-surrender and ignoble self-suppression they lie in prostrate admiration.[88]

Such admonition was unworthy of any true patriot whose plain duty, according to Blyden, is to defend and cultivate the peculiarity of his race.[89] Africans had been assigned a place in the universe; there was no room for them as something else. Of course he was aware that some Africans and their descendants assumed the disgusting posture of "cringing self-surrender" through fear of offending their European friends who might ostracise them. None the less, he considered it more honourable to be ridiculed for being oneself than applauded for aping foreigners.[90] The African at home he explained:

> needs to be surrounded by influence from abroad, not that he may change his nature, but that he may improve

[86] E. W. Blyden, *The Origin and Purpose of African Colonization* (Washington City, 1883), p. 18.

[87] Printed in *Sierra Leone Weekly News* (27 May, 1893), pp. 2-4.

[88] *ibid., passim.*

[89] *ibid.*

[90] J. Walter Cason, "E. W. Blyden's Contribution to the African Personality," *Cuttington Review* No. 3 (June, 1962).

his capacity. Hereditary qualities are fundamental, not to
be created or replaced by human agencies, but to be
assisted and improved. Nature determines the kind of
tree, environments determine the *quality* and *quantity* of
the fruit. We want the Negro's eye and ear to be trained
by culture that he may see more clearly what he does not
see, and hear more distinctly what he does not hear. We
want him to be surrounded by influence from abroad to
promote the development of his latent powers, bring the
potentiality of his being into practical or actual
operation. He has capacities and aptitudes which the
world needs, but which it will never enjoy until he is
fairly and normally trained. In the music of the universe
each shall give a different sound but necessary to the
grand symphony.[91]

Little wonder he told an annual conference of the
American Colonization Society that the young nation of
Liberia would not be a copy of the United States; she would
discover a method for her own development and it would be
different from that of the Anglo-Saxons.[92]

To prevent the European agencies from destroying the
African cultural heritage, Blyden pressed for the establishment
of a West African university as well as a West African church
to be controlled by Africans. He corresponded with J. Pope
Hennessy, Administrator-in-Chief of the British West African
Settlements, on the issue of a higher institution of learning.[93]
Blyden proposed a curriculum based on the study of the
Greece-Roman classical civilization, mathematics and African
subjects including African languages. Hennessy recommended
the scheme to Lord Kimberley, Secretary of State for the
Colonies. This led to the conversion of Fourah Bay College,
originally founded as a theological institution in the 1820s, to a
university college affiliated to Durham University, England.
In the preface to the second edition of his major work,

[91] *The African Repository* (January, 1879), p. 3-4.

[92] *The Origin and Purpose of African Colonization*, p. 18.

[93] *The West African University* (Freetown, 1872).

Christianity, Islam and the Negro Race, published after the correspondence with Hennessy, Blyden states that the book was meant for Negro youths eager to know the history, character and destiny of their race. His *African Life and Customs*, which appeared four years before he died, further stimulated interest in African traditions.

Like James Johnson, Blyden supported the idea of Africanising Christianity. Following a dispute between the C.M.S. and Samuel Ajayi Crowther, the first Anglican bishop, he called for the formation of an independent church. Such a church, he insisted, must be African, not a copy of the Anglican Church, adding that the "great incubus upon our development has been our unreasoning imitation."[94] In the same breath he warned against the danger of moving to the opposite extreme of shunning anything foreign merely because it is foreign. There were many good things in other peoples' customs; these, Africans should isolate and cherish.

Blyden's demand was among the reasons why the United Native African Church was set up in Lagos in 1891. Defending "native Christianity" at the Congress on Africa held in Atlanta (United States) four years later, Orishatuke Faduma maintained that there was no absolute connection between spiritual salvation and European usages.

Hence he discarded his foreign name, William James Davies, just as Mojola Agbebi (formerly D. B. Vincent) and the Gold Coaster S. R. B. Attoh Ahuma (formerly S. R. B. Solomon) had done. This was why Faduma demanded at the Congress "a Christian life and thought expressed in Africa, not after the manner of a Frenchman, an American, or an Englishman but assimilated to Africa."[95] It was also for this reason that Blyden sometimes preferred Islam to Christianity.

[94] For details see J. B. Webster, *op. cit.* and J. F. Ade Ajayi, *Christian Missions in Nigeria* (London: Longmans, 1965); Edward W. Blyden, *The Return of the Exiles and the West African Church* (London, 1891), pp. 25-32.

[95] J. W. E. Bowen, ed., *Africa and the American Negro: Addresses and Proceedings of the Congress on Africa* (Atlanta, 1896), pp. 25-136, *passim.*

Islam, he often remarked, "possessed inherent elements of strength suited to the African in his environment, his racial character and traditions."[96]

Finally, Edward Blyden also shared the hope of a grand African future. He conceded that suffering had been a conspicuous feature of the recent history of the African world. "But the future," he predicted confidently, "will have a different story to tell. The Cross precedes the Crown."[97] To quicken the regeneration of the continent Blyden advocated the establishment of what he called "an African Nationality." In common with most of his contemporaries he entertained no doubt that the African diaspora would ever become first class citizens in the New World. The whites had for a long time had the upper hand. The educational institutions, banks, ships and the media of propaganda belonged to them. The laws were framed and enforced by them. They also controlled the security forces. Given such an impregnable position it was impossible, so it seemed to Blyden, to dislodge them.

For him the only realistic solution was to be found in the creation of an African nationality. Africa's wealth was being appropriated by outsiders while her own sons, its legitimate owners, languished in poverty abroad. If the expertise these sons were wasting in trifling occupations were thrown into the ancestral continent the result would be a strong and respectable African power. For three hundred years, he recalled, their skill and industry had been mainly responsible for the development of the western hemisphere while in Africa herself there was still no country powerful enough to check the continual threat from European nations to the sovereignty of Haiti and Liberia. As long as Africans remained disunited, he warned, they must expect to suffer from the whims and

[96] *West Africa* (November, 1900), p. 225.
[97] *Sierra Leone Weekly News* (27 May, 1893), p. 3.

caprices of other peoples. "We need some African power," he urged:

> some great centre of the race where our physical, pecuniary and intellectual strength may be collected. We need some spot whence such an influence may go forth in behalf of the race as shall be felt by the nations. We are now so scattered and divided that we can do nothing. The imposition begun last year (1861) by a foreign power upon Haiti, and which is still persisted in, fills every black man who has heard of it with indignation, but we are not strong enough to speak out effectually for that land. When the same power attempted an outrage upon the Liberians, there was no African power strong enough to interpose. So long as we remain thus divided, we may expect impositions. So long as we live simply by the sufference of the nations, we must expect to be subject to their caprices... We must build up negro states; we must establish and maintain the various institutions; we must make and administer laws, erect and preserve churches, and support the worship of God; we must have governments; we must have legislation of our own; we must build ships and navigate them; we must ply the trades, instruct the schools, control the press, and thus aid in shaping the opinions and guiding the destinies of mankind.[98]

Implicit in Blyden's African nationality is complete autonomy in political, economic and religious affairs. His proposals anticipated much that first Marcus Garvey and later Kwame Nkrumah later advocated in the twentieth century. Perhaps it is not far-fetched to see in the proposals the thin edge of the concept of Black Power as well as the idea of an Organization for African Unity backed by a high command.

It was partly in response to Blyden's call that many an exile returned to the fatherland in general and Liberia in particular

[98] *Liberia's Offering* (New York, 1862), pp. 74-76.

during the nineteenth century. This motive is abundantly illustrated by an appeal issued in 1893 by the Afro-American colonists of Maryland County in connexion with a boundary dispute between Liberia and France. "We are not foreigners," they boasted,

> we are Africans and this is Africa. Such being the case we have certain natural rights — God-given rights — to this territory which no foreigner can have. We should have room enough, not only for our present population, but also to afford a home for our brethren in exile who may wish to return to their fatherland and help to build up this Negro nationality.[99]

The idea of a Negro nationality or an African nationality received further extension and elaboration at the hands of Timothy Thomas Fortune (1856-1928), an Afro-American publicist. Though at first he opposed the back-to-Africa campaign he became at the end of his life editor of Garveyite publications. Like Reverend James Johnson he believed that European intervention in Africa would ultimately lead to solidarity and unification of the continent.

While James Johnson saw the Native Pastorate set up by the C.M.S. in Sierra Leone as the embryo of a continental African church, the nucleus of a future African existence, Timothy Fortune foretold that the proliferation of African nationalities arising from the European partition would culminate in some sort of a united states of Africa. Speaking at the Atlanta Congress of Africa of 1895 he insisted that Africans

> will be forced into this federation in self defence, as the American colonists were. History repeats itself. The nationalization of the African confederation which is a

---

[99] Quoted in John D. Hargreaves, "Liberia: The Price of Independence," *Odu* (A Journal of West African Studies), New Series, No. 6 (October, 1971), p. 14.

foregone conclusion from the facts in the case, will be the first step toward bringing the whole continent under one system of government.... It is written in the Holy Book that Ethiopia shall stretch forth her hand to God. Is it in the power of men to make of no effect the divine prophecy? Perish the thought. There shall yet be evolved out of the conflicting race elements on the continent of Africa a civilization whose glory and whose splendour and whose strength shall eclipse all others that now are, or that have gone before.[100]

Finally we must cast a glance at the Haitian propagandist, scholar and diplomat, Benito Sylvain (1868-1915). He is important not because of any novel ideas he propounded — his ideas were essentially those of his contemporaries — but because he is an interesting personality who deserves to be better known. In his book, *Du Sort des Indigenes dans les Colonies d'exploitation* (Paris, 1901), his titles are given as *Officier de la Marine Haitienne, stagiaire de la Marine Francaise, Aide de camp de Sa Majeste l'Empereur d'Ethiopie, Docteur en Droit de la Faculte de Paris, Delegue general de L'Association Pan-Africaine.* Other publications by him include *L'Etoile Africaine: bulletin de l'Oeuvre du relevement social des noirs,* the first number of which appeared in 1906, and *L'oeuvre de la Regeneration africaine.*

Born on 21 March, 1868 at Port-de-Paix (northwest Haiti), Sylvain took courses in naval studies at College Stanislas and later at L'Ecole Saint Charles, Saint Brienne in France. Because of an 1887 edict forbidding foreigners to enter the French Naval Academy, he abandoned science in favour of philosophy for which he gained a degree after a short period of intensive study. He attained similar distinction in journalism repudiating attacks against the African race penned by the Frenchman M. Gaston Jollivet in *Le Matin* in 1888. The next

[100] "The Nationalization of Africa," in J. W. E. Bowen, ed., *Africa and the American Negro,* pp. 199-204.

year Benito Sylvain served as Secretary to the Haitian Delegation in London. On his return to France in 1890 he challenged M. Charles Canivet who had written a series of anti-African articles in *Le Soleil.*

Sylvain's replies were highly commended as a brilliant vindication of his maligned brethren and as an adequate refutation of those whom Benito Sylvain himself nick-named *"aristocrates de la peau."* As a delegate to the Brussels Anti-Slavery Convention of Paril 1891, he read a paper, "L'Evolution De La Race Noire," besprinkled with sentiment of Pan-African dimension. As the Afro-American agitator Rev. James Theodore Holly had argued thirty-four years earlier, Sylvain maintained that the Haitian Revolution conclusively demonstrated the equality of the black and white races when the odds were even. Sylvain conceded the relative backwardness of Africa vis-a-vis Europe but he maintained that this situation would not continue forever. From Africa shall radiate for the benefit of all humanity that sublime precept: Love your neighbour as yourself. Anticipating Blyden's lecture "Study and Race," Benito Sylvain assured his audience that when Africa's hour of glory arrived, Africans would not abuse the opportunity to revenge themselves by suppressing less privileged peoples. Instead, Africans would endeavour to belie the monstrous aphorism: *homo homini lupus.* Referring to the historic Scramble for Africa, he regretted that whenever Europeans thought about Africa it was to carve out portions of that continent for themselves with the result that international conferences had come to have no other purpose than to demarcate boundaries of territories the great powers had awarded themselves.

Benito Sylvain stands out as one of the last noteworthy exponents of Pan-African ideas. From 1893 onwards, politically conscious men of African blood began to summon Pan-African conferences and to organise themselves in pressure groups thus transforming Pan-African ideas into a movement.

CHAPTER 2

FROM IDEA TO MOVEMENT

The Chicago Congress on Africa of 1893 may be taken as the beginning of Pan-Africanism as a movement. W. E. B. DuBois' assertion that the Pan-African meeting summoned in London in 1900 put the word "Pan-African" in the dictionaries for the first time is largely responsible for the orthodox view that that gathering was the first Pan-African convocation ever. Actually the Chicago Congress on Africa of which our authorities appear to be unaware has a better claim. Opened on 14 August, 1893, it lasted for a whole week. Among the participants were Africans and persons of African descent in the New World notably Alexander Crummell; Yakub Pasha, presumably an Egyptian; Bishop Henry Turner, an ardent advocate of the back-to-Africa movement and founder of the African Methodist Episcopal churches in Sierra Leone and Liberia; Bishop Alexander Walters of the African Methodist Episcopal Zion Church who seven years later would chair the London Congress and the Afro-American, Frederick Perry Noble, secretary to the conference.[1] The American Colonization Society was represented by its secretary, Mr. J. Ormond Wilson, a retired educator. Other whites present included European scientists, explorers and missionaries most of whom had come to Chicago primarily for the World Columbian Exhibition held there that summer.

Edward Blyden and Booker T. Washington promised

---

[1] Frederick P. Noble, *The Chicago Congress on Africa, 1894,* a report in the *Schomburg Collection*, New York City Library, pp. 280-81.

papers; that of Reverend James Johnson was read by proxy. In all, a hundred papers were given, half of them by members of "the African race."[2] Some of the topics debated were "The Africa in America," "Liberia as a Factor in the Progress of the Negro Race" contributed by J. Ormond Wilson and "What do American Negroes Owe To Their Kin Beyond the Sea."[3] Turner seized the opportunity to urge African exiles to return to the fatherland. A few months before the Congress he had warned that French encroachments on Liberia's frontier and the general "increase of whites all along since I last visited Africa" might culminate in the capture of the only spot (besides Haiti and Abyssinia) "upon the face of the globe [where] the black man can ever hope to be in power and demonstrate the ability of self-government."[4]

Commenting on the Congress, the *Advance,* a Chicago newspaper, stated: "This great congress was unquestionably one of the most notable convocations of recent years in any country. We have had pan-Presbyterian, pan-Methodist, Pan-Anglican, pan-missionary and pan-Congregational councils... But none signified more than this pan-African conference."[5]

Anti-European feeling was also voiced at another Congress on Africa called this time in Atlanta (Georgia, U.S.A) in December, 1895 under the auspices of the Steward Missionary Foundation for Africa of Gammon Theological Seminary. Among those in attendance was the Afro-American John Henry Smyth (1844-1908), a former United States Minister Resident and Consul General to Liberia who was honoured by President Richard W. Johnson of Liberia with the title "Knight Commander of the Liberian Order of African Redemption."

[2] *ibid.,* p. 314.

[3] Edwin S. Redkey, *Black Exodus, Black Nationalist and Back-to-Africa Movements, 1890-1910* (Hartford, Conn.: Yale University Press, 1969), pp. 142, 182.

[4] Quoted in *ibid.,* p. 180. For details on Turner's back-to-Africa campaign see Chaps. 2 and 8.

[5] Frederick P. Noble, *The Chicago Congress on Africa*, p. 313.

In his address, "The African in Africa and the African in America," Smyth attributed the appalling conditions in Africa to the activities of the European adventurers. "European contact," he lamented, "has brought in its train not merely the sacrifice, amid unspeakable horrors, of the lives and liberties of twenty million Negroes for the American market alone, but political disintegration, social anarchy, moral and physical debasement."[6]

It is partly against the background of this growing anti-colonial sentiment among the African diaspora that the African Association was launched in England on 24 September, 1897 mainly through the efforts of Henry Sylvester Williams, an Afro-West Indian Barrister from Trinidad.[7] As the centre of wide imperial and missionary interests, Great Britain was a natural focus for a protest movement. The organization aimed

> to encourage a feeling of unity; to facilitate friendly intercourse among Africans in general; to promote and protect the interest of all subjects claiming African descent, wholly or in part, in British Colonies and other places especially in Africa, by circulating accurate information on all subjects affecting their rights and privileges as subjects of the British Empire, and by direct appeals to the Imperial and local Governments.[8]

The founders of the African Association were convinced that the time had come when the voice of black men should be heard independently in their own affairs and that this could be best achieved by a pressure group with headquarters in London, the metropolitan capital.[9] Three patrons served it. They were J. Otonba Payne, an ex-registrar of the Supreme

---

6 Smyth's paper is printed in J. W. E. Bowen, ed., *Africa and the American Negro* (Atlanta, 1896).

7 *The Lagos Standard* (27 July, 1898), p. 2; *The Pan-African,* Vol. 1, No. 1 (October, 1901), p. 4.

8 *The Lagos Standard* (27 July, 1898), p. 2.

9 *The Gold Coast Chronicle* (Accra) (12 August, 1898), p. 3.

Court of Lagos; Dr. Mojola Agbebi, Pastor of the United African Church, Lagos and a lawyer, D. Augustus Straker probably from the West Indies. The officers were: Reverend H. Mason Joseph, a Master of Arts from Antigua (president); H. Sylvester Williams (honorary secretary); Moses Da Rocha of Lagos (assistant secretary) and John Otonba Augustus Payne, the patron (treasurer).[10] Meetings of the organization took place at 139 Palace Chambers, Westminister, S.W.[11]

In his autobiography Bishop Alexander Walters gives the credit of conceiving the idea of summoning the London Congress to Sylvester Williams.[12] But in a letter of 8 June, 1899 to Booker T. Washington, Williams himself states that he had been "authorised by the Officers and Committee of Our Association to bring to your notice the proposed conference which you will notice in the enclosed Circular."[13] Washington was also requested to "make this known as widely as is possible."[14]

A similar letter was sent to Benito Sylvain.[15] By June, 1900 a Pan-African Conference Committee had been created with the following officers: Reverend H. Mason Joseph (chairman), Reverend Thos. L. Johnson (vice-chairman), H. Sylvester Williams (general secretary), R. E. Phipps (secretary for West Indies), Henry Plange (secretary for West Africa), F. J. Peregrino (secretary for South Africa) and Hector Macpherson (treasurer).[16]

What must now be regarded as the Second Pan-African congregation eventually took place from 23 to 25 July, 1900

[10] Henry Sylvester Williams to Booker T. Washington, 8 June, 1899 (in *Booker T. Washington Papers*, Principal's Office Correspondence, 1899, Container No. 164, Library of Congress).

[11] *ibid.*

[12] *My Life and Work* (New York, 1917), p. 253.

[13] *Booker T. Washington Papers*, Principal's Office Correspondence, 1899, Container No. 164.

[14] *ibid.*

[15] H. Sylvester Williams to Booker T. Washington, 17 July, 1899, *ibid.*

[16] H. Sylvester Williams to Booker T. Washington, 1 June, 1900, Booker T. Washington Papers, Principal's Office Correspondence, 1900, Container No. 187.

under the chairmanship of Alexander Walters in the West-minister Town Hall. The objects of the meeting were:

> First, to bring into closer touch with each other the peoples of African descent throughout the world; second to inaugurate plans to bring about a more friendly relation between the Caucasian and African races; third, to start a movement looking forward to the securing to all African races living in civilized countries their full rights and to promote their business interests.[17]

Altogether about thirty-two delegates from various sections of the African world attended — men, women and university students whose occupations or courses of study would normally place them in the middle class. Among the Afro-American contingent may be mentioned Mrs. Annie J. Cooper of the High School, Washington D.C.; Miss Anna H. Jones, a Master of Arts from Missouri and DuBois. Haiti was represented by Bishop J. F. Holly. Other notable Afro-West Indians included Reverend H. Mason Joseph; R. E. Phipps, another Trinidadian barrister; G. L. Christian of Dominica and J. E. Quinlan, a land surveyor from St. Lucia.

From Africa came about ten representatives, the most prominent being J. Otonba Payne; James Johnson; the Sierra Leonean Councillor G. W. Dove; A. Ribero, a Gold Coast barrister; F. R. S. Johnson, formerly Liberia's attorney-general, and Benito Sylvain, *Aide-de-camp* to Emperor Menelik II of Abyssinia.

The Afro-West Indian Literary Society of Edinburgh was represented by Mr. Meyer, a West Indian medical student at Edinburgh University and R. Akinwande Savage, a medical doctor from Lagos. The latter subsequently became an editor of the influential newspaper *The Gold Coast Leader* and at the end of the Great War helped J. Casely Hayford to form the National congress of British West Africa. Also in attendance were several exiles resident in England. They included John

---

[17] Alexander Walters, *My Life and Works*, p. 253.

Alcindor, a Trinidadian medical practitioner trained at the University of Edinburgh, Reverend Henry Smith about whom not much is known and H. Sylvester Williams.

Benito Sylvain and F. R. S. Johnson were made vice-chairmen of the conference.[18] Some of the sessions were attended by three English Africophils namely: Bishop Colenso of South Africa fame; Dr. R. J. Colenso, a relation of the bishop and Dr. G. B. Clark, a Liberal Member of Parliament.[19] Conspicuously absent was the veteran Pan-African theorist Edward Blyden but some of his ideas on the African past and arguments for race individuality were echoed in the course of the deliberations.

The address of welcome was delivered by Dr. Creighton, the Lord Bishop of London. He assured the delegates that they enjoyed the sympathy and support of men of goodwill throughout the realm expressing the hope that similar congresses would take place in the future. Alexander Walters opened the meeting with a paper entitled "The Trials and Achievements of the Coloured Race in America."[20] He set out the disabilities suffered by the Negroes there tracing their long struggle for the attainment of social, economic and political liberties enjoyed by their white counterparts. Every form of violence and defamation was being used by white men to prevent the advancement of the coloured population. Concluding, Walters explained that the purpose of the conference was "to organise, to better their condition, and to lay their

---

[18] The rest of the representatives as listed by Alexander Alters *ibid.,* pp. 253-54 are: C. W. French (St. Kitts), S. Coleridge Taylor (London), Pulcherie Pierre (Trinidad), Chaplain B. W. Arnett (Illinois), Prof. L. L. Love (Washington D.C.), J. Buckle (London), Hon. Henry F. Downing (U.S.A. ex-Consul, Loando, W. A.), T. J. Calloway (Washington D.C.) Rev. Henry B. Brown (Lower Canada), Counsellor Chas. P. Lee (New York) J. F. Loudin (London), A. R. Hamilton (Jamaica), Miss Barrier (Washington D.C.), Mrs J. F. Loudin (London) and Miss Ada Harris (Indiana).

[19] *The Manchester Guardian* (25 July, 1900), p. 7; *The Times* (London), (25 July, 1900), p. 15

[20] *The Daily News* (London) (24 July, 1900), p. 6.

claims before the white races, from whom they desired respect and recognition given by Benito Sylvain."[21]

In the evening the chief item was a paper, "The Necessary Concord to Be Established Between the Native Races and European Colonists."[22] The African race, he said, had successfully proved its manhood. A race which in the face of formidable obstacles blocking its path of advancement had produced such men as Toussaint L'Ouverture, Alexander Dumas, Pushkin and Emperor Menelik II deserved the respect of the rest of humanity. Britain was blamed for conniving at the abuses created by the concession systems and therefore held responsible for the anti-liberal reaction characteristic of colonial policy in the preceding fifteen years. Before many years would pass the rights of the indigenous inhabitants must be recognised by every imperial power. In the meantime, he urged the metropolitan governments to end the practice of treating their subjects as serfs maintaining that no human power could stop the Africans in their social and political development.[23]

The next day, the congress debated the topic "The Progress of Our People in the Light of Current History." Opening it, F. R. S. Johnson gave a glowing but exaggerated account of the achievements of the Afro-American colonists in Liberia. In a speech more sensational than Johnson's claims and which was undisguised counter-racism, John E. Quinlan asserted that there was scientific evidence in support of the superiority of blacks over whites both in "skin and skull."[24]

Another topic discussed during the morning sessions was "Africa, the Sphinx of History in the Light of Unsolved Problems." The first speaker on this issue was an Afro-American student, Mr. M. D. Tobias who summed up civilization as a system under which blacks slaved for the whites.[25]

21 *ibid.*
22 *The Manchester Guardian* (24 July, 1900), p. 8.
23 *The Times* (London) (24 July, 1900), p. 7.
24 *The Manchester Guardian* (25 July, 1900), p. 7.
25 *The Daily News* (London) (25 July, 1900), p. 3.

The debate was continued in the evening when two further papers were read. One with the title "Some Startling Historical Facts of the History of the Negro" was contributed by Reverend H. Smith. He dismissed as racist the theory that the black man descended from apes and monkeys. The idea is in fact not racist being part of the evolutionary doctrine of the time that all *homo sapiens* are so descended. Smith went on to claim with obvious exaggeration and oversimplification that the great and the marvellous in ancient Egyptian civilization owed its stimulus and impetus to the neighbouring southern city-states now known as Sudan, Ethiopia and Nubia. "Just as the River Nile," he proceeded, "had its source and rise in Ethiopia and its ebb and flow in Egypt, so all that was great and distinguished — architecturally, religiously, and in the sense of civilization — had its rise in the lower country."[26] Contrary to popular impression, the Negro race had a grand and noble past and he hoped that it would have a yet grander and nobler future.[27] Smith recalled that Homer in the *Iliad* sang of these Africans beyond Egypt as favourites of the gods. The other paper "A Plea for Race Individuality" was given by Miss Anna H. Jones. She contended that the Negro's nature was artistic and religious. This artistic and spiritual disposition she pleaded must not be allowed to be soiled by the ephemeral materialistic civilization of the Anglo-Saxon.[28]

Part of the session of the third and last day of the meeting was devoted to a scrutiny of the colonial policies. Both G. J. Christian and Henry Sylvester Williams condemned the native policies in South Africa and the Rhodesias and insisted on reforms.[29] The rest of the session considered and adopted a report from a committee providing for the formation of a permanent Pan-African Association apparently to replace the African Association. The objects of the new organisation were:

[26] *The Manchester Guardian* (25 July, 1900), p. 7.
[27] *ibid.*
[28] *ibid.*
[29] *The Manchester Guardian* (26 July, 1900), p. 8.

1. to secure civil and political rights for African and their descendants throughout the world:
2. to encourage friendly relations between the Caucasian and African races;
3. to encourage African peoples everywhere in educational, industrial, and commercial enterprise;
4. to approach Governments and influence legislation in the interests of the black races; and;
5. To ameliorate the condition of the oppressed Negro in Africa, America, the British Empire, and other parts of the world.[30]

A central body or secretariat located at 61-62 Chancery Lane, London was set up. Officers were elected for a term of two years as follows: Bishop Alexander Walters (president), Henry Sylvester Williams (general secretary) and Dr. R. J. Colenso (general treasurer).[31] An executive committee of four men and two women was elected to help the secretariat. Three of the members were Miss Annie J. Cooper; the musician S. Coleridge Taylor and J. R. Archer, a prominent West Indian resident in London.[32] Emperor Menelik II and the Presidents of Haiti and Liberia were made honorary members of the Pan-African Association.[33] There were provisions for the establishment of branches in different parts of Africa, the Caribbean, and United States which were to be self-governing.[34] Among the officers elected for the branches were Benito Sylvain (Abyssinia), J. Otonba Payne and N. W. Holm (Lagos), Edwin Vin Loch (Natal), J. W. Williams, and A. Lewis (Sierra Leone) and W. E. B. DuBois (United States).[35] The vacancies for Canada, Trinidad, Gold Coast, Cape Town, Orange River Colony, Transvaal and Rhodesia could not be filled during the congress.[36] The members of the branches were

[30] *The Daily News* (London) (26 July, 1900), p. 6.
[31] *ibid.* Alexander Walters, *My Life and Work,* p. 260.
[32] *ibid.*
[33] *The Daily News* (London) (26 July, 1900), p. 6.
[34] *The Manchester Guardian* (26 July, 1900), p. 8.
[35] Imanuel Geiss, "Notes on the Development of Pan-Africanism," *Journal of the Historical Society of Nigeria* Vol. III, No. 4 (June, 1967), p. 726.
[36] *ibid.*

required to pay a shilling a year to meet local expenses and each member four shillings annually to the secretariat in England.[37] A conference of the Association would be called every two years; accordingly, it was decided that the next meeting would take place in 1902 in the United States and another in Haiti in 1904.[38]

The gathering then adopted a draft statement, "To The Nations Of The World," submitted by DuBois on behalf of a sub-committee and which was despatched to sovereigns in whose territories persons of African origin might be found.[39] The problem of the twentieth century was prophetically recognised as the problem of the colour line, the problem as to how far differences of races, as manifested in skin colour and the texture of the hair, were going to be used as criteria for denying over half the population of the globe the right of sharing to their utmost ability, the blessings of modern civilization. It was conceded that the darker races of the time lagged behind their European counterpart. "This has not, however, always been the case in the past, and certainly the world's history, both ancient and modern, has given many instances of no despicable ability and capacity among the blackest races of men."[40]

Reacting against the Yellow Peril phantasy of the day, the Congress pointed out that the so-called coloured peoples were bound to exercise tremendous influence upon the world by virtue of their numerical superiority. If blacks and the other backward peoples were given the opportunity for education and self-government, this influence would be channelled along lines beneficial to all mankind. "But if, by reason of carelessness, prejudice, greed and injustice, the black world is to be exploited and ravished and degraded, the results must be deplorable, if not fatal, not simply to them but to the high

---

[37] *The Manchester Guardian* (26 July, 1900). p. 8.

[38] *The Times* (London) (26 July, 1900), p. 11.

[39] Alexander Walters, *My Life and Works,* pp. 257-260.

[40] *ibid.,* p. 258.

ideals of justice, freedom, and culture which a thousand years of Christian civilization have held before Europe."[41]

The Congress then suggested ways and means of achieving these high ideals of civilization. Discrimination on grounds of race and colour must cease. The aspirations and interests of Africans must not be subordinated to the greed for gold, "their liberties taken away, their family life debauched, their just aspirations repressed, and avenues of advancement and culture taken from them."[42] Missionary enterprise must no longer be used as a screen to hide "the ruthless economic exploitation and political downfall of less developed nations, whose chief fault has been reliance on the plighted faith of the Christian Church."[43] Great Britain was invited to complete the noble work of Wilberforce, Clarkson, Buxton, Sharp, Livingstone and Bishop Colenso by granting as soon as practicable the right of responsible government to her colonies in Africa and the Caribbean. The conscience of the United States was challenged to "rise and rebuke all dishonesty and unrighteous oppression toward the American Negro, and grant to him the right of franchise, security of person and property, and generous recognition of the great work he has accomplished in a generation toward raising nine millions of human beings from slavery to manhood."[44] France and Germany were reminded that the true worth of imperial dependencies "lies in their prosperity and progress, and that justice, impartial alike to black and white, is the first element of prosperity." The Congo Free State should become "a great central Negro State of the world" (i.e. an African nationality) whose prosperity should be measured not in terms of cash and commerce, but in the happiness and genuine advancement of its inhabitants.

Finally, the Congress made an appeal to the nations of the world on the one hand and to persons of African extraction on

[41] *ibid.*
[42] *ibid.*, p. 259.
[43] *ibid.*
[44] *ibid.*

the other. The Great Powers were requested to respect the integrity and autonomous status of Abyssinia, Haiti and Liberia. At the same time the inhabitants of these countries as well as the African diaspora were exhorted to "strive ceaselessly, and fight bravely that they may prove to the world their incontestable right to be counted among the great brotherhood of mankind."[45] A separate memorial protesting against the condition of Her Majesty's subjects in the British Empire including South Africa was sent to Queen Victoria. The British Secretary for the Colonies in a reply assured "the members of the Pan-African Conference that, in settling the lines on which the administration of the conquered territories is to be conducted, Her Majesty's Government will not overlook the interests and welfare of the native races."[46] He also stated that a copy of the memorial had been communicated to the High Commissioner for South Africa.

As an attempt to institutionalise Pan-Africanism the Pan-African Association had great symbolic value and therefore was of considerable historial significance. But the achievements of the organisation itself were short-lived. Its immediate achievement seems to be the journal, *The Pan-African,* launched in October, 1901 with the motto: Light and Liberty. Edited by Sylvester Williams, it was a monthly intended to disseminate information concerning the interests of the peoples of the African world. Though the journal promised to feature the progress and culture of the African world in subsequent issues, it did not survive the maiden number.

Earlier in March the same year Williams had travelled to the West Indies to involve his own people in the work of the Pan-African Association. A meeting was held towards the end of that month in St. George's School, Kingston (Jamaica) with the aim of starting a local branch there.[47] During his absence

---

[45] *ibid.,* pp. 259-260.
[46] *ibid.,* p. 257.
[47] *The Pan-African* (October, 1901), pp. 2-3.

from England some of his colleagues alleged there were no funds and dissolved the Pan-African Association. As a result of this arbitary action Alexander Walters and Sylvester Williams hurried to London and on 13 September announced the continuation of the organisation. The following were appointed members of the executive committee in replacement of those considered to have resigned: Bishop Small from Pennsylvania, Reverend Henry Smith, J. Otonba Payne, the South African Tengo Jabavu, Lieutenant Lazare of Trinidad and the medical practitioner, Dr. R. N. Love who was born in Nassau (Bahamas) and educated in England and on the Continent but spent many years in Jamaica fighting for the uplift of the black masses.[48] Williams was re-elected general secretary until the next congress met in 1902. The proposed conference never took place and when Sylvester Williams returned to the Caribbean the Pan-African Association lapsed into obscurity.

By including colonial reforms in their resolutions the London Congress implicitly accepted the new order of European domination as a *fait accompli*. With the collapse of the Pan-African Association individuals assumed the task of keeping Pan-African ideals alive and airing colonial grievances. During the ensuing decade the need to preserve African traditions became an obsession. Seizing the opportunity offered by the death of Miss Mary Kingsley, Blyden further elaborated the concept of the African Personality in a series of articles written for the Sierra Leone *Weekly News.* Intended as a tribute to her courageous defence of the African way of life they were subsequently reprinted in London as a pamphlet under the title: *The African Society and Miss Mary H. Kingsley.*[49] To her the African was a different kind of being from whitemen; his intelligence might even be found to be superior to theirs. But it was a different kind of intelligence

---

[48] *ibid.*
[49] See her **books** *Travels in West Africa* (London, 1897) and *West Africa Studies* (London, 1897).

incapable of moving along European lines of thought. Because of this difference it was wrong to regard Africa society as a childish groping towards the European model. "On the contrary, African religion, African morality and society were natural and proper expressions of African personality, and to try to "improve" them would produce only bastardization, corruption, and degradation."[50] No race, as a race, could make progress except along its own line of development.[51] Customs usually sneered at in Europe as a welter of cruelty, cannibalism and barbarism she examined with sympathy. She rebuked the missionaries severely for attempting to empty the African mind of its content and refill it with Christian dogma which tends to create more problems than it solved. In her last letter written on her way to South Africa and addressed to a Liberian newspaper, *The New Africa,* she complained that she had had to stand alone for two years fighting for Africa's freedom and institutions while Africans equally well and better educated in English culture had been prattling about religious matters to a pack of people who did not care about Christianity at all.[52] Africans were exhorted to defend their institutions, to refute the stay-at-home politicians who thought that Africans were all awful savages or silly children to be dealt with only on a reformatory penitentiary line, to combat the false theories of missionaries, officials and stray travellers "who for their own

[50] John E. Flint, "Miss Mary Kingsley — A Reassessment," *Journal of African History* Vol. IV, No. 1 (1963), p. 100. Flint warns that to treat her theories on a purely philosophical level is to miss their significance and argues that despite her claims, the African was not the focal-point of her thinking. "Mary Kingsley," Flint goes on, "was the intellectual and philosophic spokeswoman for the British traders to West Africa. She thought of herself as possessed of a mission to urge their views and defend their interests, resist attacks upon them, and undermine the influence of their enemies. Every argument she put forward, though usually developed logically from an analysis of African society and its needs, was directed to these ends." (p. 96)

[51] W. Blyden, *The African Society and Miss Mary H. Kingsley* (London, 1901), p. 9.

[52] Miss Kingsley's letter was also published in the *Lagos Weekly Record* (29 September, 1900), pp. 4-5.

aggrandisement exaggerate the difficulties and dangers with which they have to deal."[53]

All this Blyden recalled with great emotion. In an address delivered before the Africa Society in 1903, Blyden in answer to Miss Kingsley's strictures on the educated African maintained that if an African trained on European lines was unable or unwilling to teach the outside world something of the institutions and inner feelings of his people, "if he cannot make his friends feel the force of his racial character and sympathise with his racial aspiration, then it is evident that his education has been sadly defective, that his training by aliens has done but little for him — that his teachers have surely missed their aim and wasted their time."[54]

At this time too, Mojola Agbebi gave a sermon that won the admiration of Edward Blyden and other prominent persons of African descent in the New World. The occasion was the celebration of the first anniversary of the African Church. Under the guise of exposing the defects of the version of Christianity being offered to Africans, Agbebi drew attention to the discrepancy between the words and deeds of the imperialists. What did one think, he asked, of a "religion which points with one finger to the skies, bidding you, lay up for yourselves treasures in heaven, and while you are looking up grasps all your worldly goods with the other hand, seizes your ancestral lands, levels your forests, and places your patrimony under inexplicable legislation."[55]

With the same breath he defended the African way of life. Hymnals were unnecessary for the propagation of the Christian faith. A hymn which induced solemnity in St. Paul's

---

[53] E. W. Blyden, *The African Society and Miss Mary H. Kingsley,* p. 7.

[54] Edward W. Blyden, *African Life and Customs* (London: African Publication Society, 1908), p. 16 (page reference to 1969 edition).

[55] *Inaugural Sermon Delivered at the Celebration of the First Anniversary of the "African Church,"* Lagos, West Africa, December 21, 1902. There is a copy in the *Schomburg Collection,* New York City Public Library.

Cathedral, England might merely excite disgust in a church among the Kru of Liberia. The fact that every one calls barbarian what is not his own usage reinforced his conviction that English hymns were actually unsuited to African aspirations; hence he thought it undesirable that Africans should dance to foreign music in their social festivities, sing to foreign music in their churches, march to foreign music in their funerals and use foreign models to cultivate their musical talents.[56] Prayer books, harmonium dedications, pew constructions, surpliced choir, the white man's style, the white man's name, the white man's dress, all he dismissed as superfluities. For him the proper vehicle of thought of any country was to be found in its vernacular dialect. Africans must therefore cultivate an effective use of their mother tongue(s). Was not the grace bestowed on the day of Pentecost considered marvellous because every man heard in his native language the wonderful works of God?

The publication of Mojola Agbebi's sermon in the Sierra Leone *Weekly News* for 14 March, 1903 provoked widespread comment. "This is the first time," exclaimed Blyden, "I have known of a native African, racy of his soil, inbued with European culture, uttering views so radically different from the course of his training, but intrinsically African and so valuable for the guidance of his people."[57] The Afro-American journalist, John Edward Bruce (1856-1923), who as a filing clerk in the 1880s first met Blyden in the rooms of the American Colonization Society, Washington, D.C., was no less impressed. Considering the sermon worthy of wider notice than it was likely to receive in the West African press, he republished it in the United States. In a congratulatory letter to Agbebi he wrote:

> I thank you with all my heart, dear good sir, and wish it were possible for me to shake your hand and tell you how

[56] *ibid.,* p. 7.
[57] Blyden to Mojola Agbebi. Printed in *ibid.,* pp. 17-20.

proud I am of one, who is unquestionably an honour to
the African Church and the African race.... I am black all
over, and am as proud of my beautiful black skin, and
that of my forbears, as the *blackest* man in Africa.[58]

The cult of the African Personality reached its zenith in
Edward Blyden's series of articles on "African Life and
Customs" in the Sierra Leone *Weekly News* from where they
were reprinted in London in 1908 in book form under the same
title. The articles represent a passionate analysis of the social,
economic and political arrangements evolved by the un-
Europeanised African and under which he had lived and
thrived from generation to generation. Under the African
socio-economic system "All work for each, and each works for
all."[59] This communistic or socialistic order was not the result
of an accident. Born of centuries of experience and the
outcome of philosophical and faultless logic, its idea among all
the ethnic groups was enshrined in proverbs. "Among the
Veys, for example, a proverb runs thus, 'What belongs to *me* is
destroyable by water or fire; what belongs to *us* is destroyable
neither by water nor fire.' Again: 'What is *mine* goes; what is
ours abides.'"[60]

Consequently the surplus wealth accumulated under the
native system by co-operative labour was regularly and in the
most orderly manner shared among all concerned.[61] Compulsory spinsterhood was unknown and its recent introduction "is
destined, wherever it seems to exist in practice, to disappear as
an unscientific interference of good meaning foreign
philanthropists with the natural conditions of the country."[62] If
we are to trust the evidence of contemporary English
periodicals, there were a little over five million unmarried

[58] (16 April, 1903), reprinted in *ibid.*, p. 27.
[59] Edward W. Blyden, *African Life and Customs,* p. 11.
[60] *ibid.,* p. 39.
[61] *ibid.,* p. 46.
[62] *ibid.,* p. 11.

women in Great Britain and the number was increasing. In London alone, there were 80,000 professional outcasts.[63]

Under the African social system, Blyden boasted, there were no "women of the under world," no "slaves of the abyss." Every woman was above ground, sheltered and protected. The "Bundo" and "Porroh" institutions were held up for the emulation of Europeans. A Bundo society or school gives instruction in the normal and abnormal complaints females, particularly wives and mothers, were liable to suffer. All known remedies or sedatives for such aliments were taught, thus enabling a young girl to take care of herself in emergencies whether in the bush or in the town. The Porroh order was a similar society for males. By practising polygamy, which enabled a mother's womb to recuperate for three years after each birth and ensured the production of a virile and vigorous race, Africa solved the marriage question for herself thousands of years ago. It has needed no revision and no amendment, because "it was founded upon the law of Nature and not upon the *dictum* of any ecclesiastical hierarchy."[64]

In reply to the charges of blood-thirstiness and human sacrifice frequently levelled against African society, Blyden declared that those acquainted with history would agree that in her most brilliant period, Rome, who gave law to the civilised world, practised extremely brutal customs. At that time, after Virgil and Cicero and Horace had lived and the reign of universal peace had prevailed under Augustus, hundreds of highly civilised Romans gazed upon combats of men with men, between whom no emnity existed, or of men with beasts. "Roman spectators encouraged men to butcher each other, not under the influence of any cause so respectable as superstition, but from a morbid love of amusement at the sight of blood."[65]

Even after the impact of Christianity had penetrated Southern Europe, highly cultivated Spanish Christians

[63] *ibid.,* p. 25.
[64] *ibid.,* p. 21.
[65] *ibid.,* p. 59.

62

delighted in shedding blood, sometimes on behalf of Christianity itself (i.e. the Spanish Inquisition), not to mention bullfights in the list of entertainments at Seville or an *auto-da-fe* in the square of Toledo. Compared with such scenes, Blyden emphasised, the alleged blood-thirst of the Africans appeared insignificant, the occasional blood spilt at human sacrifices a mere drop in the ocean, the public execution of criminals a mere child's play.

With regard to the punishment of crimes, the policy in Africa was to exterminate them as well as their perpetrators. Under the European system, so Blyden contended, the worst criminals were locked up for a few months and then released to continue to poison the moral and social atmosphere. The intention seemed to be not to eliminate the burglar but to invent instruments to defeat his enterprise. "Every day, then, hundreds of foes to the interests and peace of the community are turned loose, only to return to a career of war upon society."[66] The "75,000 thieves known to the Police in London" were of course ex-convicts who had undergone discipline or retribution in the prisons.[67]

The African method produced a deterent effect upon the populace at the same time ridding the society of the pernicious influence of a permanent criminal class. The universal absence of theft in the hinterland of the continent had been abundantly testified to by European travellers themselves. Blyden considered it a sad commentary on social conditions in Europe that some 2,000 or 3,000 homeless poor existed in the city of London.[68] Such a state of affairs could never be found in any part of Africa. "The African believes that the earth is the Lord's and the fulness thereof, and the sheep and the goats and the cows are all communal property, and no sheep would be

---

[66] *ibid.,* p. 56.
[67] *ibid.*
[68] *ibid.,* p. 50.

allowed to go about bleating with filth and disease without being cared for."[69]

It was in defence of his institutions that the African fought internal wars resisting men of his own community bent on aggrandising themselves at the expense of the larger whole. "His wars against Europeans have also been in defence of his native Institutions which he regards as sacred."[70] Africans did not wish to see their communistic and co-operative system disturbed by indiscriminate foreign invasion. "And here we would ask those who have done us the honour to follow us thus far in this discussion, whether in social, economic, or industrial life, Europe has anything better to offer to the African than the system he has constructed for himself."[71]

Embedded in Blyden's analysis are germs of the now familiar concept of African Socialism. In appreciation of the articles also published in the Sierra Leone *Weekly News,*[72] Casely Hayford seized the opportunity to castigate the Europeanized African. In his opinion such a man was useless in the task of directing African life and African idiosyncracies along the line of natural and healthy development. "The superfine African gentleman, who at the end of every second or third year, talks of a run to Europe, lest there should be a nervous break-down, may be serious or not, but is bound in time to be refined off the face of the African continent."[73] Like Blyden and Africanus Horton, Hayford saw a university rooted in African soil as "the means of revising erroneous current ideas regarding the African; of raising him in self-respect; and of making him an efficient co-worker in the uplifting of men to nobler effort." He considered professorships in African languages to be the safest road to self-preservation. Casely Hayford subsequently expanded these

69 *ibid.*
70 *ibid.,* p. 46.
71 *ibid.,* pp. 52-53.
72 Reprinted in *ibid.*
73 *ibid.,* p. 85.

into the African past were canalised in the Negro Society for Historical Research. Launched in the United States in 1911, the year Casely Hayford's book appeared in London by John E. Bruce and Arthur A. Schomburg, a Puerto Rican of African origin, the Society seems to have been inspired by the American Negro Academy started by Alexander Crummell on 5 March, 1897.[74] In fact, Bruce and Schomburg were associated with the American Negro Academy. At one time the former was an executive member, the latter a president of the Academy. Among the New World members of the Negro Society for Historical Research may be mentioned the philosopher Alain Locke, the first black American Rhodes Scholar at Oxford, editor of the anthology *The New Negro*[75] and a leading spirit of the Harlem Renaissance;[76] W. E. B. DuBois; Mrs. Marie Du Chatellier of Panama; Reverend William Forde from Costa Rica and J. S. Moore of Bahia (Brazil).[77]

If Henry Sylvester Williams had not died the same year he would probably have supported the new organisation. The African members included King Lewanika of Barotseland (now an integral part of Zambia) who was made honorary president, Edward Blyden, Casely Hayford, Mojola Agbebi, Moses Da Rocha; the South African F. Z. S. Peregrino. ideas into a book *Ethiopia Unbound, Studies in Race Emancipation.*

This growing racial awakening and the sporadic excursions

[74] The objects of the Academy were: the promotion of literature, science and arts, the culture of a form of intellectual taste, the fostering of higher education, the publication of scholarly works and the defence of the Negro against vicious assault. Occasional Papers No. 20, American Negro Academy, Washington D.C., 1920.

[75] (Albert and Charles Boni, Inc., 1925). Page references are to the Atheneum, New York, 1969 edition.

[76] The Harlem Renaissance also known as the New Negro movement had no formal organisation being essentially aesthetic, philosophical or metaphysical rather than political. Not surprisingly its leading spirits tended to be hostile to Marcus Garvey. See Alain Locke, *The New Negro.*

[77] For a full list of the foundation members see A. C. Hill and Martin Kilson, *op. cit.,* pp. 176-177.

presumably one of the organisers of the London Congress, and Duse Mohamed Effendi (later Duse Mohamed Ali).

Educated at King's College, London University where he read History, Duse Mohamed was the son of an Egyptian army officer and his Sudanese wife. Offended by a statement on Egypt by Theodore Roosevelt of America, Duse Mohamed wrote his only book *In the Land of the Pharaohs: A Short History of Egypt from the Fall of Ismail to the Assassination of Boutros Pasha* acclaimed by the English press as the first book on Egypt by an Egyptian.[78] "His new fame got him the job to organise the entertainment for the First Universal Races Congress, which apparently he did with great success."[79] The Races Congress sat in London from 26 to 29 July, 1911 to discuss the relations between the so-called white and coloured peoples with a view to fostering friendlier feelings and a heartier co-operation.[80] Among the participants were John Tengo Jabavu, DuBois, Mojola Agbebi and Edward Blyden. In their papers the first two analysed the Negro problem while Agbebi passionately defended African customs and institutions.

It is true that the Universal Races Congress, as its title attests, was no Pan-African conclave. Nevertheless it has some relevance, however marginal, to the Pan-African movement. Its aim harmonises with an aspiration of the London Pan-African Congress to improve the relations between the black and Caucasian peoples. Agbebi, Blyden, Jabavu and DuBois probably attended the Races Congress mainly to fulfil this objective of the 1900 Pan-African meeting.

It was the Races Congress which inspired Duse Mohamed to launch a journal in collaboration with Casely Hayford.

[78] Duse Mohamed Ali, *In the Land of the Pharaohs: A Short History of Egypt from the Fall of Ismail to the Assassination of Boutros Pasha,* 2nd ed. (London: Frank Cass, 1968).

[79] Imanuel Geiss, *The Pan-African Movement* (London: Methuen and Co., 1974), p. 730.

[80] G. Spiller, ed., *Papers on Inter-Racial Problems Communicated to the First Universal Races Congress held at the University of London,* 1911, p. v.

Called *The African Times and Orient Review: politics, litera-*
ture, art and commerce: a monthly journal devoted to the
interests of the Coloured races of the World, it ran for six years
beginning in July, 1912 and enjoyed a wide circulation in the
United States, the West Indies, Egypt, East and West Africa as
well as Europe and a number of Asian countries including
India and Japan. Its chief support, however, came from West
Africa and it is believed that Casely Hayford made substantial
financial contributions to keep it in existence. African exiles
like John Edward Bruce, Booker T. Washington and William
H. Ferris (author of *The African Abroad*) contributed articles.
Biographies of such prominent men of African origin as
Mensah Sarbah of the Gold Coast, the Egyptian nationalist,
Mustapha Kamil, J. E. K. Aggrey and the Afro-American
scholar, William Scarborough, as well as the musician, Samuel
Taylor-Coleridge formed a feature of the magazine. Another
feature was the day to day reports and speeches on Africa
made in the British Parliament.

The year Duse Mohamed launched his magazine was also
the year Edward Blyden died in Sierra Leone. With the death
of Blyden the stage was cleared for the appearance of new
leaders. The first leader of his stature to emerge was Marcus
Garvey. It was he more than any other person who introduced
the ideas of an African Nationality and the African Personality, hitherto restricted to a handful of intellectuals, to the
uninformed masses in the villages and streets of the African
world.

After a sound elementary school education supplemented
by a pupil-teachers' course in the coastal town of St. Ann's Bay,
Jamaica where he was born on 17 August, 1887, he joined
Benjamin's Printery in Kingston. He was so proficient that at
twenty he became master printer and foreman of one of the
largest local firms. This in itself constituted a spectacular
achievement since printing was a first-class trade in Jamaica at
that time and some of the foremen of the big plants were
imported from England and Canada. To keep pace with the

ever rising cost of living the printers union went on strike in 1909. Though Garvey was promised an increase in pay he led the strike. "He did the job efficiently, organized public meetings and for the first time demonstrated those oratorical talents which were to magnetize the Negro people and stir the world."[81] The agitators received money from sympathetic American printers but the union treasurer absconded with it, thereby shattering the morale of the strikers. As a result Garvey went to work at the Government Printing Office.

Still dissatisfied with the plight of the blacks around him he gave up his new job to embark on an extensive tour that took him to about a dozen countries in South and Central America. The places he visited before returning to his native Jamaica in 1911 included Costa Rica, Panama, Ecuador, Nicaragua, Spanish Honduras, Colombia and Venezuela. In Costa Rica and Panama he started the newspapers *La Nacionale* (which soon wound up) and *La Prensa* respectively. The conditions under which men of African blood in Costa Rica and Ecuador toiled drove him to protest to the British Council in each place. The British representative in Costa Rica told him nonchalantly that as consul he was powerless to change conditions there. The consul's indifference shook Garvey's being, leading him to the conclusion that the whites did not consider the lives of black people to be as valuable as theirs and had no intention of protecting blacks or removing their disabilities.[82] During his travels he also learnt about indescribable conditions in the ancestral continent itself from Jamaican and Barbadian ex-service men. As members of the West India Regiment these soldiers had been used by the British to subdue Africans and take their territories.[83]

[81] Claude McKay, *Harlem: Negro Metropolis* (New York: E. P. Dutton, 1940), p. 145; see also Theodore G. Vincent, *Black Power and the Garvey Movement* (Berkeley: Ramparts Press, 1971).

[82] Amy Jacques Garvey, *Garvey and Garveyism* (London: Collier-Macmillan, 1970), p. 10.

[83] *ibid.*

All this made an indelible impression on his mind so that he become possessed of a determination to end the white man's duplicity once and for all. In 1912 he went to England travelling through Spain and France. While in Britain he joined the staff of *The African Times and Orient Review* just launched by Duse Mohamed. In an article he wrote for the journal, Garvey predicted that West Indians would be the instrument of uniting the African race "who before the close of many centuries will found an Empire"; to those who might laugh at his statement he posed the question: "Would Caesar have believed that the country he was invading in 55 B.C. would be the seat of the greatest Empire of the world."[84]

It cannot be doubted that conversations with Duse Mohamed as well as specimens of ancient African art he saw in the British Museum together with his voluminous reading on the fatherland helped to stir the Africanism in Marcus Garvey. Nor can one completely discount the influence on Garvey of the African Movement of the West African Chief Alfred Sam of the Gold Coast and Orishatuke Faduma which caused considerable excitement in West Africa and the United States between 1914 and 1916. Among other things the African Movement aimed at the maintenance of the cultural integrity of the African world and its economic independence; it sought to develop Africa industrially, to encourage the emigration of the best Afro-American farmers and technicians to West Africa, to develop banking and mining there, to build and acquire ships for transportation and dredging and to establish institutions of higher learning on modern lines.

Whatever Garvey owes to the African Movement and his association with Duse Mohamed seem to be out-weighed by the inspiration he derived from his catholic reading and travels and from men like Dr. R. N. Love. In her recent privileged account, *Garvey and Garveyism*,[85] Mrs. Amy Jacques Garvey

[84] (October, 1913).
[85] (London: Collier-Macmillan, 1970).

points to Dr. Love as the first man of African blood to make a deep impression on her husband. A native of the Bahamas and executive member of the defunct Pan-African Association, Dr. Love was based in Jamaica where he edited a paper called *The Advocate*. "Courageous and outspoken, he spent all his time and means in this work, and in the practice of medicine, especially among the poor."[86]

It was during his 1912-13 sojourn in England that Marcus Garvey formulated his plan of liberating the Negro race on a permanent basis.[87] He was conscious, as Blyden had been, that the members of the African world were unorganised with no meaningful commercial and industrial enterprises unlike the Jews. "And what people could hold their own in these competitive days against groups and communities that had vast accumulated reserves and therefore immense sustaining power?"[88] His travels had revealed that whether in the western hemisphere or Europe or even Africa the Negro was treated like an animal possessing no political and economic rights. Would not a Negro National State, an African Nationality, located in the fatherland and controlled by men of African blood solve all the problems of the members of the race wherever they might be? Would it not protect and give impetus to Negro commerce and industry "unfettered by any other motives but those of the welfare of the Negro race?" [89] Would the black man, then, not rise to any height merited by his ability instead of by the grace of his oppressors and detractors? For Garvey a people without authority and power was a race without respect. Also like Blyden, Garvey realised that it was impossible to erect such a nationality or polity without the rehabilitation of African values. Garvey therefore wanted the

[86] *ibid.*
[87] Hucheshwar G. Mudgal, *Marcus Garvey: Is He the True Redeemer of the Negro?* (New York City: The African Publication Society, 1932), p.5.
[88] *ibid.*
[89] *ibid.*

Negro to cultivate self-respect, race pride, love of his dark skin, woolly hair, broad nose and thick lips.

After presenting his ideas to some English liberals who approved of them,[90] he went back to Jamaica in July, 1914. With the support of a Dr. J. A. Thorne the plan of redeeming the African people was laid before the public. The following month Garvey launched the Universal Negro Improvement and Conservation Association and African Communities' League[91] which subsequently attracted world attention as the Universal Negro Improvement Association. In a leaflet bearing the former title, Marcus Garvey explained that in "view of the universal disunity existing among the people of the Negro or African race, and the apparent danger which must follow the continuance of such a spirit, it has been deemed fit and opportune to found a Society with a universal programme, for the purpose of drawing the people of the race together, hence the organization above-named."[92] All persons of Negro or African parentage were requested to support the organisation for the propagation and achievement of the following general objects:

> To establish a Universal Confraternity among the race.
> To promote the spirit of race pride and love.
> To reclaim the fallen of the race.
> To administer to and assist the needy.
> To assist in civilizing the backward tribes of Africa.
> To strengthen the imperialism of independent African States.
> To establish Commissionaries or Agencies in the principal countries of the world for the protection of all Negroes, irrespective of nationality.
> To promote a conscientious Christian worship among the native tribes of Africa.

[90] *ibid.*

[91] This is the title of the letter-head with which Garvey wrote Booker T. Washington on 12 April, 1915. See *Booker T. Washington Papers,* Miscellaneous Correspondence, 1915, Container No. 939.

[92] *ibid.*

> To establish Universities, Colleges and Secondary
> Schools for the further education and culture of the boys
> and girls of the race.
> To conduct a world-wide commercial and industrial
> intercourse.[93]

Though Garvey met with little enthusiasm in his native island and received little support from his English friends who were now pre-occupied with the great War, he did not feel discouraged. "He, however, kept on agitating single-handed and with his limited means, until the end of 1916 when he sailed for New York to try his luck in Harlem."[94] Exploiting the contemporary excitement about the doctrines of "democracy" and "self-determination" which war-aims propaganda, especially Woodrow Wilson's famous Fourteen Points, had precipitated, Garvey put forward his plans for freeing Africa.

Garvey's ideas won immediate approval partly because of the fearless personality of the revolutionary and partly because the circumstances were propitious. During the Great War British and American spokemen claimed that it was being fought in order to make the world safe for democracy. But with the end of hostilities they appeared to be unaware of the oppressive conditions facing the demobilised soldiers of African blood and their countries. Marcus Garvey only needed to open his mouth for the disillusioned masses to embrace him.

Thus the Universal Negro Improvement Association of New York fame was born. In January, 1918 its organ, the *Negro World,* a weekly, appeared, remaining in circulation until 1933 when the *Blackman* succeeded it. In its first years the *Negro World* was published in English, French and Spanish. Timothy Thomas Fortune became chief-editor; Hucheshwar G. Mudgal, author of an important booklet *Marcus Garvey: Is He The True Redeemer Of the Negro?*[95] served as editor, William

[93] *ibid.*
[94] H. G. Mudgal, *Marcus Garvey,* pp. 5-6.
[95] *ibid.*

Ferris started a poetry section while the Jamaican writers Claude McKay, John E. Bruce and Duse Mohamed Ali functioned as columnists. Another newspaper *The Daily Negro Times* was soon launched. A flag for the race — a horizontal tricolour of red, black and green — was adopted. An African National Anthem set to martial music was produced:

> Ethiopia, thou land of our fathers,
> Thou land where the gods loved to be,
> As storm cloud at night sudden gathers
> Our armies come rushing to thee.
> We must in the fight be victorious
> When swords are thrust outward to gleam.
> For us will the victory be glorious
> When led by the red, black and green.

> *Chorus*

> Advance, advance to victory,
> Let Africa be free;
> Advance to meet the foe
> With the might
> Of the red, the black and the green.

> Ethiopia, the tyrant's falling,
> Who smote thee upon thy knees,
> And the children are lustily calling
> From over the distant seas.
> Jehovah, the Great One has heard us,
> Has noted our sighs and our tears,
> With His Spirit of Love has stirred us
> To be one through the coming years.

> O, Jehovah, Thou God of the ages
> Grant unto our sons that lead
> The wisdom Thou gave to Thy sages
> When Israel was sore in need.

Thy voice thro' the dim past has spoken,
Ethiopia shall stretch forth her hand
By thee shall all fetters be broken
And Heaven bless our dear Motherland.[96]

Marcus Garvey struck African Redemption medals and created orders of chivalry with such titles as: Duke of the Nile; Earl of the Congo; Viscount of the Niger; Baron of the Zambesi; Knights of the Distinguished Service Order of Ethiopia, Ashanti and Mozambique. Though a born Catholic, Garvey set up an African Orthodox Church with Archbishop Alexander McGuire, a West Indian theologian, at the head. On the request of West African farmers and producers he created a Black Star Steamship Company to carry African merchandise to the United States.[97] Some African businessmen had complained of victimisation alleging that white shipping agencies as well as produce dealers invariably offered them very low prices for their goods.[98]

Africa for the Africans. Ethiopia Awake. Back to Africa. A Black Star Line. These were the slogans Garvey employed to capture the heart of the Negroes. In the jungles of the Congo in Central Africa villagers described him as an African who had been lost in America but was about to return in order to save his brethren. The story is well known of how the King of Swaziland in Southern Africa told a friend that he knew the names of only two black men in the western hemisphere: the boxer Jack Johnson who defeated his white opponent and Marcus Garvey. When the Governor of British Honduras banned the *Negro World* Garveyites staged the July, 1919 uprising at Belize.[99] In the United States, Hubert Harrison, journalist and founder of the Liberty League of Negro Americans, declared in a tract *When Africa Awakes* (1920) that

[96] Quoted in Amy Jacques Garvey, *Garvey and Garveyism,* pp. 31-32.
[97] *ibid.,* p. xiii.
[98] *ibid.*
[99] Theodore G. Vincent, *Black Power and the Garvey Movement,* p. 128.

the majority of the races would not acquiesce indefinitely in white supremacy and domination.[100] He advised the whites that whenever they read about the activities of the Mullah, Casely Hayford and the Egyptian nationalist, Zaghlul Pasha, or heard about Indian nationalist uprisings, of Black Star Lines and West Indian "seditions" they should remember that those fruits sprang from the seeds of their own sowing.[101]

By 1919 Garvey had formed branches of the U.N.I.A. all over the world. These branches held themselves in readiness for what was commonly but wrongly believed would be the first international convention of the Negro peoples of the globe. Plans for the convention included the drafting of grievances and a Declaration of Rights, the election of international officers and the discussion of special reports on political and economic aspects of the African problem.

The convention eventually took place throughout the month of August, 1920 in Madison Square Garden the largest auditorium in New York City. Delegates came from different regions of Africa, Brazil, Colombia, Haiti, Panama, the West Indies as well as Canada, England and France. About 25,000 representatives were inside the auditorium and thousands who could not be seated overflowed into the adjoining streets. In a long special address, punctuated with applause, Garvey presented his case for African Redemption. After five hundred years of oppression, Negroes were determined to suffer no longer. Despite promises made to Africans and their descendants during the Great War, they were deprived of all the democracy for which they had shed their blood. Black American soldiers returning from the battlefield of Europe were beaten up or lynched in their uniforms in many a Southern States.[102] Since the other races had countries of their own, it was time the four hundred million Negroes of the world

[100] J. Ayodele Langley, *Pan-Africanism and Nationalism in West Africa, 1900-1945* (London: Oxford University Press, 1973), p. 36.

[101] *ibid.*

[102] Amy Jacques Garvey, *Garvey and Garveyism,* p. 53.

claimed Africa for themselves. If Europe was for the Europeans, Africa should belong to Africans and their descendents. Concluding, he warned that the African exiles were poised to return to their fatherland. He gave notice to the tenant, the European imperialists and colonists, to quit or face forcible eviction.

Officers of the Supreme Executive Council were then elected. The position of potentate, titular head of all the black people of the world, was ear-marked for an African residing in the continent. The Mayor of Liberia, Mr. Gabriel Johnson, was chosen in view of the plans of the U.N.I.A. to send the first batch of repatriates there.[103] Mr. George O. Marke, a Sierra Leonean civil servant educated at Oxford, became deputy potentate.[104] The office of Provisional President went to Garvey.

Similar conventions took place between 1920 and 1925. During the quinquennium two major deputations were despatched. One went to Liberia to secure land for the settlement of the diaspora. The other delegation was sent in September, 1922 with a five-page petition to the League of Nations, Geneva.[105] Signed by the executive officers of the U.N.I.A. on behalf of the Third Annual Convention of the Negro Peoples of the World, the petition recalled that the service rendered by the black race during the war of 1914-18 enabled the Allies "to defeat Germany in German East Africa, in German South-West Africa, in Togoland, the Cameroons, and other parts of the continent, as well as to defeat the common foe in Europe." As a reward for this "splendid service" the U.N.I.A. prayed the League to surrender to them "for the purpose of racial development, the mandates now given to the Union of South Africa; namely, German East

---

[103] Theodore G. Vincent, *Black Power and the Garvey Movement*, p. 120.
[104] *ibid.*
[105] There is a copy of the Petition in *The Reginald Bridgeman Collection* (in owner's possession).

Africa, and German South-West Africa."[106] The petitioners were confident that if the territories were ceded as requested the U.N.I.A. would be able to bring them within two decades to a level of development that would "prove to the world and to the League our ability to govern ourselves."[107]

Overcome by impatience a West African Garveyite unilaterally issued a circular dated December 6, 1922 to the European metropolitan governments affirming that "The Expression 'Africa for the Africans' is not merely a statement of fact but one of truth"[108] and deploring white supremacy as detrimental to the interest, peace and happiness of the subject races. In the interest of world peace there should be a turning point. On the assumption that this was happening he deemed

> it necessary to point out that the whole Continent of Africa should come under a Monarchical Government having one "Common flag," a Union African Flag flying throughout the length and breadth of the Continent and replacing every other flag. An African Empire creates a position of an African King and Emperor which position should be assumed, and be done by an African Prince.

> There being none feeling himself called to do so I John H. Davies of 51 formally [*sic*] 43 Liverpool Street Freetown, Sierra Leone do hereby declare and make it known throughout the world that I have now done so.[109]

Having appointed himself King and Emperor of Africa, Mr. John H. Davies ordered all foreigners, with the exception of those lawfully married to men or women of African blood, to leave. Colonial administrations were also ordered to hand over

---

[106] *ibid.* It should be noted that Tanganika was not given to South Africa.
[107] *ibid.*
[108] *Archives du Senegal* (Dakar), File No. 4F14(31).
[109] *ibid.*

to "African Natives and Afro-Americans [*sic*] equal to the various positions."[110]

This circular was passed on to Sir A. R. Slater, the Governor of Sierra Leone, by the Governor-General of French West Africa asking the former to look into the matter.[111] In a reply, Governor Slater dismissed John Davies as a deranged mind who was not responsible for his actions adding that steps had been taken to prevent the repetition of that offence.[112]

The fate of John Davies' Circular foreshadowed the failure of the diplomatic initiative launched by the U.N.I.A. and the imminent decline of the movement itself. Despite its fantastic following, Garveyism was bound to suffer a set-back mainly because of the unfavourable international political situation of the time. Threats to expel the imperialists from Africa by force naturally alarmed the western powers even though the Provisional President of the continent was unlikely to muster enough warships, submarines and tanks to make good his boast. The French and British colonial authorities began to suppress *The Negro World*. To possess any Garveyite publication became a serious offence punishable by imprisonment. Yielding to pressure from the United States and the metropolitan powers, Liberia, which the U.N.I.A. had planned to use as a nucleus for the proposed Negro National State suddenly dissociated herself from the Garvey movement.

Marcus Garvey also paid dearly for underestimating the machinations of several Afro-American intellectuals, most of whom envied his worldwide popularity and boldness. When these intellectuals, among them well-known Harlem journalists, began to demand an investigation of his ventures, Garvey completely ignored them. Instead he concentrated his energy on demonstrating the moral and material benefits that

110 *ibid.*

111 Enclosure to a letter dated February 7, 1923, *ibid.*

112 Gov. A. R. Slater to Governor-General of French West Africa, 29 March, 1923, *ibid.*

the black world could derive from running steamships of their own. Prominent Afro-Americans of Harlem were also among the first to demand his arrest. Such men included George W. Harris, editor of the *News* (Harlem), Williams Pickens and Robert W. Bagnal, officials of the National Association for the Advancement of Colored People as well as Robert S. Abbott, editor-publisher of the *Chicago Defender*.[113] After serving a short prison sentence, allegedly for misusing the United States mail, he was deported to his native Jamaica where he encountered even greater intrigues and harassment from the local black elite.

With the removal of the redeemer from the United States, Garveyism suffered a set-back from which it is only just beginning to recover, thanks to the changed world political situation. In the words of Claude McKay "Marcus Garvey had dreamed of a vast model colony in Liberia. But it was Harvey Firestone who realized the dream with his extensive [rubber] plantations."[114]

Nonetheless it would be mistaken to suppose that Marcus Garvey achieved nothing. Apart from rehabilitating the colour "black" he shook the black masses of the diaspora into an awareness of their African origin. Without setting foot on African soil he created for the first time a real feeling of international solidarity among Africans and persons of African stock.

This feeling of solidarity had already begun to manifest itself as early as 1917 when West Indian and West African students in London formed a Union for Students of African Descent primarily for literary and social activities.[115] An organisation called the African Progress Union also based in

113 Claude McKay, *Harlem,* p. 170.

114 *ibid.,* p. 168.

115 *West Africa* (25 October, 1924), pp. 1178-80. Between 1921 and 1924 the membership of the Union for Students of African Descent rose from 25 to 120.

London appeared the next year with the aim of promoting the social and economic welfare of the Africans of the world.[116] Among the members of the A.P.U. were Duse Mohamed Ali and Councillor J. R. Archer, an influential West Indian in the Battersea District of London.

It was also partly against the impact of Garveyism. Though he disapproved of its propaganda tactics, W. E. B. DuBois convened a series of Pan-African meetings between 1919 and 1927. Following the procedure adopted by Henry Sylvester Williams in connexion with the 1900 Pan-African Conference, DuBois addressed a memorandum on New Years Day 1919 to prominent personalities of African blood, among them the Senegalese, Blaise Diagne, on the necessity for a Pan-African Congress.[117] The proposed congress was expected to consider reports on the conditions of the Negroes in various parts of the globe, to "obtain authoritative statements of policy toward the Negro race from the Great Powers," to make representations on behalf of the Negro people to the Paris Peace Conference and to lay down principles for the development of the Negro race. The principles were political rights for all educated persons of African extraction and their children, economic development in the colonies primarily for the benefit of the indigenous inhabitants, political reforms based on local traditions "with the object of inaugurating gradually an Africa for the Africans," recognition of the sovereign status of Haiti, Abyssinia and Liberia and the development of the former German dependencies under the supervision of the League of Nations.[118] The proposed conference was also expected to set up a permanent secretariat with headquarters in Paris charged with the task of "collating" the history of the Negro race, encouraging the appreciation of Negro art and literature, following political, social and economic developments in the

[116] *The Sierra Leone Weekly News* (3 September, 1921), p. 11.

[117] For a full text of the memorandum see *The Crisis* (March, 1919), pp. 224-225.

[118] *ibid.*

African world; publishing articles, pamphlets and proceedings of the congress under discussion, and organising another Pan-African meeting in 1920.[119] Finally, the memorandum suggested that a preliminary conference be held at once to consider the proposals just outlined and others that might be advanced. "This plan was acceptable not only to the representatives of the various Negro peoples gathered in France, but it was also welcomed by the French [Government]"[120] thanks to the influence of Diagne who during the Great War was a cabinet minister in the French Government headed by M. Clemenceau.

DuBois eventually called a Pan-African meeting in Paris. Held from 19 to 21 February, 1919 in the Grand Hotel, Boulevard des Capucines, it was attended by fifty-seven delegates drawn from different sections of the African world.[121] Fifteen territories were represented, notably Abyssinia, Liberia, Haiti, the United States, San Domingo (Dominican Republic), French Caribbean, British Africa, French Africa, Egypt and the Belgian Congo.[122] Also in attendance was J. R. Archer, a participant at the 1900 Pan-African Congress and president of the African Progress Union. The importance which the European colonial administrations attached to the Paris gathering was reflected by the high calibre of their representatives. France was represented by the Chairman of her Foreign Affairs Committee; Belgium by M. Van Overgergh, a member of the Belgian Peace Delegation; Portugal by M. Freire d'Andrade, formerly Minister of Foreign Affairs.[123] The United States Government sent Messrs William E. Walling and Charles Edward Russell.[124]

As chairman and one recently elevated by the French Government to the position of Commissioner-General of

119 *ibid.*
120 *ibid.,* p. 225.
121 *The Crisis* (April, 1919), p. 271.
122 *ibid.*
123 *ibid.*
124 *ibid.*

Native Affairs and who had married into one of France's most distinguished families, Blaise Diagne not surprisingly opened the proceedings with praise for the French colonial system. Mr. C. D. B. King, president-elect of Liberia and Liberian delegate to the Paris Peace Conference, gave an inspiring account of his country's aspirations and accomplishments expressing the hope that the people of African descent would feel proud of that republic. "Let us," he concluded, "be considered a home for the darker race in Africa."[125] The representatives of the American Government as well as M. Gratien Candace, deputy from Guadeloupe in the French Chamber, unequivocally condemned discrimination on grounds of race. Two other deputies from the West Indies, M. Boisneuf (Guadeloupe) and M. Lagrosilliere (Martinique) expressed disappointment at the refusal of white Americans to treat as equals black men "who in common with themselves were giving their lives for democracy and injustice."[126] While the delegates of the Belgian and Portuguese colonial authorities talked about imminent reforms, the Chairman of the French Foreign Affairs Committee claimed that his country adopted the policy of equality and liberty for all men regardless of race even before the French Revolution boasting that there were no less than six coloured deputies in the French Parliament, among them the chairman of the Congress who also served on his committee.[127]

In compliance with DuBois' pre-conference memorandum, resolutions were passed providing for another Pan-African meeting and demanding reforms. The Great Powers were asked to issue an international code, similar to that being proposed for labour, for the protection of Africans.[128] A

[125] *ibid.*

[126] *ibid.*

[127] For a critical reassessment of French colonial policy see Martin D. Lewis, "One Hundred Million Frenchmen: The 'Assimilation' Theory in French Colonial Policy," *Comparative Studies in Society and History,* Vol. IV (1961-62), pp. 129-153.

[128] W. E. B. DuBois, *The World and Africa, An Inquiry into the Part which Africa has Played in World History,* enlarged ed. (New York, 1965), p. 11.

permanent bureau should be set up by the League of Nations to ensure the enforcement of the code. The inhabitants of Africa and the peoples of African descent must henceforth be governed according to certain principles. These included the abolition of forced labour; the right of Africans "to participate in the government as fast as their development permits, in conformity with the principle that the government exists for the natives, and not the natives for the government"; to the right of every child to learn to read and write in his language; the regulation of capital investment and concessions to prevent explicitation of the African people and the holding of land with its mineral resources in trust for the community who at all times should have effective ownership of as much land as they could profitably develop.[129] Viewed against the contemporary obsession with the doctrine of self-determination as expressed in Woodrow Wilson's Fourteen Points, these demands seem moderate.

More radical and therefore more in tune with the post-war agitation for freedom were the resolutions adopted at the 1921 London Pan-African Congress held at the Central Hall, Westminster from 27 to 29 August with further sessions in Brussels and Paris the next month. In attendance were medical doctors like the Sierra Leonean, Ojo Olaribigde, practising in England, and Vitallian, a former physician to Emperor Menelik II; seasoned trade unionists like Albert Marryshaw from Grenada who later became member of the Legislative Council there; diplomats like Mrs. Helen Curtis, Liberian Consul to Brussels, and M. Dantes Bellegarde of the Haitian Delegation, Paris; students and dons like the Nigerian under-graduate Ibidunni Morondipe Obadende and Jose de Magalhaes of Angola, a professor at the Lisbon School of Tropical Medicine, deputy for Sao Thome in the Portuguese Parliament and president of an African pressure group called the *Liga Africana;*[130] businessmen like the Nigerian, Peter

---

[129] *ibid.*, pp. 11-12.
[130] Alain Locke, *The New Negro,* pp. 386-87.

Thomas and Nicola de Santos-Pinto, a mulatto planter also from Sao Thome and member of the *Liga Africana*. Morocco was represented by a certain Mr. Arnold, an English liberal familiar with the social and political conditions there; South Africa by Mr. and Mrs. J. L. Dube; East Africa by Dr. Norman Maclean Leys, a British medical officer well known for his anti-settler views and opposition to colonial rule;[131] and the Belgian Congo by Mfum Paul Panda, leader of the *Union Congolaise* and "spokesman for black Belgium."[132] M. Gratien Candace, described by DuBois as "more French than the French,"[133] and M. Isaac Beton, a school teacher in Paris represented Guadeloupe; Jean Razaief, Madagascar (now Malagasy). The British Government sent two observers, namely: Colonel Beckles Wilson, Publicity Agent of the Gold Coast, and Captain Fitzpatrick of the Nigerian Political Service. The delegates of the A.P.U., which made the arrangements for the London sessions, included Dr. John Alcindor and Mr. J. R. Archer both of whom attended the 1900 Congress as well as the Liberian, Robert Broadhurst, secretary of the A.P.U., and J. A. Barbour-James (British Guyana) who had served in the Gold Coast as a surveyor.

Among the representatives of the N.A.A.C.P. may be mentioned DuBois, Mr. Walter F. White, an Afro-American journalist and graduate of Atlanta University (Georgia, U.S.A.) and Miss Jessie Redmon Fauset, trained at Cornell University and the Sorbonne and literary editor of *The Crisis,* organ of the N.A.A.C.P. Unlike the American participants, those who came from West Africa did so mostly as individuals and not as the representatives of organizations. Other persons came from Swaziland, Jamaica, Martinique, French Congo, Trinidad, the Philippines and Liberia.[134] Altogether a hundred

---

[131] See his books *Kenya* (London, 1925) and *The Colour Bar in East Africa* (London, 1941).
[132] Alain Locke ed., *The New Negro*, p. 390.
[133] *ibid.,* p. 392.
[134] *The Crisis* (December, 1921), p. 69.

and ten delegates took part in the 1921 Pan-African meeting and in addition to these there were no less than 1000 visitors.[135] Compared with the Pan-African Convention summoned in New York the previous year by Marcus Garvey, the attendance at the 1921 Conference appears unimpressive.

Dr. Alcindor, Chairman of the A.P.U., presided over the opening session in London. In his address he thanked the American delegates "who had financed the conference, and travelled thousands of miles to maintain an entente cordiale between the Africans and African-descended people."[136] They would ventilate their grievances and devise ways and means of removing them. The enemies of the African race were very often the Africans themselves who he thought lacked character, education and cohesion. Observers were beginning to see that "all was not well with Africa and the Africans." It was the duty of the African to speed up this awakening of public conscience and galvanize it into activity by means of a wise propaganda.[137]

Then followed an account by DuBois of the Pan-African Movement since 1900 and the numerous obstacles that had to be surmounted. It was of the utmost importance that Negro leaders of thought should come together and inform themselves of the different aspects of the Negro problem. The conference had been called to discuss segregation, the racial problem of America and South Africa, the land question especially in Africa and the methods of co-operation among the peoples of the African world. In view of the reluctance of the Great Powers to allow a discussion of their domestic problem in the countries, the French and the British authorities had been assured that the gathering was neither "directed towards revolution" nor financed by the Soviet Union as was

---

135 For a list of the delegates see *ibid.*, pp. 68-69.
136 *West Africa* (3 September, 1921), p. 988.
137 *ibid.*

then commonly assumed that any movement of that nature must be.[138]

Of the many speeches on race relations, the most touching was that contributed by Peter Thomas. Little children in the streets of London embarrassed him with shouts of "There's the nigger." Though he did not feel insulted, he wanted that expression expurgated from the English language. Harmony between the races in the British Empire demanded that children should be taught from their cradle days to respect fellow human beings regardless of their complexion. As a loyal British subject, he deprecated the metropolitan government's habit of misinterpreting any articulation of grievances by subjects on "a seething, underground current of disloyalty."[139]

Turning to segregation, he argued that "it meant separating one class of mankind from another." On the steamer an observant stranger would notice how West Africans were confined to one side. Probably unaware that European domination was largely imposed by superior force of arms, Peter Thomas lamented that if West Africans had not received Europeans with kindness, the invaders would not have had the power to introduce the vicious policy of segregation. "With their intense spiritual nature they were prepared to forget a wrong, and to forgive, but they could not go on forgiving."[140] Recalling that the riches of West Africa were used to develop Liverpool, he urged the authorities to increase the educational and industrial facilities so as to improve the standard of living of the people.[141]

Presenting the case of East Africa where he worked as a medical officer for sixteen years, Dr. Norman Leys described how the indigenous inhabitants of Rhodesia, Nyasaland, Uganda and Kenya (the first two are in Central Africa) were being dispossessed of their lands. In these places, practically no

---

[138] *ibid.*
[139] *ibid.*, p. 990.
[140] *ibid.*
[141] *ibid.*

African had any legal right of ownership or security of tenure in communal or even individual land. In Kenya, alone, the land already alienated to white settlers amounted to nearly five million acres. It was the policy of the imperial regime to induce those living on lands that had been alienated to leave their homes and work for the white settlers. That policy was carried out by the influence of the colonial government over local chiefs, who were in their pay, thus enabling the Secretary of State for the Colonies in London to deny that forced labour was being used in British dominions. Wages were fixed by the joint action of the white employers. The standard wage was six shillings a month or two pounds of rice or maize a day. If the congress wanted to defend the interests of the East Africans, Dr. Leys advised, now was the time to do so.

Two concrete proposals stood out clearly in the welter of ideas exchanged: one concerned co-operation among the peoples of African stock, the other dealt with their political future. With regard to the question of co-operation, Albert Marryshaw (Grenada) warned that what was needed was not dazzling oratory but actions. Men of African blood must be prepared to dip their hands into their pockets; they must make financial sacrifice to help one another.[142] A Nigerian lawyer, Mr. L. B. Augusto, urged that a start could be made by going to the aid of Liberia who appealed to the United States for a loan of five million dollars in January, 1918.[143] "Let us," he pressed, "lend the solid weight of the newly conscious black world towards its development."[144]

Combining the League of Nations idea with the political aspirations of the N.C.B.W.A. and the back-to-Africa movement of Marcus Garvey, Ibidunni M. Obadende (Nigerian) advocated the formation of a League of the Negroes of the World with headquarters in Liberia and branches in other

[142] *The Crisis* (November, 1921), p. 13.
[143] *ibid.;* R. L. Buell, *The Native Problem in Africa,* Vol. II (New York: Macmillan, 1928).
[144] *The Crisis* (November, 1921), p. 13.

parts of the globe where persons of African descent might be found. From this League was to emerge a union of all "the West African countries, extending from Senegal to Portuguese West Africa, including [the] Belgian Congo, or as far as possible under the name of the United States of West Africa on the basis of alliance with the European Powers who have helped in developing those Colonies and Protectorates."[145]

Thus Obadende's "African Programme" in the end turned out to be a charter for West Africa only. The programme itself rested on the naîve assumption that the imperialists would eagerly surrender their acquisitions. Despite its naîveté the scheme was significant for it showed what kind of future some of the delegates envisaged for Africa: a united Africa, free of alien influence. It is important to note that something of Obadende's programme was reflected in the resolutions.

The resolutions may be divided into four main sections as follows: a general criticism of the colonial system and relations between the "coloured" and "white" races; detailed criticisms of the major imperialist powers; a plea for the continued respect for the sovereignity of Abyssinia, Haiti and Liberia; and lastly a challenge to the rest of the world. The first part of the manifesto regretted that relations between the various groups of humanity were determined principally by the degree in which one could subject the other to its service "uprooting ruthlessly religion and customs, and destroying government, so that the favoured few may luxuriate in the toil of the tortured many."[146] What was needed was a fair distribution of world income between the exploiting and the exploited peoples.

A second part of the document contained criticisms of some aspects of the colonial activities of Belgium, Great Britain, Portugal, Spain and France. France was commended for placing "her cultured black citizens on a plane of absolute legal and social equality with her white, and [for having] given

[145] Obadende's paper, "An African Programme," was published in *The Crisis* (May, 1922), p. 33.

[146] *The Crisis* (November, 1921), p. 6.

them representatives in her highest legislature."[147] At the same time she was urged to widen the political basis of her native government, to restore "to her indigenes the ownership of the soil" and rebuked for exposing African labour to the "aggression of established capital" and for "compelling black men without a voice in their government to fight for France."

A third section of the manifesto warned that the continued existence of the autonomous Negro states was "absolutely necessary to any sustained belief of the black folk in the sincerity and honesty of the white."[148] The continued occupation of Haiti by the United States was condemned.

Finally, the resolutions called upon the rest of the world to choose one of the following alternatives:

> either the complete assimilation of Africa with two or three of the great world states, with political, civil and social power and privileges absolutely equal for its black and white citizens, or the rise of a great black African State founded in Peace and Goodwill, based on popular education, natural art and industry and freedom of trade; autonomous and sovereign in its internal policy, but from its beginning a part of a great society of peoples in which it takes its place with others as co-rulers of the world.[149]

Commenting on the Conference, a London journalist paid tribute to the humour that marked its proceedings.[150] This cordial atmosphere was absent in the Brussels sessions held from 31 August to 2 September, 1921. The resolutions passed unanimously at the London meeting aroused opposition when DuBois proposed their adoption.[151] As chairman, Blaise Diagne, whose co-operation in 1919 had made the Paris

---

147 *ibid.,* p. 8.
148 *ibid.*
149 *ibid.,* pp. 8-9.
150 *The African World* (3 September, 1921), p. 177.
151 *The African World* (10 September, 1921), p. 211.

Congress possible, now refused to submit DuBois' motion to the vote. The Senegalese politician was determined to see that nothing revolutionary was done by the gathering. Ignoring the overwhelming majority support for DuBois' motion, he proclaimed adopting a declaration submitted by the Belgian liberal, M. Otlet. The convocation did not break up in confusion thanks to the restraint of DuBois who desisted from pressing the matter. The Otlet manifesto was, at bottom, a diversionary document demanding among other things the establishment of scientific institutes to investigate the development of the Negroes.[152]

At the Paris session the London resolutions were substantially rephrased on the insistence of Blaise Diagne who rejected blunt references to the metropolitan powers. With the end of the deliberations in September, the Congress sent a committee, among them DuBois and the Haitian diplomat, Dantes Bellegarde, to Geneva to present a petition to the League of Nations.[153]

What was the reaction of the Europeans to the 1921 pan-African meeting? It was a mixed one. The fact that so many black men of consequence from remote corners of the globe were exchanging ideas on disabilities imposed by white arrogance and intolerances not surprisingly aroused suspicion of a revolution and fear of black domination. As Walter White relates, there were secret agents of the British Colonial Office at the London sessions "and the same surveillance was encountered in Belgium and France."[154] The *Manchester Despatch* commented that the white people did not naturally look forward with joyful emotions to the day when a prolific black race would rise to power "but the time may come when we shall have to submit ourselves to the tender mercies of our

---

[152] *ibid.*
[153] W. E. B. DuBois, *The World and Africa,* pp. 240-41.
[154] *A Man Called White: The Autobiography of Walter White* (New York: the Viking Press, 1948), p. 61.

dusky conquerors."[155] Reflecting the post-war disillusionment with European civilization, the *Public Opinion* of London declared that no white man could have attended the conference and retained his smug complacency; the days of the super-race were numbered; the theory of the permanent and necessary inferiority of the Negro seemed then to be untrue from a practical, as it had always been from a Christian, standpoint.[156]

Several newspapers took a less gloomy view. *Humanite* of Paris remarked that the black and mulatto intelligensia proved by its very existence that the black race was not inherently inferior. How could Europeans consider inferior to white men these orators with their clear thought and their ready words? asked the paper.[157] It was the Pan-Africanists' sincerity of purpose that most impressed many a European commentator. According to *The Daily Graphic* (London) the delegates

> were so intensely in earnest, both the men and women, so absolutely convinced of the justice of their cause, their right to a citizen's franchise, to representation in the world's councils, to everything in fact, that civilized humanity offers to the sons, regardless of race, colour and creed.[158]

Nearly all the newspaper correspondents paid a glowing tribute to the exertions and eloquence of DuBois. For instance, the Belgian *Echo de la Bourse* was convinced that whether one liked him and his programme or not one must "bow to his brilliant intellect and his devotion to the black race."[159] The fact that he impressed most of the foreign journalists who generally recognised him as "the moving spirit of the Congress" may account for the origin of the notion that he is the

[155] Reprinted in *The Crisis* (December, 1921), p. 65.
[156] (September, 1921), p. 248.
[157] *The Crisis* (December, 1921), p. 63.
[158] Reprinted in *ibid.*, p. 63.
[159] *ibid.*, p. 67.

"father" of Pan-Africanism. Whatever the origins of that belief may be, most contemporary observers expected him to win significant concessions for the movement in the very near future. This speculation seemed to be borne out by the revival of the Pan-African Association at the end of the 1921 Congress.

Based in Paris, the Pan-African Association held periodical meetings for four years and was run by three French-speaking West Indians and an Afro-American. These were Gratien Candace, Isaac Beton (secretary), Camile Mortenol (treasurer), about whom not much is known and the black American, Rayford Logan (assistant secretary), then resident in Paris and who later became a professor of History at Howard University (Washington, D.C.).[160]

The first major assignment of the Pan-African Association was the summoning of a Pan-African conference in 1923. The London sessions lasted two days, from 7 to 8 November, and were held in Denison House. Among the participants were Dr. Alcindor, Chief Amoah III of the Gold Coast, Rayford Logan as well as Kamba Simango, an Angolan educated in the United States. Also present were some distinguished members of the British Labour Party namely: Harold Laski, Sidney Olivier and H. G. Wells.

In his opening speech, DuBois, the Chairman, said that it had not been possible to meet in Lisbon on the date originally announced. The reason was due to the unilateral postponement of it by Isaac Beton on financial grounds.[161] This unauthorised action had to be reversed since it was considered more beneficial to hold a congress, even if only a handful attended, than to have none at all. Because the conference was originally intended to meet in Lisbon they must keep faith with the world by having a further session there.[162]

---

[160] Rayford Logan, "The Historical Aspects of Pan-Africanism: A Personal Chronicle," *African Forum* Vol. 1, No. 1 (1965), p. 97.

[161] *The Crisis* (December, 1923), p. 57.

[162] *West Africa* (10 November, 1923), p. 1352.

Decisions taken included the establishment, at the earliest opportunity, of Pan-African committees in England, British West Africa, British Caribbean, Brazil, Haiti, Liberia, South Africa, Portugal and the United States; the Pan-African Association located in Paris was to continue but as a Pan-African committee for France and her colonies.[163] The committees were charged with the duty of spreading information about the black world and to organise a Pan-African convocation in 1925.

On 9 November, the delegates issued a statement setting out what they believed to be the "eight general and irreducible needs" of Africans and their descendants. The first was a voice in their own government; the second, access to the land and its resources; the third, trial by jury; the fourth, free elementary education for all, broad training in modern industrial technique, and higher training of selected talent; the fifth, the development of Africa for the benefit of Africans, and not merely for the profit of Europeans; the sixth, the abolition of the slave trade and the traffic in liquor; the seventh, world disarmament; and the eighth, the organization of commerce and industry so as to make the main objects of capital and labour the welfare of the many, rather than the enriching of the few.[164]

The socialist economic policy advocated by the delegates was robbed of considerable force when they proceeded to demand specifically for "the civilised British subjects in West Africa and in the West Indies the institution of home rule and responsible government."[165]

The "uncivilised" colonial subjects of Northern Nigeria, Uganda and Basutoland (now Lesotho) should be prepared for "home rule and economic independence, and for eventual participation in the general government of the land."[166]

[163] *The Crisis* (January, 1924), p. 122.
[164] *West Africa* (17 November, 1923), p. 1377.
[165] *ibid.*
[166] *ibid.*

Citizenship rights of voting and representation in the French Parliament enjoyed by Senegal and the French Caribbean should be extended to other sections of the French Empire. The white settler minorities in Kenya, Rhodesia and South Africa were admonished to surrender "native" land alienated to them; there was no "other road to peace and progress."[167]In each of these places there should be an end to "the pretension of a white minority to dominate a black majority"; nothing could be more ironical than the spectacle of "the official head of a great South African State [General Smuts]"; striving blindly to build peace and goodwill in Europe by "standing on the necks and hearts of million of black Africans."[168]

For the black Americans, the document demanded full civil rights and the suppression of lynching. With regard to the autonomous nations of Liberia, Ethiopia and Haiti, the delegates urged not only respect for their political integrity but also "their emancipation from the grip of economic monopoly and usury at the hands of the moneymasters of the world."[169] Britain was asked to hand over the Egyptian Sudan to Egypt, now independent. Finally, persons of African ancestry in Brazil and Central America were told to be no longer satisfied with a solution of the Negro problem involving their assimilation by another race without fully recognizing their "manhood."

These resolutions were adopted without amendments at the Lisbon session jointly organised by Jose de Magalhaes and Rayford Logan. Eleven nations and colonial territories were represented, the largest contingent being that of Portuguese Africa; also in attendance were two former Portuguese colonial administrators.[170]

The decision to set up Pan-African committees in different

[167] *ibid.*
[168] *ibid.*
[169] *ibid.*
[170] *The Crisis* (February, 1924), p. 170.

parts of the world, first taken at the 1900 Congress, never materialised. Nor was the proposed 1925 Pan-African conference held. Arrangements to hold it in the West Indies had to be abandoned "on account of the difficulty of transport"; a meeting did take place in New York in August, 1927 and it called for reforms demanded in previous gatherings.[171] After the New York Congress the initiative passed from black Americans in the New World to Africans and West Indians in England and France.

With the death of Dr. Alcindor in the mid-1920s, the A.P.U. lapsed into obscurity clearing the way for the appearance of more dynamic pressure groups. The first such organisation to emerge was the West African Students' Union. We must however not suppose that the W.A.S.U. owed its existence solely to the ineffectiveness of the A.P.U. A more important factor was the colour prejudice that marked British society of the time. Most men of African blood went to England with an idealised concept of the mother country with her reputation for justice and fair play. But daily life there often fell short of these ideals. Their admiration of the mother country and their pride in membership of the British Empire proved to be empty and hollow if not misguided.

Kobina Sekyi, a Gold Coast philosophy student at University College, London, conveyed his impressions in a series of articles entitled "The Anglo-Fanti."[172] It did not take the African long, Sekyi observed, to discover that he was regarded as a savage even by the starving unemployed who begged him for alms. Amusing questions were frquently put to him as to whether he wore clothes before his voyage to England, whether it was safe for Europeans to visit his country since the climate was unsuitable for civilised people, and whether wild animals roamed about in his village.

Among Africans who went to Britain in 1922 to study Law

---

[171] *The Crisis* (October, 1927), pp. 263-65.
[172] *West Africa* (25 May-28 September, 1918).

was Ladipo Solanke, a Nigerian from Abeokuta and graduate of Fourah Bay College, Freetown. Like Kobina Sekyi and Peter Thomas he found race relations in the imperial capital deplorable. As a result he was seized with a determination to unite Africans and fight the colour bar.[173] Discussions with other West Africans culminated in a meeting held in London on 7 August, 1925. Speakers regretted that after seven years of existence the A.P.U. could not boast of a single concrete achievement; finally, it was resolved to launch the W.A.S.U.[174]

At a subsequent meeting officers were elected as follows: president, W. Davidson Carrol, a Gambian lawyer educated at Oxford; vice-president, J. B. Danquah of the United Gold Coast Convention fame; honorary secretary, Ladipo Solanke; treasurer and financial secretary, a Nigerian medical student called Joseph Akanni Doherty.[175] An important member of the W.A.S.U. worth noting is the Sierra Leonean London undergraduate who subsequently became a vice-president of the Union and Governor-General of his country, H. J. Lightfoot· Boston. Another is J. W. de Graft Johnson from the Gold Coast, also a London University student.

The W.A.S.U. had nine aims, namely: to establish a hostel; to foster the spirit of national consciousness and racial pride among all African peoples; to serve "as a Bureau of Information on African history, customs and institutions"; to "act as a centre for Research on all subjects appertaining to Africa and its development"; to "present to the world a true picture of African life and philosophy, thereby making a definitely African contribution towards the progress of civilisation"; to foster co-operation and the spirit of true leadership among its members; to "promote, through regular contacts, the spirit of goodwill, better understanding and brotherhood between all persons of African descent and other races of mankind"; to

[173] Ladipo Solanke, *A History of W.A.S.U.* (manuscript in British Museum [n.d.]), p. 1.
[174] *West Africa* (15 August, 1925), p. 1002.
[175] *West Africa* (12 September, 1925), p. 1176.

publish a monthly called *Wasu*; and finally, to "raise necessary funds for the carrying out of the above-named objects."[176]

None of these aspirations is new in the history of Pan-Africanism. Four years before the inauguration of the W.A.S.U., the A.P.U. had discussed the necessity for a hostel.[177] The case for a new interpretation by Africans of their past to replace the unreliable accounts of racist anthropologists, missionaries and travellers had been eloquently made by Edward Wilmot Blyden. Not only did Solanke endorse the arguments of Blyden on this matter, he also showered praises on patriots like Mensah Sarbah and Casely Hayford who produced *Fanti Customary Laws* (London, 1897) and *Gold Coast Native Institutions* (London, 1903) respectively.[178] Speculating on the future of West Africa, J. H. Lightfoot-Boston stressed that it "was in consequence of the recognition of the need for co-operation that the West African Congress N.C.B.W.A. was formed."[179] He confirmed that "the same spirit was responsible for the formation of the West African Students' Union."[180] Similarly the attempt to use a journal to publicise the history, culture and aspirations of the African world goes back to the turn of the twentieth century, if not earlier, when Henry Sylvester Williams' Pan-African Association started *The Pan-African.*

The first object of the W.A.S.U. to materialise was the launching in March, 1926 of *Wasu* with a Sierra Leonean student, Melville Marke, as editor. Its sub-editors were J. W. de Graft Johnson and Julius Ojo-Cole, a Nigerian undergraduate at King's College, London. From the beginning *Wasu* secured a circulation that extended beyond the United Kingdom, Africa and continental Europe to the New World and even

---

[176] *Wasu* (March, 1926); *Wasu* (May-July, 1936).
[177] *Sierra Leone Weekly News,* (3 September, 1921), p. 11.
[178] *Wasu* (March, 1926), pp. 11-15.
[179] *ibid.,* pp. 15-19.
[180] He confirmed that "the same spirit was responsible for the formation of the West African Students' Union."

Asia.[181] Except on a few occasions, the magazine was issued as a quarterly, instead of as a monthly, owing to financial difficulties. A society known as The Rising Ethiopian Development Association (Chicago) and the African Patriotic Students' Club (New York) served as agents for its distribution in America.

Far from constituting a new and distinct Pan-African movement led by men with unorthodox ideas, the W.A.S.U. represents a continuation of existing Pan-African traditions and goals. It was neither West African nor a students' union. Not West African because, according to its constitution,[182] membership was open to any African and African descendants. In fact, the East African, Jomo Kenyatta, as well as the West Indian, H. Bereford Wooding[183] were among its members and in 1935 the famous black American singer Paul Robeson succeeded Casely Hayford as one of the Union's patrons.

The W.A.S.U. was not primarily a students' union because its aims reflected not the academic and personal problems of African students in England but a concern for the predicament of the Negro race and the future of Africa. It is significant that the Freetown Branch had five lawyers, a medical practitioner and a lecturer at Fourah Bay College.[184] Similarly, most of the branches in Nigeria had as members barristers, doctors, chiefs, clergymen and teachers.[185] In Kano, the Chief of Sabon Gari assisted by two Yoruba clerics led the branch; the Prince, later the *Oni* of Ife was an active member of the Ile-Ife branch while the paramount chief, Oba Alaiyeluwa Ademola II, the *Alake* of Abeokuta, served as a patron.[186]

Note should be taken of the impact which the exertions and

[181] Gamell to Editor, *Wasu* (30 June, 1933).

[182] For a text of the W.A.S.U. Constitution see *Wasu* (May-July, 1936)

[183] *Wasu* (March-June, 1927), p. 7.

[184] Philip Garigue, "The West African Students' Union: A Study in Culture Contact," *Africa* (Journal of the Royal African Institute), Vol. XXIII (1953), pp. 55-69.

[185] *ibid.*

[186] *ibid.*

ideas of Casely Hayford, J. E. Kweggyir Aggrey and Marcus Garvey had on the W.A.S.U. during its formative period. Addressing its members on 5 November, 1926, scarcely three months after its inauguration, Casely Hayford described the aspiration of the African as the "attainment of nationality, the possibility of raising his head among the other peoples of the world, and of commanding his national and racial opportunity."[187] Unless the African did his own thinking and produced his own leaders in all walks of life "he would always remain a hewer of wood and drawer of water."[188] The members of the Union were portrayed as the flower of African intelligence. It was their duty to continue the work of correcting wrong impressions about men of African extraction and to assume the burden of "looking after West African's prosperity in the coming generation."[189] The audience now took its leadership role as confirmed by Hayford more seriously and saw themselves as the means of enhancing the status and prestige of West Africans in particular and persons of African ancestry in general.

The sayings of Kweggyir Aggrey also exercised considerable influence on the W.A.S.U. Indeed, they did much to raise the opinion of many persons of African descent of their race and potentialities and to rehabilitate the word "black" which had been devalued especially by nineteenth-century racists. An early convert to Christianity, he went to the United States in 1898 where he obtained over a dozen degrees within the next quarter of a century. Aggrey's work on the two Phelps-Stokes Education Commissions to Africa[190] earned him recognition in his native Gold Coast; but it was love for his own black race as

---

[187] *Wasu* (December, 1926), pp. 23-28.

[188] *ibid.*

[189] *ibid.*

[190] For details see Kenneth King, "The American Background of the Phelps-Stokes Commissions and their Influence on Education in East Africa especially in Kenya," Edinburgh Ph. D. Thesis, 1968.

expressed in his aphorisms that won him international fame. Among his famous sayings are:

> I am proud of my colour; whoever is not proud of his colour is not fit to live.
> If I went to heaven and God said, "Aggrey, I am going to send you back, would you like to go as a white man?" I should reply, "No, send me back as a black man, yes completely black." "Because I have [*sic*] work to do as black man that no white man can do. Please send me back as black as you can make me."[191]

The W.A.S.U.'s object to promote understanding and brotherhood between Africans and the other branches of humanity may partly have derived from Aggrey's famous simile of the need for both black and white keys on the piano for the production of musical harmony. "His sudden death in New York in 1927 while engaged on a thesis on racial interpretations robbed the Gold Coast of a valuable son and the world of a work that would have been founded on experience of the African in many environments."[192] The *Wasu'* editorial comment on his death and the memorial service held in his honour by the W.A.S.U. are a measure of the man's influence on the Union.[193]

A third celebrity of African origin whose racial and political philosophy affected the W.A.S.U. was Marcus Garvey. After his release from Atlanta Prison in 1927, the year Kweggyir Aggrey died, he emigrated to England the following year. On his arrival, Garvey acquired an office designated "European Headquarters" at 57 Castleton Road, West Kensington, London, W.14. The facilities of this Office were for some time also used by the W.A.S.U. Though the Black Star Line and the Back to Africa schemes were wrecked by his imprisonment, his massive propaganda for pride in the black

---

[191] Quoted in E. W. Smith, *Aggrey of Africa* (London, 1930), pp. 2, 4.
[192] *West Africa* (23 July, 1932), p. 748.
[193] *Wasu* (September, 1927).

skin left an indelible mark on African nationalism everywhere despite the criticisms made against him by white men and influential persons of African stock, notably W. E. B. DuBois.

From his London base, Marcus Garvey attempted to revive the campaign for justice and respect for Africans and their descendants and for their re-settlement in the fatherland. On 6 June, 1928 he delivered at Royal Albert Hall, London a long and passionate speech with the title "The Case of the Negro for International Racial Adjustment, Before the English People."[194] He had been jailed, he explained, because an auxiliary of the U.N.I.A. "posted a letter to somebody; in the evidence an envelope was presented to the witness which he identified as addressed to him, but he could not identify any letter contained in the envelope, and the prosecuting attorney presented it in evidence as a fair assumption that the envelope bore mailed matter from the Black Star Line, of which I was President, and because of that — an empty envelope — I was sent to prison in America for five years."[195]

Arguing that "being imprisoned in the United States of America is not like being imprisoned in England, where you have morality and principle and justice and law before you can take away the name of a man and deprive him of his character," he appealed to the British public not to jump to any hasty conclusion about his character challenging any man in the world to say that he had ever defrauded him of even a single penny.[196] Garvey then recalled how the British West India Regiment was used to incorporate most of West Africa to the British Empire and how, during the Great War, the valour of black-skinned soldiers ensured the defeat of Germany thereby making it possible for France and Britain to take over the imperial acquisitions of the vanquished.

---

[194] Printed by Poets' and Painters' Press, 146 Bridge Arch., Sutton Walk, London, 1968 with an introductory biographical sketch by G. K. Osei. Page references are to this ed.

[195] *ibid.,* p. 12.

[196] *ibid.,* p. 21.

Not only had Africans and their descendants fought to extend the boundaries of the British Empire, they had also fought for the American nation. The first man who shed his blood in America for the independence of the American Colonies was a black man on Boston Common named Crispus Attucks. During the Civil War, black soldiers saved the day many a time. The great Theodore Roosevelt was saved to serve his country and humanity not by his own Rough Riders but by black men.[197] Did his audience, he asked:

> know that we have gladly borne your burdens for four hundreds of years? The cotton mills of Lancashire, the great shipping port of Liverpool, tell the tale of what we have done as black men for the British Empire. The cotton that you consume and use in keeping your mills going has for centuries come from the Southern States of United States; it is the product of negro labour. Upon that cotton your industry has prospered and you have been able to build a great Empire to-day.[198]

Although black men had received unfair treatment in the colonies, they did not hate the whites since God intended humanity to live in common brotherhood. What blacks were demanding was a fair chance, a fair opportunity to live in peace and develop their talents.

Marcus Garvey followed up this speech with a letter of 5 September, 1928 addressed to Reginald Bridgeman,[199] a former British diplomat and now international secretary of the League Against Imperialism launched in Brussels the previous year. Garvey outlined in the form of questions, twenty-two in number, the grievances and aspirations of the peoples of the African world. Did Bridgeman accept Africa to be the "proper, moral and legal home of the black race?" Did he think the Negro was entitled to all the rights of other human beings? Was he satisfied that the Negro had been given in modern

[197] *ibid.,* pp. 16-17.
[198] *ibid.,* p. 17.
[199] In *Bridgeman Collection.*

times a fair chance to develop himself? Did he believe that the Negro could best develop himself under the tutelage and direction of the other races? Did he think that the black Republics of Haiti and Liberia had been given a fair chance to develop as proof of the ability of the Negro for self-government? When the time came for the repatriation of the African diaspora to their ancestral home, would he help to make the venture a success? Did he believe that because of the "higher cultural attainments" of the Negroes of the Western World and those of West Africa, "they should be the real and only missionaries to their own people in Africa?" In the concluding section of the letter, Marcus Garvey re-affirmed the aims and objects of his organisation, the U.N.I.A.

Also in 1928, Marcus Garvey submitted a petition to the League of Nations on behalf of the U.N.I.A. Incorporating the earlier petition (1922), the document was published in London the same year as a thirty-page booklet.[200] It enumerated the disabilities imposed on black men since the Atlantic slave trade and condemned South Africa's native policy, the horrors of the Belgian Congo and the mandate system. Also severely attacked were the alienation of lands belonging to Africans to white settlers and the Firestone Agreement negotiated between the Liberian Government and the American Firestone rubber Company in 1926. Points raised in his speech at Royal Albert Hall, in his Petitions to the League of Nations as well as in his letter to Bridgeman, all these were kept alive by a journal started in the early 1930s by Garvey and called *The Black Man*.

Despite his exertions, he found it impossible to recapture his former following. In the opinion of George Padmore, the black population in Britain proved too scanty to provide any substantial organizational strength and too poor to contribute the funds needed if the U.N.I.A. was to be resuscitated on a

[200] A copy can be found in *ibid.*

global scale.[201] As a result, Padmore further explains, the Black Redeemer "spent his declining years addressing small crowds of English people in Hyde Park, boasting of his former glory."[202]

The declining fortunes of Garveyism enabled the W.A.S.U. to flourish and other Pan-African pressure groups to emerge. From the beginning, the W.A.S.U. operated from its secretary's lodgings from where it moved in 1928 to premises offered by Garvey. The use of a whole house proved so effective in increasing both the Union's activities and membership that when the lease expired a year later, it was decided that funds should be raised to secure another house. Consequently, the W.A.S.U. authorised Ladipo Solanke to go to West Africa and appeal for funds. From October, 1929 to September, 1932 he visited several West African cities and towns. Chiefs and other influential leaders were approached. The tour yielded about £1,381 enabling a hostel to be opened in January, 1933 in Camden Town in the St. Pancras District of London.[203]

Besides furnishing money for the hostel scheme, the tour provided an opportunity for the formation of branch unions where none already existed. Among the branches started as a direct consequence of the tour were those of Cape Coast, Elmina, Nsawam, and Sekondi in the Gold Coast; Aba, Abeokuta, Ebute Metta, Enugu, Jos, Port Harcourt and Zaria in Nigeria. The first branch to be established was in Accra followed in 1928 by another in the Belgian Congo. The Freetown, Accra and Lagos branches included many foundation members of the parent union and, in several cases,

[201] *Pan-Africanism or Communism? The Coming Struggle for Africa* (London, 1956), p. 102.

[202] *ibid.*

[203] See "The Official Report of the W.A.S.U. Mission, 1929-1932," *Wasu* (August-November, 1935).

as in Lagos the branches were inaugurated by former members of the parent union themselves.

Meanwhile there appeared in London in December, 1931 an organisation styled the League of Africans whose aim was "to promote mutual understanding and to maintain sincere, friendly relationships among the Native races of South, East and West Africa, Egyptians and other Native races of North Africa."[204] Officers were elected as follows: president, A. H. Koi, a Gold Coast medical student who subsequently became a member of Kwame Nkrumah's first administration; vice-president, T. Deressa from Abyssinia; treasurer, Jomo Kenyatta; general-secretary, Miss M. Faro of Transvaal (South Africa); assistant secretary, the Gold Coaster Jukius S. Adoo.[205] The League of Africans seems to have barely survived its inaugural meeting for there is scarcely any evidence of its activities in British journals like *West Africa* and *The African World* nor is it mentioned by the W.A.S.U. and the League of Coloured Peoples, another Pan-African pressure group launched earlier the same year. The League of Africans was probably an off-shoot of the League of Coloured Peoples whose name would logically make Asians eligible for membership.

The League of Coloured Peoples was started chiefly due to the efforts of the Jamaican, Harold Arundel Moody (1882-1947), a devout Christian trained at King's College, London where he obtained the degree of Doctor of Medicine in 1919. His scientific studies could not suppress his religious disposition, for Christianity continued to loom large in both his private and public life. During the 1930s he became president of the Christian Endeavour Union of Great Britain and Ireland as well as an executive member of the British and Foreign Bible Society.

However, he did not allow his deepening involvement in

---

[204] *West Africa* (26 December, 1931), p. 1606.
[205] *ibid.*

spiritual matters to overshadow the Negro Question. Like Ladipo Solanke, Moody "also was very conscious of the need to bring together all the members of his own race resident in Great Britain for personal intercourse and consultation."[206] His chance came during the great depression when Dr. Charles Wesley gave a talk to the Young Men's Christian Association, London. Harold Moody naturally attended and before the large gathering of persons of African descent he seized the opportunity to unfold his ideas. The ideas won the approval of Dr. Wesley for, as we have already noted, he was himself not only a leading spirit of the new Negro movement then in vogue but had also taken part in the New York Pan-African Conference. A special meeting was summoned on 13 March, 1931 in the Y.M.C.A. Hall.

It was at this meeting that the League of Coloured Peoples was launched with Harold Moody as president. Among those present were Stephen Petter Thomas, a Nigerian law student and his sister, Stella Thomas, who in 1933 became the first African female barrister. Their father, Peter Thomas had attended the 1921 London Congress. Also present at the inaugural meeting was the British Guianese, J. A. Barbour James, also a participant at the 1921 London Congress.

The objects of the L.C.P. were:

> To promote and protect the Social, Educational, Economic and Political Interests of its members;
>
> To interest members in the Welfare of Coloured Peoples in all parts of the World;
>
> To improve relations between the Races;
>
> To co-operate and affiliate with organisations sympathetic to Coloured Peoples;
>
> To render such financial assistance to Coloured Peoples in distress as lies within its capacity.[207]

[206] D. A. Vaughan, *Negro Victory: The Life Story of Dr. Harold Moody* (London, 1950), p. 52.

[207] *The Keys* (July, 1933), back cover. The last object was a later addition.

Compared with those of the W.A.S.U., the aims of the L.C.P. are definitely more political.

For about two years the L.C.P. possessed no official means of publicity. Money had been a problem right from the start since many of its members were students. But in July, 1933 it launched an organ with the title *The Keys*, a name inspired by the aphorismes of J. E. Kweggyir Aggrey who maintained that the fullest musical harmony can be achieved only by the combined use of the black and white keys of the piano. Like the *Wasu, The Keys* secured a wide readership; unlike the *Wasu*, it frequently changed its name. After September, 1939 it assumed the designation *News Notes*, finally adopting the title *League of Coloured Peoples Review*.

At first the L.C.P. operated from Harold Moody's house in Peckman but the volume of its membership soon underlined the urgent need for better arrangements. In October, 1936 decisions were taken to establish permanent headquarters and to engage a full-time salaried secretary. Accordingly, the headquarters moved from the President's lodging to Farrington Street (London). A few months later five committees were created including the Colonial Questions Committee, the Editorial Committee and the Finance Committee.[208]

A feature of the association was its acceptance of white members, presumably as a way of fulfilling one of its objects: the improvement of race relations. Although the white members freely participated in debates and conferences, they were excluded from the executive committee. In an address delivered at an L.C.P. Conference on "The Negro in the World To-Day" held in Memorial Hall, London from 13 to 15 July, 1934, Harold Moody argued that if the Negro was to be emancipated, the emancipator must come from within. Thus, during the year April, 1933 to March, 1934, officers of the society were three West Indians (excluding Harold Moody) and three Africans, while in the executive committee there

[208] *The Keys* (April-June, 1937), p. 56.

were eight West Indians, two Africans, two Afro-Americans and one Indian.[209] In the year 1936-37, Africans accounted for eight out of the thirteen executive members.[210] The next year four West Indians and two Africans formed the executive committee.[211]

That members were future leaders of their people and that the purpose of the League was to provide training in leadership were statements that the President often made and stressed. In a speech, "The Duty of the Educated African," given at the Third Annual Conference of the L.C.P. held from 3 to 5 April, 1936, Moody declared that:

> The task of building up a new Africa fell most appropriately on the young educated African. It was for him to equip himself thoroughly with knowledge, not merely in such subjects as medicine, chemistry or engineering, but also in the social sciences, sociology, economics, ethnology, etc. Secondly he should steep himself in the history of his own people so as to have that sense of racial pride and unity without personal sacrifice; the individual must be willing to subjugate his own interests to the good of the whole race.[212]

The League of Coloured Peoples was hardly four years old when disintegration threatened it. One cause of the misunderstanding is to be found in the interpretation of the phrase "Coloured Peoples." To the President it meant Africans and their descendants in the New World.[213] Indeed, the very first editorial in *"The Keys"* announced that the aim of the L.C.P. was to state the cause of the Black Man. None the less, some members felt that the Indians' interests ought also to be catered for. They cited the Indian presence in Africa and the fact that forty per cent of the population of British Guiana was

---

209 *The Keys* (July, 1933), back cover.
210 *The Keys* (July-September, 1936), back cover.
211 *The Keys* (January-March, 1938), back cover.
212 *The Keys* (July-September, 1936), p. 14.
213 D. A. Vaughan, *op. cit.,* p. 65.

Indian. Harold Moody's interpretation eventually prevailed but there were still members who remained unconvinced.

Much more serious was the challenge to the president's leadership itself. Many of the members were young men fascinated by the revolutionary ideas of Karl Marx and Lenin. Interested though he was in what was happening in the Soviet Union, the foundation for all things, Moody insisted, was Christianity.

But the most important cause of the opposition was the groundless suspicion that he was collaborating with the British Colonial Office to stifle the growing nationalism of African students.[214] As early as 1932 an anonymous appeal in *The Negro Worker*, a left-wing journal edited by George Padmore, was addressed to all coloured students "to break with the sycophantic leadership of Dr. Harold Moody, a typical 'Uncle Tom.' "[215]

By the beginning of 1935 the situation had become so bad that Moody offered to resign. But the break never came. The offer was withdrawn and at the annual general meeting summoned in the same year he was re-elected president, an office he held without interruption until his sudden death after the Second World War.

Between 1924 and 1936, African exiles in France formed pressure groups there, notably the *Ligue Universelle pour la défence de la Race Noir,* the *Comité de la défense de la Race Nègre* and the *Ligue de la défense de la Race Nègre* led by the Dahomeyan, Touvalou Houénou, the Senegalese, Lamine Senghor and the Sudanese, Tiémoho Garon Kouyaté, respectively.[216] The *Ligue Universelle* rejected "the idea of racial

[214] *West Africa* (3 February, 1934), pp. 109-110; *West Africa* (7 April, 1934), p. 350.

[215] Reprinted in Nancy Cunard, ed., *Negro Anthology* (London, 1934), p. 555.

[216] J. Ayodele Langley, *Pan-Africanism and Nationalism in West Africa,* p. 287.

inferiority," stood for the solidarity of the African race, advocated the establishment of educational and economic institutions, pledging itself to protect the territorial integrity and independence of Liberia, Haiti, Abyssinia and San Domingo.[217]

Condemnations of the controversial Senegalese politician, Blaise Diagne, as a traitor to the black race proved fatal for the *Ligue Universelle*; weakened by the harassment of Diagne, the organisation collapsed in 1926, barely two years after the inauguration, and was succeeded by the *Comité*. With the death of Lamine Senghor the following year, the *Comité* was in turn reconstituted as the *Ligue de la défense de la Race Nègre*. By espousing the cause of the North African nationalist movement, *L'Étoile Nord-Africaine*, led by Messali Hadj, and by contemptuously alluding to men like Diagne and Gratien Candace from Martinique, as the agents of imperialism, the *Ligue* antagonised the French authorities who suppressed it in 1937.

Unlike the Pan-African associations launched in England, notably the West African Students' Union, the League of Coloured People, and the International African Service Bureau, those of France were short-lived and, as a consequence, could not make a sustained and meaningful impact. Launched in the heyday of Garveyism from which they derived most of their inspiration, the French pressure groups collapsed before the death of Marcus Garvey himself in 1940. It appears that Dr. J. Ayodele Langley, who has examined their activities in considerable detail, has exaggerated their importance.[218] It was chiefly the Pan-African pressure groups in Britain that would keep alive the ideals of the movement from the mid-1930s to the end of the Second World War.

---

[217] *ibid.,* p. 296.

[218] *ibid.,* Chapter VII: "The Movement and Thought of Francophone Pan-Negroism, 1924-1936."

CHAPTER 3

THE IMPACT OF THE ABYSSINIAN CRISIS AND WORLD WAR II

The Abyssinian question and the Second World War which were to have a far-reaching influence on the development of Pan-Africanism was preceded by the Liberian "scandal." The scandal itself served as a pointer of black feelings in a white dominated world.

Frustration caused by colour prejudice and the persistence of racial myths partly account for the exiles' apparent connivance at the charges of slavery and forced labour levelled against Liberia during the great slump. In 1929 the League of Nations appointed a commission of inquiry headed by an Englishman, Dr. Cuthbert Christy, assisted by Mr. C. S. Johnson and Arthur Barclay representing the United States and Liberia respectively. The Commission's Report, published the next year, found that although "classic slavery" with slave markets and slave dealers no longer existed, a considerable measure of inter- and intra-tribal domestic slavery flourished.[1] It accused some American Liberians (i.e. Afro-American settlers) of taking some indigenous inhabitants as pawns and of criminally abusing the system for their personal ends.[2] It also

---

[1] League of Nations, *International Commission of Enquiry in Liberia*, Geneva, 1930, pp. 83-84.

[2] Under the system indigenous children were adopted into "civilised" Liberian families for purposes of education. Among other things, it facilitated inter-marriage between the Afro-American colonists and the aboriginal population and the participation of aboriginal elements in the government of the country. For further details, see H. L. Buell, *The Native Problem in Africa* Vol. 2 (New York: Macmillan, 1928).

confirmed that members of the aboriginal population were being recruited and sent to Fernando Po and French Gabon under conditions of criminal compulsion scarcely distinguishable from slave raiding and slave trading. However, the Commission was satisfied that domestic slavery received no encouragement from the Liberian Government and that there was no evidence that leading citizens participated in it.

Despite the cautious tone of its findings, many white critics, among them several liberals, saw the Report as a confirmation of the earlier allegations that the Liberian Government had reduced the indigenous people to oppression and servitude. The results was that condemnations of Liberia increased in volume and bitterness. So widespread and sometimes sweeping were the accusations that several observers openly demanded that the country be placed under the control of a foreign commission; in other words, Liberia should become a mandated territory. The demand was repeated during the House of Lords debate in March, 1932.[3]

No doubt, some of the critics of Liberia's domestic policy like John Harris of the Aborigines' Rights Protection Society (England) were motivated by humanitarianism. But conditions in South Africa, the Portuguese colonies and the Belgian Congo, where whites were in charge, made their well-meaning attacks appear hypocritical if not racist. Hence, an incensed African, who signed himself "Africanus," could argue that Africa's lapses were not unique and that mismanagement prevailed everywhere, insisting that abuses in Liberia must not be "unduly magnified, because the delinquent happens to be a struggling African republic."[4]

The suspicion that the allegations of the European critics stemmed from racial prejudice was reinforced by the fear that a bad reputation for Liberia would be exploited by racists to further discredit peoples of African extraction and to prove

[3] *Parliamentary Debates,* House of Lords, Fifth Series, Vol. 83, 1931-32, pp. 912-38.
[4] *West Africa* (17 October, 1931), p. 1259.

their incapacity for self-government. This seems clear from an article, "The Future of Liberia: Proposed League Control," which Harold Moody as leader of the L.C.P. wrote in an English daily. With the great scramble in mind, he accused the whites of scheming to annex the only remaining spot (besides Abyssinia) which the black man could call his country.[5] The record of Portugal in Africa made anything but cheerful reading but the League of Nations had made no efforts to expose the facts or to suggest that Portugal be advised as to the way to govern the African subjects humanely. Moody regretted that whereas a century ago, Wilberforce fought for the emancipation of slaves, his countrymen were today seeking to deprive the descendants of those slaves of the little vestige of freedom left to them. No man "is free who has not a country of his own which he may direct according to his will"; it was undesirable that "one branch of the human family however noble and however wonderful may have been its achievements should direct the destiny of every other branch of that family."[6] No race was strong enough, he believed, to lord it over the other indefinitely. Anticipating Kwame Nkrumah, Moody maintained that it was better to do wrong in liberty than to do right in chains. In his opinion, the full development and independence of the black man was essential for the moral and spiritual good of the white man and of humanity at large.[7] Moody revealed that he had had several talks with Mr. L. A. Grimes, Liberia's Secretary of State, and had received from him documents presenting the case of the Liberian Government.[8] Moody rejected the League of Nations' Plan of Assistance for Liberia as a proposition that no self-respecting nation would countenance. The Plan, among other things, provided for a financial adviser to be nominated by the United States and approved by the President of Liberia.

[5] *The Manchester Guardian* (30 October, 1933).
[6] *ibid.*
[7] *ibid.*
[8] *West Africa* (1 July, 1933), p. 640.

Concluding, Harold Moody expressed the hope that the white man would adopt "a more liberal attitude which must result in the discovery of, new argosies of cultural exchange' for the universal good of man."[9] Coming from a man of conservative temperament, this article was a measure of the feelings of nationalism which the debate on the Liberian Crisis engendered in the African diaspora. Such a public controversy could hardly fail to foster a corresponding feeling of solidarity among the exiles for it was conducted on racial lines.

At the end of the Second Annual Conference of the L.C.P. held in High Leigh, Hoddesdon from 23 to 25 March, 1934, a resolution was passed and sent to the British Colonial Secretary. It condemned, as Moody had done the year before, the League of Nations Plan of Assistance as a violation of the sovereign status of Liberia.[10] Convinced that the Liberian Government was not faultless and thrifty enough, W. E. B. DuBois approved of expert advice in principle. What he opposed was expert advice from the whites; such advice accompanied by invested capital, meant loss of political power. And Liberia was jealous of her independence.[11] Liberia's chief crime, he went on, "is to be black and poor in a rich, white world; and in precisely that portion of the world in

[9] *The Manchester Guardian* (30 October, 1933).

[10] *The Keys* (April-June, 1934). For details of the League of Nations Plan of Assistance see *The African World* (15 October, 1938), p. 412. In November, 1934 Charles Roden Buxton, a grandson of the great abolitionist and member of the L.C.P. toured West Africa. At the request of the L.C.P. he visited Liberia. His personal observations and discussions with high government officials led him to the conclusion that the alleged irregularities had been exaggerated. What many a critic did not know was that the Christy Commission took place in the midst of a presidential election campaign. As Buxton explains, "The President's opponents were well organised and produced Native witnesses to support charges which were, in fact, an important factor in the campaign." (Charles R. Buxton, *Impressions of Liberia, November 1934: A Report to the League of Coloured Peoples* (L.C.P. Publication, n.d.).

[11] *Foreign Affairs* (July, 1933), p. 682.

which colour is ruthlessly exploited as a foundation for American and European wealth."[12]

Interest in Liberia was almost completely overshadowed as from the middle of 1935 by Mussolini's preparations to attack Ethiopia, then better known as Abyssinia. At that time, the exiles, as Jomo Kenyatta put it, regarded Abyssinia as "the remaining relic of the greatness of an Africa that once was."[13] In anticipation of the Italian invasion, several persons of African origin formed in August, 1935 an organization known as the International African Friends of Abyssinia with an office at 62 New Oxford Street, London (W.C.1).[14] A statement issued by Jomo Kenyatta said that the object of the I.A.F.A. was to assist by all means in their power, in the maintenance of Abyssinia.[15] The release explained that the organisation had on its committee and among its officers representatives of the Gold Coast, Somaliland and East Africa. The names of the representatives, apart from Jomo Kenyatta's, were however not given. But a letter of 14 August, 1935 from Kenyatta to the famous suffragette, Miss Sylvia Pankhurst, contained them.[16] The officers were: chairman, C. L. R. James; vice-chairman, Dr. Peter Milliard, a medical practitioner from British Guiana; a second vice-chairman, Albert Marryshaw, who attended the 1921 London Pan-African Congress; honorary secretary, Jomo Kenyatta; treasurer, Mrs. Amy Ashwood Garvey, an ex-wife of Marcus Garvey; and secretary for propaganda, Samuel Manning of Trinidad.

The committee members were Muhammed Said from Somaliland; John Payne, an Afro-American; J. B. Danquah, G. E. Moore and S. R. Wood. The last three were members of two political missions from the Gold Coast that came to Britain

[12] *ibid.,* p. 695.
[13] *The Labour Monthly* (September, 1935), p. 536.
[14] *ibid.,* p. 532; *New Times and Ethiopia News* (30 January, 1954), p. 3.
[15] *The Labour Monthly* (September, 1935), p. 532.
[16] Printed in *New Times and Ethiopia News* (30 January, 1954), p. 3.

in 1934 to demand constitutional reform. One mission representing the traditional rulers and unofficial members of the Legislative Council was led by Nana Sir Ofori Atta with J. B. Danquah as secretary. The other mission was comprised by G. E. Moore and S. R. Wood, both of them officers of the Gold Coast A.R.P.S. When George Padmore came to England towards the end of 1935 to settle there permanently, he joined the International African Friends of Abyssinia. Though he did not form the I.A.F.A., contrary to popular impression, he eventually dominated it.

Also in anticipation of the Italian invasion, the L.C.P. summoned a general meeting held in Memorial Hall on 4 September, 1935. The crowded meeting unanimously passed a resolution which not only expressed an opinion upon the imminent crisis but also laid down a policy concerning the future of Africa as a whole.[17] The L.C.P. offered its utmost co-operation to the Abyssinians in the deep shadow of war hanging over their beloved country. Mussolini's policy was denounced as expressive of a deep-rooted conviction in the minds of most Europeans that Africans were ordained to be their serfs.[18] Europeans were urged to abandon this idea and invited to begin to recognise the African peoples as equal partners with them in the noble task of human advancement and to desist from looking upon Africa as a continent designed for ruthless exploitation. Finally, the resolution warned the metropolitan powers and the League of Nations that the time was "now ripe for them to consider a plan for the future of Africa which plan should be nothing less than the ultimate and complete freedom of Africa from any external domination whatsoever."[19]

The following month, October, 1935, the Italians attacked Abyssinia. In their attempt to "raise Abyssinia to the level of

[17] *The Keys* (January-March, 1936), p. 31; D. Vaughan, *Negro Victory* (London, 1950).
[18] *ibid.*
[19] *ibid.*

other civilised nations" the fascist invaders violated a series of international agreements, notably the League of Nations Covenant (Articles XII, XIII and XV) and the Kellogg Pact (1928) both of which renounced war as an instrument of national policy as well as the Italo-Ethiopian Treaty of Perpetual Friendship also signed in 1928. By bombing and spraying poisonous gas over the beleaguered population, Italy contravened yet another international convention namely: the Geneva Protocol of 1925. At a time when pacifism had won the hearts of many, the unprovoked barbarities that marked the fascist campaign naturally engendered global sympathy for the Ethiopians.

For Africans and their descendants at home and abroad, the Italian adventure amounted to another rape of the fatherland. The reaction of Kwame Nkrumah who was passing through England from the Gold Coast to the United States was typical. When he saw the poster, "MUSSOLINI INVADES ETHIOPIA," he was overwhelmed by emotion. In his own words: "At that time, it was almost as if the whole of London had suddenly declared war on me personally."[20]

The West African press reacted in a similar manner. "We in West Africa," a Sierra Leonean weekly commented, "are not disinterested in this Italo-Abyssinian question, for our past experience has taught us that though out of the 'heats,' we cannot escape the 'finals.' "[21] A Gold Coast newspaper asserted that the conflict was revealing, especially to the African race, what was at the back of the minds of the European powers in their dealings with the weaker peoples of the world and was teaching the members of the African race never to rely "on the most solemn promise or in the most sacred treaty made by a European power with a subject race."[22] "What we would like to impress on the inhabitants of this

---

[20] *Ghana: The Autobiography of Kwame Nkrumah* (Edinburgh: Thomas Nelson, 1961), p. 22.

[21] *Sierra Leone Weekly News* (3 August, 1935).

[22] *Vox Populi* (11 September, 1935).

country," the paper later declared, "is that war with Abyssinia is our war."[23]

Ethiopian Defence Committees were set up in various parts of West Africa. In London, the W.A.S.U. also formed an Ethiopian Defence Committee. In France the *Ligue de la défence de la Race Nègre* held joint meetings with *L'Étoile Nord-Africaine* "on behalf of Ethiopia and as a demonstration of racial solidarity."[24] Statements expressing support for Abyssinia were issued by *L'Étoile Nord-Africaine* and by Negro workers in Holland and the French Caribbean.[25]

When the Ethiopian Emperor, His Majesty Haile Selassie, and the other members of the royal family arrived in England in 1936 to spend years of exile there, the I.A.F.A. gave a reception for them.[26] In an article "Abyssinia and the Imperialist," apparently addressed to Europeanised blacks, C. L. R. James as chairman of the I.A.F.A. declared:

> Africans and people of African descent, especially those who have been poisoned by British Imperialist education, needed a lesson. They have got it. Every succeeding day shows exactly the real motives which move Imperialism in its contact with Africa, shows the incredible savagery and duplicity of European Imperialism in its quest for markets and raw materials.[27]

The I.A.F.A. was disbanded when a number of European liberals, including admirers of the Emperor, formed pressure groups to work on behalf of Ethiopia. In France a *Comité International pour la défense du peuple Ethiopien et de la Paix* was inaugurated with headquarters in Paris. In Holland there appeared *Nederlandsche Vereeniging voor de Vrijmaking Abessynie* (Dutch Society for the Liberation of Abyssinia)

[23] *Vox Populi* (9 October, 1935).

[24] J. Ayodele Langley, *Pan-Africanism and Nationalism in West Africa*, p. 324.

[25] *New Times and Ethiopia News* (30 May, 1936), p. 3.

[26] George Padmore, *Pan-Africanism or Communism?*, p. 145.

[27] *The Keys* (January-March, 1936).

based at The Hague. Similarly the Venezuelans started a society known as the Friends of Abyssinia.

In Britain alone, over a dozen organizations worked on behalf of the besieged African monarchy of which the most effective were the Friends of Abyssinia (Ethiopia) League having as its Patroness Princess Tsahai, daughter of the Ethiopian Emperor and the distinguished scholar Dr. Ernest Baker among its honorary members; the Circles for the Liberation of Ethiopia (Essex) and the Abyssinia Association. The Circles for the Liberation of Ethiopia, founded on the initiative of the suffragette, Miss Sylvia Pankhurst, published a weekly *New Times and Ethiopia News* with a world-wide circulation. The Abyssinia Association began as a group of English persons particularly interested in Abyssinia, most of them having lived there or visited the country. The Association aimed "to diffuse correct information about Ethiopia in lectures and the press; and to urge in every way action by the League of Nations to save the country from Italian conquest."[28] Among its foundation members were Sir George Paish (chairman). Major Neil Hunter (honorary treasurer) and the economist, Professor H. Stanley Jevons (secretary). Other persons who later joined the society included the pacifist, Norman Angell of *The Great Illusions*[29] fame, the Dean of Winchester, Miss Eleanor Rathbone M.P., Mr. Philip Noel-Baker M.P. and Miss Muriel Blundell who subsequently replaced Stanley Jevons as secretary. Compared with the more recent unilateral declaration of independence by the white settler minority in the Rhodesia colony, the Italian invasion evoked an equal, if not greater, amount of concern in the white world for the African victims.

The vehement protest of the British populace against the policy of their Government as reflected in the Hoare-Laval Plan resembled the vigorous opposition in the eighteenth and

[28] *New Times and Ethiopia News* (16 May, 1936), p. 4.
[29] (London, 1910). See also his *The Fruits of Victory* (London, 1921) and *This Have and Have Not Business* (London, 1936).

nineteenth centuries of the British abolitionists to the Atlantic slave trade. Drawn up by Sir Samuel Hoare, the British Foreign Secretary, and M. Laval, the Prime Minister of France, the proposals were extremely favourable to Italy and would have compromised Ethiopia's independence had they been implemented, which they never were, thanks to the outcry of the British public.[30] It was suggested, among other things, that Italy should receive Eastern Tigre (included Adowa but not Aksum) and the Donakil area except for the territory in the Ogaden. In a protest memorandum to the League of Nations, the Ethiopian Administration rejected the proposals as an invitation to Abyssinia, the victim of an act of aggression, first: to cede to her Italian aggressor, under the pretext of exchange of territories, about half of her national territory to enable the aggressor to settle part of her population there; and second, to agree that the League of Nations should confer upon the invader control over the other half of Ethiopian territory pending future annexation.[31]

The unexpected dogged resistance to the fascist adventurers offered boundless opportunities for the ventilation of patriotic sentiments and demonstration of solidarity with Abyssinia as well as the glorification of her history and culture. Besides furnishing the exiles with material that gave enormous scope for the propagation of Pan-African aspirations, the prolonged resistance showed that in the defence of the fatherland no sacrifice could be too great. It was more honourable to die a free man than move under a foreign yoke. In the popularisation of the virtues of patriotism, the Abyssinia Association made a significant contribution. Not only did some of its pamphlets reprint from time to time quotations emphasising the inalienable right of all human beings to

[30] A full text of the Hoare-Laval Proposals was published in *The Times* (London) (14 December, 1935), p. 12. For reaction of the British people see *The Tragedy of Abyssinia*, League of Nations Union Publication, London, 1936.

[31] *The Times,* (London) (14 December, 1935), p. 12.

liberty and justice, but the Association itself frequently paid tribute to the memory of "Those Ethiopians Who Died for Freedom."

At a memorial service of the organisation held in London on 18 March, 1937, the preacher, the Dean of Winchester, reminded the congregation that what was at stake was "the issue between Right and Wrong, Freedom and Oppression."[32] Four months later a similar service was conducted in New Church, Owo (Nigeria) with Reverend Africanus Mensah, founder of the Church, as preacher. Though the text of his sermon was "Ethiopia shall soon stretch forth her hands unto God," his comments were more political than religious. He traced the history of the country from the reign of Queen Sheba to the eruption of the crisis. The exertions of Miss Sylvia Pankhurst received high commendation and the League of Nations was severely rebuked for lifting oil sanctions on Italy barely a year after their imposition.[33]

Many observers the world over shared Africanus Mensah's views that the League had been partial in its handling of the conflict. Nehru made it clear that the Congress Party was not enamoured of the League and that the people of India objected to "this suppression of the Abyssinian people or to any recognition of the aggressor nation."[34] A conference of the West African Youth League, an anti-imperialist movement launched and led by the Sierra Leonean agitator I.T.A. Wallace Johnson, also called upon the League to denounce the aggressor in a more practical form by enforcing an oil

[32] *Nemesis* (Abyssinia Association Pamphlet), London, 1939. On the front page of the pamphlet are the following excerpts:
"We believe in liberty ... We assert the right of all nations to live their own lives." (Mr. Arthur Greenwood, M.P., 3.9.39).
"The British Government and the British people are profoundly convinced that every nation has its contribution to make to the common civilisation of humanity, but that no nation, great or small, can do itself justice unless it be free." *The Times* (London) (5 September, 1939).
[33] *New Times and Ethiopia News* (3 July, 1937), p. 2.
[34] *New Times and Ethiopia News* (9 October, 1937), p. 5.

embargo.[35] An article "Has the African a God" written by Wallace Johnson for the *African Morning Post* (Accra)[36] deploring Italian atrocities gave the British colonial authorities in the Gold Coast an opportunity to charge him with sedition. But he escaped to Britain where he helped to form more Pan-African pressure groups.

Though the League of Nations disapproved of Italy's intervention in Ethiopia, it failed to enforce economic sanctions on the culprit. The readiness with which European leaders accepted and even aided the Italian incursion drove many men of African blood to the conclusion that they were immoral and unscrupulous politicians united by instinct and interest against the blacks. This view is well brought out in an editorial comment in the *Gold Coast Spectator:*

> Force, the white man's god, is again supreme. Addis Ababa is occupied ... Poison gas, British oil, and the white man's duplicity all combined to make the Italian advance victorious .... After the Great War [World War I] the League lent money to some of the small Central Powers to rehabilitate them. But these are white. The League refused funds to Ethiopia, even though Article XVI stipulates it. Ethiopia, being black, could not be supported, even in affliction, and her financial solicitations were treated with derision. This is the Christian nations at work![37]

As in West Africa so in the Caribbean, the much vaunted values of European civilisation began to come under fire as is clear from the following outburst of the West Indian, Mr. C. C. Belgrave:

> The cold, hard inhuman attitude, which the European Powers have assumed towards Ethiopia, has taught black men that somehow or other, there is a difference in

[35] *Wallace Johnson Collection,* Institute of African Studies Library, Legon (University of Ghana).
[36] (May 15, 1936).
[37] (May 9, 1936).

justice; there is one kind of justice for the white folk, and another kind for black. We wonder if the European Powers still profess to be Christians.[38]

"Rest assured Ethiopia," a Gold Coast patriot consoled, "your territory will be freed once again, as was that of the Poles and Belgians. When that day comes, you will rebuild a strong Empire and negotiate international alliances with Liberia and Haiti."[39]

Erosion of confidence in the League of Nations and the moral integrity of European statesmen compelled the African race to draw closer together for more reliable means of defending their interests. Early in 1937 two Pan-African associations were established in the United States. One was the United Aid for Peoples of African Descent.[40] The organisation sent a message of solidarity to the Emperor as well as letters of protest to the American President, Mr. Franklin D. Roosevelt, the Italian Ambassador to the United States, the former British Prime Minister, Mr. David Lloyd George and the Pope (Pius XI).[41] The other pressure group was the Congress of the African Peoples of the World War Two of whose aims were "To make Liberia one of the Great Powers of the World" and "To help in the hard fight for Ethiopian independence."[42] The Congress announced that plans were "under way for a General Conference to be held in Africa" sometime in 1937 but there is no evidence that it took place.

In Britain, frustration engendered by the role of the League drove some members of the now defunct I.A.F.A., assisted by newcomers, to inaugurate an organisation called the International African Service Bureau. Among the newcomers were T. Ras Makonnen, a British Guianese of Ethiopian extraction formerly known as Mr. Thomas Griffiths, and Wallace

---

[38] *New Times and Ethiopia News* (16 January, 1937), p. 3.
[39] *New Times and Ethiopia News* (14 August, 1937), p. 6.
[40] *New Times and Ethiopia News* (6 March, 1937), p. 8.
[41] *New Times and Ethiopia News* (19 June, 1937), p. 8.
[42] *New Times and Ethiopia News* (7 April, 1937), p. 7.

Johnson. The one was made treasurer, the other general secretary. The other officers were: George Padmore (chairman); Jomo Kenyatta (assistant secretary) and the Barbadian trade unionist, Chris Jones (organising secretary).[43] "The executive committee included Chris Jones, J. J. Ocquaye (Gold Coast), L. Mbanefo (Nigeria), K. Sallie Tamba (Sierra Leone), Garan Kouyaté (Soudan), N. Azikiwe (Nigeria), Gilbert Coka (South Africa). Among its Patrons were Nancy Cunard, Dorothy Woodman, D. N. Pritt, Noel Baker, A. Creech Jones, Victor Gollenz, F. A. Ridley, Sylvia Pankhurst, and Max Yergan."[44]

Like the W.A.S.U. and the L.C.P., the I.A.S.B. provided itself with an organ. Called the *International African Opinion*,[45] the journal was launched in July, 1938 under the editorship of C.L.R. James assisted by the Afro-American, William Harrison, a research student at the London School of Economics and Political Science. That the leaders of the I.A.S.B. were bent on achieving concrete results is clear from the editorial in the maiden issue of its organ. The purpose of the groups was "to assist by all means in their power the unco-ordinated struggle of Africans and people of African descent against oppression which they suffer in every country." The members of the society recognised that their position in London made them more immediately aware of the problem of the Negroes in British dependencies. Nevertheless, their appeal was directed to Negroes everywhere — in the colonial empires, South America and the United States. Though the I.A.S.B. also realised that problems differed from place to place, they were convinced that there existed a common bond of oppression, and as the Ethiopian struggle had shown, blacks everywhere were beginning to see the necessity for international organization and unification of their scattered efforts.

[43] George Padmore, *Pan-Africanism or Communism?*

[44] J. Ayodele Langley, *Pan-Africanism and Nationalism in West Africa,* p. 338.

[45] There is a complete file in the *Schomburg Collection.*

The nature of the struggle before them was becoming clearer and they were determined to fight to the end "until economically, politically and socially, the black man was everywhere as free as other men were." The founders of I.S.A.B. were realistic enough to appreciate that they could "not liberate the millions of Africans and peoples of African descent from their servitude and oppression. That task no one can do but the black people themselves. But we can help to stipulate the growing consciousness." In a release entitled "What Is The International African Service Bureau?", Wallace Johnson further explained that the I.A.S.B. was a "non-party" organization that owed no allegiance or affiliation to any political party or group in Europe.[46] Active membership was confined to Africans and persons of African stock regardless of their political and religious persuasions. Such members were however required to accept the aims of the association. Non-Africans who sympathised with the aspiration of the Bureau and desired to demonstrate their interest in Africans and their descendants in a practical way were permitted to be associate members.

In one respect, the I.A.S.B. differed from the other exile pressure groups in Britain for it sought

> to co-ordinate and centralize the activities of the various organisations be they Political, Trade Union, Co-operative, Fraternal, Cultural, etc. which at present exist in different parts of the black world, and in this way bring them into closer fraternal relation with one another, as well as sympathetic organizations in Great Britain and other countries, so as to arouse concerted action upon all questions affecting the common economic, political, social and educational well-being of the Africans and peoples of African descent.[47]

To see the Italo-Ethiopian conflict as the sole cause of the

---

[46] Reprinted on the inside pages of cover of *Hands Off the Protectorates* (I.A.S.E. Publication), London, 1938.
[47] *ibid.*

establishment of the I.A.S.B. would however be an over-simplification of a complex situation. Other factors were also at work, notably the growth of articulate racialism even in Britain and the protracted debate on the German and the Italian colonial demands. The significance for African nationalism of the Italo-German colonial ambitions in particular, and the debate in general, can be gleaned from a letter of October, 1938, which Padmore wrote to the Gold Coast A.R.P.S. In that letter he emphasized that the colonial question was coming up before the politicians of Europe as a result of the demands of Hitler and that it was necessary for men of African blood to be on their guard.[48] "In this respect," he concluded, "the closest collaboration of our Bureau and the Aborigines' Rights Protection Society would be of tremendous importance in making the voice of Africa heard in the councils of the nations."[49]

One suggestion advanced to meet the German and Italian claims advocated the return to Germany of her former dependencies and the cession to dissatisfied powers of some others. A leading exponent of this idea was Lord Lothian who, as private secretary to Lloyd George, helped in the wording of those clauses of the Versailles Treaty providing for the mandate system.

The most widely discussed proposal and wish which met with considerable support in liberal circles was the remedy prescribed by Sir J. A. Salter (later Baron), a former director of the Finance and Economic Section of the League of Nations. Salter's solution was first put forward at a conference on "Peace and Colonial Problem" summoned by the National Peace Council (London) and held on 29 October, 1935 in Livingstone Hall, Westminster.[50] J. A. Salter recommended first, that whether or not other countries took the same step,

---

[48] Padmore to W. Essuman-Gwira Sekyi, 4 October, 1938 in *Gold Coast A.R.P.S. Papers*, Acc. No. 156/1965.

[49] *ibid.*

[50] *Peace and Colonial Problem,* London, 1935.

Britain should return to her traditional policy of equal opportunity for all nations in her colonies; and, second, that she should offer to join with other imperial powers in placing her dependencies under the mandate system and international control.[51] He also suggested a reform of the mandate system itself so as to make it possible for representatives of the Permanent Mandates Commission to visit mandated territories in order to verify statements in the annual reports of the mandatories. The terms of the mandate would remain the same but instead of applying exclusively to the territories taken from Germany and Turkey after the Great War, the system would cover all the colonies.

Arnold Ward, Secretary of the Negro Welfare Association, was present at the conference. Repudiating the trusteeship principle on which the mandate system rested, he said that co-operation between the whites and the blacks could only be put on a lasting basis by the emancipation of the colonial peoples. The interests of the subject inhabitants and of the dissatisfied powers, he concluded, were incompatible.[52]

Harold Moody echoed Arnold Ward's views adding that it was immoral for one race to seek to dominate another.[53] In a resolution passed at an annual general meeting held in March, 1938, the L.C.P. reminded the British Government that when Britain was assigned dependencies previously under German control, the purpose of this was that these territories should be developed primarily for the benefit of their indigenous inhabitants and with a view to their self-government. Such development and the goal of freedom would be more readily attained if these colonies remained in the trust of democratic countries with a parliamentary form of government. On the other hand, the L.C.P. felt that these objectives would be

---

[51] *Economic Policies and Peace* (Metterns Lecture) London, 1936, pp. 30-31.

[52] *Peace and Colonial Problem,* p. 51.

[53] *Peace* (London) (December, 1935), p. 144.

impossible of achievement if the territories concerned were handed over to countries ruled by despots.

Finally, the resolution called upon the British Government and Parliament "to refuse to consider such transfer of these territories, the more strongly that the League is confident that if the indigenous population were consulted they would refuse to consent to such transfer."[54]

The I.A.S.B. also opposed the transfer but for a different reason. In an editorial the Bureau's organ explained that if Africans opposed transfer to Hitler, it was not because they envisaged any fundamental difference in treatment. It was because they refused any longer to be bandied about from one European power to another.[55]

Side by side with the debate on the German and Italian demand for colonial equality went another discussion on a request by the Union of South Africa for an early transfer to her of the protectorates of Basutoland, Bechuanaland and Swaziland. When the self-governing territories of Cape Colony, Natal, Orange Free State and Transvaal were merged by the Act of Union (1909), the three protectorates just enumerated remained under the control of the British Government. Their eventual incorporation in the Union of South African was however envisaged and safeguards for the rights of blacks, though vague, were set out in the Preamble and Schedule to the act. It was also provided that the time of transfer was to be settled by agreement between the governments of Britain and South Africa. Early in the thirties, reports from South Africa hinted that the Union Government was about to press for immediate transfer; this revelation caused Harold Moody to address a letter to Mr. J. H. Thomas, British Secretary of State for Dominion Affairs, opposing the transfer plan on the ground that it would amount to an "extension of

---

[54] *The Keys* (April-June, 1938), pp. 85-86.
[55] *International African Opinion* (7 November, 1938).

the present South African method of dealing with native races."[56]

In November 1934 General Smuts paid a visit to England. At a dinner given in his honour at the Savoy Hotel (London) by the South African Club, the General threatened that if incorporation was unduly delayed the Union might decline to take over the protectorates with consequent damage to their economic interests.[57] No doubt, the Union served them as a market for their agricultural products and livestock but Smuts conveniently ignored the fact that the protectorates equally supplied the Union with much needed cheap labour for her mines and farms. The shortage of labour for the Union's mining and agricultural industries was intensified by the drying up of labour supplies from Portuguese Africa; hence the Union was anxious to have the protectorates under her control.

It was argued by some writers that the protectorates should be handed over because of the invaluable services rendered by South Africans, Generals Smuts and Botha in particular, during the Great War. Many however realised that the enactment of the Statute of Westminster in 1931 and of the Status of South Africa Act three years later meant that the safeguards set out in the South Africa Act of 1909 could in the event of incorporation be replaced or amended by the Union Government without reference to the British Parliament. Such persons included Lord Lugard who held that the time for transfer had not arrived and that when the time came transfer should be effected by a tripartite agreement or treaty which, while giving assurance to the natives against unilateral change, would associate them in the transaction.[58] The signatories on their behalf would be really representatives of the people and

---

[56] *Sunday Times* (Johannesburg) (18 June, 1933); *The Keys* (October, 1933), p. 36, (April-June 1935), p. 86. See also the articles of Mr. Lionel Curtis, *The Times* (London) (13-15 May, 1935).

[57] *The Times* (London) (7 November, 1934), p. 18.

[58] *The Manchester Guardian* (28 May, 1935), pp. 11-12.

not merely the hereditary and generally conservative chiefs who then wielded enormous influence. Meanwhile the British Government should undertake to improve the conditions of the black inhabitants by introducing administrative, educational and economic reforms.

This proposal was rejected by both the I.A.S.B. and the L.C.P. for different reasons. In a petition to the Secretary for Dominion Affairs, the I.A.S.B. condemned the projected handing over of the protectorates to the South African Government for three reasons. First, because Africans and Africa were not property to be bartered between one imperialist regime and another; second, because the policy of South Africa toward the indigenous population was objectionable and third because the African inhabitants concerned were not represented in the British Parliament whose views must be heard before transfer could take place.[59] A booklet, *Hands Off the Protectorates* written by George Padmore but published in 1938 under the name of the I.A.S.B., opposed the proposal on the ground that the black Africans concerned did not approve of it.[60] A main objection of the L.C.P. to the proposal was the anxiety of black South Africans that "their brothers of the High Commission Territories [i.e. the protectorates] should not share the unhappiness and misfortune of their situation in the Union."[61]

The debates on the South African, German and Italian colonial ambitions served to bring the exiles closer together. This growing solidarity was demonstrated by the joint memorandum submitted in 1938 on the West Indies to the British Colonial Secretary by the League of Coloured Peoples, the International African Service Bureau and the Negro

[59] *International African Opinion* (July, 1938), pp. 4-5.
[60] See for e.g. *A Statement to the British Parliament and People* (London, 1935) by Tshekedi Khama, Chief and Regent of Bechuanaland setting out his people's reasons for opposing incorporation.
[61] *The Keys* (April-June, 1938), pp. 85-86.

Welfare Association. Disturbances had broken out in Trinidad and Barbados in July, 1937 and continued with violent strikes in Jamaica and St. Lucia spreading to Antigua and British Guiana. Riots involving casualties had occurred in Jamaica, St. Kitts and St. Vincent two years before but the unrest of 1937 was clearly more serious if only because it appeared to affect every section of the British Caribbean. Towards the end of May, 1938 riots broke out again in Jamaica; consequently, the L.C.P. and the I.A.S.B. took up the matter.

The following month both the I.A.S.B. and the L.C.P., organised protest meetings in London condemning the brutality with which the strikers had been treated and demanding far-reaching reforms including: the immediate release of the strike leaders, land settlement schemes, improvement of housing conditions, a self-government Federation of the West Indies and fully democratic institutions.[62] A Royal Commission of Enquiry was appointed the next month under the chairmanship of Lord Moyne. Despite its initial hostility to the Commission, the I.A.S.B. in collaboration with the L.C.P. and the Negro Welfare Association seized the opportunity to present a joint memorandum laying down a minimum programme of change and development to be adopted at once.[63]

The memorandum was in the main an elaboration of the June Resolutions. It stressed the political requisite for better conditions as being the abandonment of the crown colony system of government and urged that property qualifications for the right to vote and hold office be discarded as a first step toward democratic rule in these islands.[64] It demanded the rescinding of all sedition ordinances and emphasised the need to confer on the people the right to form trade unions. Among

[62] *The People* (Trinidad) (30 July, 1938); *International African Opinion,* (August, 1938), p. 16; *The Keys* (July-Sept., 1938), p. 10.

[63] At first the I.A.S.B. denounced the Commission as a bluff in view of the metropolitan government's failure to implement recommendations of previous Commissions (Editorial, *International African Opinion,* August, 1938).

[64] *International African Opinion* (October, 1938), p. 7.

specific proposals suggested to the Commission were: the launching of a $10 million housing scheme; the introduction of compulsory free primary and secondary education as well as the establishment of a West Indian university; the removal of racial discrimination in the colonial civil service and the provision of social welfare measures. Before the Commission left for the West Indies, Harold Moody and Peter Blackman gave evidence before them.[65]

In a pamphlet with the title *The West Indies Today* (1938), the I.A.S.B. advised West Indian dockers, oil and sugar plantation labourers to build up powerful trade unions. Though the I.A.S.B. placed in the forefront of the immediate tasks the question of trade unionism as the primary weapon in the fight for economic emancipation, it urged the workers to realise that their economic struggles could not be divorced from their political aspirations; there was still need for independent working-class political action.

In December, 1939 the Royal Commission submitted a report which emphasised the urgency for considerable extension in the public social services arguing a case for a general scheme for social reconstruction of the Caribbean. The most important recommendation was the establishment of a West Indies Welfare Fund from which the large expenditure envisaged on welfare services and development could be met.[66] The proposed Fund was to be financed by an annual grant of $1 million from the British Treasury for a period of twenty years.

The L.C.P. was invited by the British Colonial Secretary to submit a memorandum setting out its views on the recommendations. But at a meeting on 22 May, 1940, summoned by the L.C.P. to discuss the recommendations as well as British colonial policy, George Padmore and Peter

[65] L.C.P., *Eight Annual Report* (March, 1939), p. 4.
[66] The Recommendations of the Royal Commission were published separately as *Cmd. 6174*, 1940. The full Report was published in October, 1945 (*Cmd. 6607*).

Blackman representing the I.A.S.B. and the Negro Welfare Association, respectively, were present.[67] The three organisations found themselves in substantial agreement with the Commission on such matters as education, public health, housing, industrial legislation and transport. They considered the treatment of the economic and political issues altogether unsatisfactory. In expressing their opinion, the organisations were handicapped by the refusal of the metropolitan government to publish the Report on which the Recommendations were based. Protesting against the secrecy, they maintained that if the Caribbean countries were to make any meaningful progress, it was their own people guided by their own leaders who would play the major part. To withhold from the people and their leaders a report in which the fundamentals of future policy were discussed by a commission of experts could only, in their view, be a blow to West Indian advancement.

Turning to the Welfare Fund, the pressure groups pointed out that West Indians did not wish to be permanent recipients of charity from England. The aim should be to make their countries economically self-supporting so that they could finance new welfare measures without external assistance. The sections of the recommendations concerning industrial development came under heavy fire. It was the view of the Pan-Africanists that if the West Indians were to prosper, they must acquire industrial skill. They possessed oil, raw materials and easy access to the markets of North and South America. Advantage should be taken of the services of the highly skilled persons fleeing from the wrath of the Nazis. Though the organisations accepted the educational proposals, they regretted the lack of any reference to the contribution a university could make to the social, cultural and economic life of the West Indies.

Attention was also drawn to the fact that the Commission's recommendations failed to emphasise the need for economic

[67] *News Notes* (July, 1940), pp. 64-66. The reply of the three organisations is reproduced *in extenso* in D. Vaughan, *op. cit.*, pp. 107-111.

equality. The student of West Indian affairs could not but be struck by the extent to which the social pattern of the old slave society still remained stamped upon these islands. It was a pattern in which a handful of people owned most of the wealth while the vast majority of the population laboured in poverty on the landed property of the rich white minority.[68] Problems which were essentially economic acquired racial overtones because the class structure tended to coincide with racial divisions. The L.C.P., I.A.S.B. and the Negro Welfare Association felt that the solution to the problem of economic inequality lay in the extension of social services and scholarships, the development of trade unionism, the control of monopolies in the sugar and fruit industries, the redistribution of wealth by taxing the richer classes more heavily and land reform.

With regard to the political question, the Pan-Africanists advocated the establishment of an administrative federation of the islands. They also demanded fuller self-government with an extension of the franchise and other electoral reforms such as would place real power in the hands of the masses.

Subsequent events, among them the establishment of the University of the West Indies and the attempt, albeit abortive, to form a West Indian Federation show that the suggestions of the L.C.P., I.A.S.B. and the Negro Welfare Association were in tune with the realities of the situation. In addition to the Welfare Fund set up for the West Indies, a more general scheme was envisaged for all the colonies in the metropolitan government's *Statement of Policy on Colonial Development and Welfare,*[69] issued during the Second World War largely as a result of the recommendations of the Royal Commission of Enquiry.

What was the attitude of the exiles to the Second World War? There was no single concerted approach. The attitude

[68] See for e.g. David Lowenthal, *West Indian Societies* (London: Oxford University Press, 1972).

[69] *Cmd.* 6175, 1940.

adopted by the followers of Harold Moody in many respects differed from that for the Padmore group.

Disappointed by the role of European leaders in the Italo-Ethiopian crisis, the L.C.P. was at first not inclined to support either the Allied or Axis Powers. A meeting of 27 September, 1939 sponsored by the L.C.P. and held in Aggrey House (47 Doughty Street London, W.C.1) took the view that "We must remember that we are Africans first and British subjects after."[70] This position was confirmed in March, 1940 by W. Arthur Lewis, then a lecturer at the London School of Economics and former editor of *The Keys*. In his view, decent people everywhere "know that where one race sets out to exploit another there can be no peace in society; freedom and equality for all, whatever their race, colour or creed, is an essential pillar of civilisation."[71]

Going a step further, Padmore linked up the crusade against Hitlerism with colonial freedom. In an article "To Defeat Nazism We Must Free Colonials," Padmore among other things stated that self-determination was an inalienable right of every people regardless of the stage of their social and cultural development.[72]

These statements by Arthur Lewis and George Padmore clearly anticipated the Atlantic Charter. But as the War got under way, the L.C.P. modified its attitude and supported the Allied Powers. At a general meeting of the organisation convened on 22 May, 1940 and attended by Padmore, Arthur Lewis and Peter Blackman, Harold Moody declared that men of African blood could have no interest in a German victory.[73] Such a victory, he went on "could mean for us of the Colonial Empire the loss of justice, freedom and equality."[74] Moody's apparent *volte face* naturally leads one to expect from the

---

[70] *News Notes* (November, 1939), pp. 4-5.
[71] *New Notes* (March, 1940), pp. 1-2.
[72] *The New Leader* (London) (July, 1940), p. 5.
[73] *New Notes* (July, 1940), p. 64.
[74] *ibid.*

L.C.P. little or no harsh criticism of colonial rule, at least during the duration of hostilities. But the exact opposite turned out to be the case. This fact plainly contradicts the stereotype that Harold Moody was an Uncle Tom whose sole ambition lay in a modest improvement of the relations between the blacks and the whites.

The War itself brought to a focus objects of long standing agitation as well as new issues some of which served to intensify the militancy of the exiles. It raised in sharp outline such questions as the nature of liberty, the powers of the State, the rights of the individual and racial prejudice. With the eruption of hostilities, spokesmen of the British Government made speeches denouncing the racial policies of Nazi Germany and claiming that the British Empire stood for racial equality. It seemed to the L.C.P. that the time had come once more to draw that Government's attention to its own racial policies and if possible to get these sanctimonious declarations crystalised into action.[75]

A target that immediately come under fresh fire was the policy on recruitment into the British colonial medical service. On 14 December, 1939, a deputation armed with a memorandum as well as a copy of the current number of the *British Medical Journal* which contained an advertisement stating that applicants must be of European origin, called on Malcolm MacDonald, the Colonial Secretary.[76]

Among the members of the delegation were W. Arthur Lewis; J. H. Christian, a barrister for the Gold Coast; Charles E. Collet from Seychelles, then secretary of the L.C.P. and Dr. H. Dingwall of British Guaina and vice-president of the L.C.P. MacDonald appreciated the opportunity of hearing the grievances of the organisation and promised to consider whether any general restatement of policy regarding the

[75] *News Notes* (August, 1941), p. 99.
[76] *News Notes* (January, 1940), p. 3; (August, 1941), pp. 100-101.

engagement of coloured people in the unified services should be made.

MacDonald was soon succeeded by Lord Lloyd who in turn was replaced by Lord Moyne. Yet nothing seemed to be happening. Indeed a subsequent advertisement repeated the condition that applicants to the British medical colonial service must be of European stock. Consequently, Harold Moody wrote to Lord Moyne reminding him of the promise made by MacDonald. This letter opened a long correspondence between the two men.[77]

Moyne denied that there was any barrier to prevent the appointment of any inhabitant of a colony whether European or non-European adding that a substantial number of the members of those services was non-European.[78] Moody referred the Colonial Secretary to an issue of an unnamed paper "just to hand" complaining that some of the advertisements coming from His Majesty's Dockyard and Admiralty were most offensive to coloured people.[79] In a separate letter to Moyne, Moody further referred him to a passage in the *Nigerian Eastern Mail* for 22 April, 1940 expressing the hope that "one or other of our elected Legco. [Legislative Council] Members will not fail to ask at the next session of the Council, why in view of the Government's promise re the appointment of Africans to higher posts, an African was not elevated to the Bench when this vacancy occurred."[80] The newspaper was referring to the transfer from Uganda of Mr. C. C. Francis to fill the post of puisne judge in Nigeria. The Colonial Secretary explained that this post was among those normally filled by selecting the most suitable candidate from the colonial legal service.[81] Though direct appointments from the local bar to judicial posts in a dependency could be and were sometimes

---

[77] Published in *News Notes* (August, 1941), pp. 101-119.
[78] Moyne to Moody, 4 April, 1941.
[79] Moody to Moyne, 24 April, 1941.
[80] Moody to Moyne, 26 April, 1941.
[81] Moyne to Moody, 5 May, 1941.

made when circumstances justified this course, Moyne argued, it would not be in the public interest to regard this as the normal procedure.

In his answer Moody said that early in the year the attention of the L.C.P. had been drawn to a notice posted on a board of an unnamed British university inviting applications for the colonial civil service. On making further inquiries the L.C.P. discovered that the advertisement was based not on a circular but on an ordinary letter enclosing a memorandum entitled "General Information Regarding Colonial Appointments." This printed document was issued by the British Colonial Office in March, 1939. Moody thought that page sixty-four of the document proved beyond doubt the unwillingness of the Colonial Secretary to consider applications from persons not of European extraction. In view of this document Moody neither saw how Moyne could deny the existence of the regulation nor understood what purpose such a denial would serve.[82]

Moyne countered with the quibble that under those regulations, he and his predecessors had specifically reserved to themselves the right to admit to the membership of any of the unified colonial services anyone born or ordinarily resident in any of the dependencies irrespective of colour or race. Though the policy laid down by the regulations was well established, Moyne felt that they could be simplified so as to make their meaning clearer to persons unfamiliar with the organisation of the colonial civil service. He had therefore approved a revised form of words which applied to the unified colonial services as a whole. The revised form, a copy of which was sent to Moody, stated that a candidate must be "a British subject or a British protected person, and (a) is of European descent, or (b) was born, or is ordinarily resident in a Colony, Protectorate, or Mandated Territory, or is a child of a person so born or resident."[83]

[82] Moody to Moyne, 21 May, 1941.
[83] Moyne to Moody, 30 May, 1941.

Though Moody agreed with the Colonial Secretary that the regulations needed to be changed, he considered the Colonial Secretary's amendments unsatisfactory. Since the position remained unclear, Moody demanded from the Colonial Secretary "a final letter announcing that all distinction between European and non-European is now to disappear."[84] To this Moyne replied that the regulation already provided for the admission to membership of the unified services of persons born or ordinarily resident in a colony and so on and that the regulations had been revised so as to remove any doubt which might have been thought to exist as to their effect. Moreover in the revised regulations the opportunity had been seized to extend legibility to the children of persons born or ordinarily resident in one of the territories concerned.[85]

Commenting on the correspondence between Moody and Moyne, Arthur Lewis stressed that whatever might be the shortcomings of the French imperial system they did not include racial prejudice.[86] In the French Empire any man, including members of the subject population, might rise to the highest position merited by his ability. Hence, the appointment of a Negro governor was regarded as a matter of course. Lewis is here referring to the French Guianese, Felix Eboue[87] who was made Governor-General of French Equatorial Africa during the Second World War. But in the British Empire, Arthur Lewis lamented, there could be no black governor because the maintenance of white prestige was considered to be an essential prop of the imperial regime. Men of African blood were not allowed to hold posts of distinction and responsibility. The L.C.P. would not rest, Arthur Lewis finally warned, until such an iniquitous system was abolished.

The publication of the Moody-Moyne correspondence in

[84] Moody to Moyne, 12 June, 1941.

[85] Moyne to Moody, 20 June, 1941.

[86] *News Notes* (August, 1941), pp. 117-119.

[87] For his biography see Brian Weinstein, *Eboue* (London: Oxford University Press, 1972).

the organ of the L.C.P. provoked further comments in the British press and *The New Statement and Nation* sympathetically remarked that the amendment still separated Europeans from others.[88] The duty of the imperial administration, the journal contended "is to obtain Africans for self-government and room must be found for educated and patriotic Africans." Similar encouraging comments were received from such well-known figures as Mr. Vernon Bartlett, the left-wing lawyer, Mr. D.N. Pritt, Mr. Arthur Creech Jones and Dr. Temple, the Archbishop of York.[89] These press and personal comments show that the publications of the L.C.P. were not without effect and that a number of highly placed persons were following the activities of the exiles with keen interest.

More striking than the public interest the correspondence aroused was the fact that Moyne appeared to be going out of his way to thrash the matter out. Coming from a colonial secretary, the number of letters seems unusual and it is clear that Moyne regarded this as an important political issue of a delicate nature.

Viewed in the context of the Pan-African movement, the number of letters exchanged represented a measure of the growing strength of the phenomenon. Indeed, a remarkable feature of the Pan-African organisations in general and of the L.C.P. in particular during the War was the frequency with which they communicated with the British authorities. Scarcely had two months elapsed after the correspondence with Moyne than Moody initiated another in protest against the passage in August that year (1941) of the Southern Rhodesia Land Apportionment Act under which most of the fertile lands were reserved for the white settler minority.[90] In

---

[88] (August 16, 1941), p. 150. See also *The Manchester Guardian* (1 August, 1941), p. 2; *Western Mail* (Cardiff) (1 August, 1941), p. 2; *The Yorkshire and Leeds Mercury* (1 August, 1941), p. 3 and *West Africa* (2 August, 1941), p. 741.

[89] *News Notes* (September, 1941), pp. 121-122.

[90] *News Notes* (December, 1941), pp. 55-63. Moody to Moyne, 20 August,

1942 alone, no less than six sets of correspondence were conducted with the metropolitan government on matters ranging from the Abyssinian question to constitutional problems in the Caribbean.[91]

Inundating the British Colonial Office with letters of protest and criticism was by no means the only way in which the L.C.P. expressed its mounting opposition to the political subjugation of Africans and persons of African origin. Review of books on the colonial system formed another medium through which it aired its grievances. One example was W. Arthur Lewis' comments on *Africa and British Rule* (1941) written by Miss Margery Perham. As Perham explained in the preface, she wrote the book with Africans in mind as an answer to their questions concerning the irregularities associated with British rule in their countries. Her contention may be summarised as follows: Africans were "savages" as the English once were. The high state of "civilisation" which the English now enjoyed took several centuries to evolve and was attained mainly due to the efforts of conquerors like the ancient Romans and the Normans as well as the wise statemenship of the Tudor Dynasty (1485-1603). The four hundred years from the Norman conquest to the Tudor period witnessed the building of a strong central government and the forging of one nation out of a multiplicity of tribes and potentates. In the sixteenth century the Tudor monarchs destroyed what remained of the power of the feudal nobility. Africans were so backward at the time of their "discovery" by the British that the latter wondered whether the former were not really an

1941; Moyne to Moody, 22 August, 1941; Cransborne (Dominions Secretary) to Moody, 28 August, 1941; Moody to Cransborne, 4 November, 1941. See also League of Coloured Peoples, *Eleventh Annual Report* (March, 1942).

[91] League of Coloured Peoples, *Twelfth Annual Report* (March, 1943), p. 6. The list of letters include those written to: Mr. Anthony Eden (Foreign Secretary) on the Abyssinian affair; Mr. Harold Macmillan (Under-Secretary of State for Colonies) on forced labour in Nigeria and the West African medical services as well as to Lord Moyne on the Jamaica Constitution.

inferior biological specimen incapable of advancement. "Subjection was the only way by which, on account of her backwardness, and the nature of Europe's nineteenth-century system, Africans could have been brought into the civilised world." It was natural that, like Indians, Africans should desire the full British form of representative parliamentary democracy. "So did the Italians, Germans, Russians and many other people who have now found that it is quite unsuited to their traditions and character."Africans must therefore be content to improve their tribal organisations even though the English had to eliminate tribal governments and unify the country before progress was possible. She defended the colour bar, especially in East and Central Africa, with the specious argument that the handful of white settlers needed to be shielded from "barbarism."

In her concluding chapter, "Education and the Future," Perham, in accordance with the belief popular among the conservatives of the time, asserted that Africans "must have foreign rulers, and for a long time to come."[92] She did not and could not have foreseen the Suez Crisis of 1956, the granting of independence to the Gold Coast the following year, and the consequent "wind of change" that was to sweep over Africa and compel the imperialist powers to disburden themselves of colonies, some of which had become liabilities rather than assets.

Despite Perham's sparkling style, Arthur Lewis detected that she had in fact avoided answering the questions Africans were asking and that her book altogether amounted to an apologia for imperialism. Lewis, writing very much from the viewpoint of conditions in Eastern and Southern Africa or the West Indies, argued that, as a boy, an African discovered that his school was a shambles compared with that reserved for his

---

[92] She expressed a similar view in her article "The British Problem in Africa," *Foreign Affairs* Vol. XXIX (July, 1951).

white counterpart.[93] As he grew up he realised how inadequate were the lands on which his people depended for their livelihood and learnt how they had been driven into infertile "native reserves" to make room for white settlers. He found his father a tenant on a European farm, compelled by law like a mediaeval serf, to work for at least three months on this farm in lieu of rent.

As a young man, he went away from his village to work in mines, and discovered that however competent he showed himself to be, a colour bar, whether enforced by law as in South Africa or by custom as in the Rhodesias, prevented him from acquiring a skilled job. He discovered too that if he attempted to organise any protest he was branded a communist agitator and imprisoned. It did not take him long to see that if he had accidentally been born of white parents in Africa all doors would have been open to him.

Africans were seeking to know the reason for these irregularities which plainly contradicted the avowed altruistic motives of the imperialists. Rejecting Perham's rationalisation that European subjugation of Africa was a historical necessity destined to last "for a long time to come," Arthur Lewis pointed out that the exploitation of Africans could never be justified on the *a priori* ground that they were "inferior" and "barbarious." Accepting the existence of African "cultural backwardness," he argued that this went hand in hand with her economic backwardness. Confusing industrialisation with "civilisation," Arthur Lewis asserted that to civilise the continent, its human (black and white) and material resources must be utilised. Neither the present haphazard development in Africa by European shareholders, nor the measures envisaged in the *Statement of Policy on Colonial Development and Welfare* could bring "civilisation" to "savage" Africa except as a slow and uncertain by-product of private profit. And if this

[93] W. Arthur Lewis' review was printed in *News Notes* (September, 1941), pp. 125-130.

was all the development the colonies were likely to get under British rule, then Perham must be right in saying that Africa was bound to remain backward for many generations. In that case, Africans would still be more right to question whether this uncertain fringe benefit was worth the price they were paying. The time had come to critically examine not only the aims but also the methods of imperial rule. Before the colonial civil service could become an adequate instrument of a "civilising mission," its aims and traditions would require a sweeping revision. Lewis maintained that instead of speculating on the supposed inferiority of Africans and condoning racial prejudice, Margery Perham should have addressed herself to the task of how to sweep away the abuses of imperial rule. Finally, he dismissed her book as mere propaganda for the British cause.[94]

Arthur Lewis' review provoked a reply from Miss M. M. Green of the School of Oriental and African Studies, University of London.[95] Green thought that those who shared Arthur Lewis' desire for a solution of the problems of Africans under British rule must be puzzled and unhappy about his assessment of Perham's book. Arthur Lewis, she went on, wrote as though "it were a time bomb dropped by an enemy rather than a constructive piece of work by one of the most sincere and able of the champions of African advancement."

An examination of the book, chapter by chapter, led Green to a different interpretation and to the surprising conclusion that Arthur Lewis had not read the book at all. In his answer, Arthur Lewis said that since Green apparently had never heard of the numerous disabilities the Africans were made to suffer, including the alienation of their lands, Green naturally admired a work which flattered her pride as a member of the governing race and ignored what to the subject peoples were the unpleasant facts thay came up against every day.[96]

---

[94] *ibid.*
[95] *News Notes* (October, 1941), pp. 7-8.
[96] *ibid.*

The tenor of Arthur Lewis's review article reflected the belief, widely held at the time, that the end of the War would usher in a new order in which liberty and equality would replace racism and imperialism. It was an expectation stimulated, at the onset of the War, by the declarations of the British authorities sanctioned by the famous Atlantic Charter and sustained by the anti-colonial utterances of several of the leading American citizens of the day, notably Wendell Willkie.[97]

Signed on 12 August, 1941 by President Roosevelt of America and the British Premier, Winston Churchill, the terms of the Atlantic Charter were given in a broadcast to the world by Clement Attlee two days later. At the heart of the joint declaration was the principle that all people had the right "to choose the form of government under which they will live" and to determine their political destiny. Whatever were the intentions of the signatories, this principle implied a repudiation of colonialism. Since Churchill had not yet returned from the Atlantic meeting, the W.A.S.U. invited Clement Attlee, his deputy, to confirm that the Charter also covered the colonies. In a statement made on 15 August to the W.A.S.U., Attlee said:

> You will not find in the declarations which have been made on behalf of the Government of this country on the war any suggestion that the freedom and social security for which we fight should be denied to any of the races of mankind.
> We fight this war not just for ourselves alone, but for all peoples.[98]

There was nothing equivocal about Attlee's speech. As a result, the *Daily Herald* in reporting it gave it the front-page headline: "The Atlantic Charter: *it means dark races too.*" [99]

---

[97] See his book *One World* (London: Cassel and Co., 1943).
[98] *Daily Herald* (16 August, 1941), p. 1.
[99] *ibid.*

The high hopes which both the Charter and the assurance of Attlee had raised in the minds of the exiles (as well as colonials elsewhere) soon suffered a shock — a shock which made the exiles as bitter as ever. When Churchill finally returned from the Atlantic meeting, he explained in the House of Commons that clause three of the Charter — "the right of all peoples to choose the form of government under which they will live" applied only to the white peoples of Europe then living under the Nazi yoke. That was quite a separate problem, he went on, "from the progressive evolution of self-governing institutions in the regions and peoples who owe allegiance to the British Crown."[100]

Churchill's interpretation of the joint declaration inevitably sparked off a public debate on the ideas of equality and liberty. Commenting on Churchill's explanation, a Nigerian daily, *The West African Pilot*, for 5 November wondered how a British premier could utter such a statement "during an unparalleled destructive war which has cost colonial peoples their material resources and manpower."

This observation seemed borne out barely three months later by the surprising indifference displayed by most of the natives of Burma, Malaya and Singapore in the face of Japanese aggression. The explanation offered by *The Times* Singapore correspondent for this indifference was repeated *ad nauseam* by most British and American observers. In his dispatch, the correspondent revealed that the colonial government had no roots in the life of the native population and that the British residents were completely out of touch with the people.[101] The result was that "British rule and culture and the small British community formed no more than a thin and brittle veneer."[102]

An editorial of *The Times* for 28 February, 1942 is a good illustration of the popular desire, even shared by some

---

[100] House of Commons, *Debates,* 9 September, 1941.

[101] *The Times* (18 February, 1942).

[102] *ibid.*

conservative imperialists, for a "foreward colonial policy."[103] British dominion in the Far East, the editorial bluntly asserted, could never be restored in its former guise, and that it was undesirable to do so even if it were possible. But defeats must serve, it counselled, "just as defeat in the American war of independence served, as the starting point to a fresh advance in which, adapting herself to changed needs, Great Britain may once more become a pioneer of new policies and a new outlook." Some of the articles seized the opportunity to demand immediate colonial reforms; some to question the wisdom of continued colonial rule and others to challenge the rightness of colonial rule itself.

It was in the midst of public condemnations of British colonial methods as unrealistic, that the W.A.S.U. in a resolution passed on 4 April, 1942, demanded for British West Africa immediate internal self-government with a definite guarantee of complete independence within five years after the War.[104] The demand was made "in the interests of Freedom, Justice and true Democracy, and in view of the lessons of Malaya and Burma, as well as the obvious needs of giving the peoples of the Empire something to fight for."[105] The W.A.S.U. was convinced that "constitutional advancement and economic progress must move forward hand in hand together before a FREE AFRICA, which is the goal of our ambition, could be achieved."[106]

George Padmore inevitably took advantage of Britain's difficulties in the Far East to denounce not only imperialism but also the British Labour Movement which he accused of defending British imperial interests whenever they were threa-

---

[103] See for e.g. Margery Perham's two articles "The Colonial Empire," *The Times* (13-14 March, 1942), p. 5; the editorial "The Colonial Future," *The Times* (14 March 1942) and Lord Samuel's "Parliament and The Colonies: Closer Contact," *The Times* (8 August, 1942), p. 5.

[104] *West Africa* (18 April, 1942), p. 359; *News Notes* (May, 1942), p. 37.

[105] *West Africa* (18 April, 1942), p. 359.

[106] *News Notes* (May, 1942), p. 37.

tened.[107] "We desire to help the Englishman," declared Harold Moody, "to wake up to the true position as it is today. His day of domination has gone for ever.... We mean to govern ourselves and decide our own fate and our own future."[108]

Allegations of forced labour in Nigeria were promptly taken up by the L.C.P. with the Colonial Office. In a letter of 30 June, 1942 to Harold Macmillan, the colonial under-secretary, Moody deplored the use of forced labour in the West Indies and West Africa.[109] The letter desired "it to be recognised that the people of Africa cannot and must not be treated in any way less liberal than the people of Britain."

In a lengthy reply, the colonial under-secretary explained that it had become imperative since the loss of Malaya for the output of the Nigerian tin mines to be increased to the utmost as part of the war effort.[110] It had not been found practicable to do this effectively without recourse to some degree of compulsion. The colonial under-secretary then enumerated provisions which had been made for the welfare of labourers so far called upon for work. Among the provisions were prior medical examination and free transport to and from the minefields. Concluding, Harold Macmillan assured Moody that "the matter will be very carefully considered before compulsion is applied in other cases, either in Nigeria or elsewhere in the Colonies and that wherever it has to be resorted to, every effort will be made to ensure adequate provisions for the welfare of the workers concerned."

The impact of the Atlantic Charter and the Far Eastern crisis also caused a conference summoned by the Fabian Colonial Bureau and held on 15 November, 1942 to make far-reaching demands.[111] Those present at the gathering

[107] *Forward* (May, 1942), pp. 5-7.

[108] *News Letter* (May, 1942), pp. 25-32.

[109] *News Notes* (September, 1942), pp. 145-46.

[110] Harold Macmillan to Moody, 31 July, 1942. Macmillan's letter is reproduced in full in *ibid.*, pp. 146-149.

[111] *The Manchester Guardian* (16 November, 1942), p. 6.

included the Labour Members of Parliament, Reginald Sorenson and Arthur Creech Jones[112]; Beoku Betts, president of the W.A.S.U. and the West Indian member of the L.C.P., Miss Doris Morant. Harold Moody, who was chairman, stressed the need "for a united colonial agreement" to strengthen the Atlantic Charter which, in common with other contemporary commentators, he criticised as vague.[113] Colonial status, he again rejected as "a dead conception to be buried for ever," a thesis he further developed in two booklets *Christianity and Race Relations* and *Freedom For All Men* published in London in 1943. Reginald Sorenson feared that the statements of Churchill, as shown in his reply on the position of India in relation to the Atlantic Charter, might be endorsed by many working-class people who were more imperialist than was sometimes realised.[114] "We must proceed during the war to clarify our ideas and guarantee that in measurable time those areas subject to us should be free and independent," he concluded.

The conference finally adopted a resolution demanding that the coloured peoples should not be excluded from the terms of the Atlantic Charter and that a "Special Charter... be formulated, giving specific guarantees to British dependencies that "Colonial status" shall be immediately abolished."[115]

In his pamphlet, *Freedom For All Men,* Harold Moody emphasised the need not only "to adjust ourselves to a world in which there is freedom and equality for all" but also "to remove from ourselves every vestige of race-superiority."[116] Relations between the various races were, indeed, among the

[112] Both of them were also members of the L.C.P.

[113] *The Manchester Guardian* (16 November, 1942), p. 6.

[114] See for instance *The Manchester Guardian* (10 September, 1941), p. 2 where Churchill declared that the Atlantic Charter "did not qualify in any way the various statements of policy which have been made from time to time about the development of constitutional government in India."

[115] *The Manchester Guardian* (16 November, 1942), p. 6. For the text of the resolution see *News Notes* (February, 1943), p. 148.

[116] (London, 1943), p. 15.

issues brought to a focus by the War. During the War, the exiles showed themselves extremely sensitive to expressions which could be interpreted as offensive to black people, partly due to the presence of American soldiers in Britain. The attitude of the L.C.P. to the word "nigger" was shown in a communication to the British Broadcasting Corporation complaining about its use by an announcer.[117] A reply acknowledged the mistake and expressed the hope that the League "would accept the B.B.C.'s apology for this slip, which is sincerely regretted."[118]

And in 1943 the W.A.S.U. actually succeeded in having the script of a proposed film revised. In preparation for the shooting of the film, "Men of Two Worlds," Two Cities Film Limited had asked the W.A.S.U. to recommend to them some African girls as extras. The W.A.S.U. felt unable to do so without seeing the script which was eventually submitted. After a careful study of it, the W.A.S.U. decided that it should either be re-cast or dropped on the ground that it amounted to a misrepresentation of African life and aspirations. Meanwhile it was discovered that the Colonial Office had already approved the script. Thereupon, the W.A.S.U. passed a resolution of protest, copies of which were delivered to the Colonial Secretary, Colonel Stanley, with comments and suggestions attached.[119] The resolution contended that the film represented a distortion of the African "social system"; that it cast a slur on the prestige of African peoples and the British empire. In the attachments, the W.A.S.U. among other things objected to the use of the term "witch-doctor." After the exchange of a series of letters between the W.A.S.U., the Colonial Office and Company, the script was substantially revised on the lines suggested by the W.A.S.U.[120]

[117] *News Notes* (June, 1940), p. 39.
[118] *ibid.*
[119] Solanke to Colonial Secretary, 27 July, 1943, p. 11.
[120] The correspondence between the W.A.S.U., the C.O. and the Company were published in *Wasu* (June, 1944), pp. 11-15.

Meanwhile the public discussion on the Atlantic Charter had continued unabated. The year 1943, which saw the publication of *Freedom For All Men* by Moody, was also the year in which Nancy Cunard and George Padmore jointly produced in London a monograph with the title *The White Man's Duty: An Analysis of the Colonial Question in the Light of the Atlantic Charter.* The application of clause three of the Charter to all peoples regardless of the stage of their social development and the organisation of colonial economies for the benefit of the native inhabitants were envisaged as the ideal post-war solution of the colonial problem. Suggestions as to how this ideal solution could be carried out were given in a proposed "Charter for the Colonies" which formed the concluding chapter of the monograph. Notable among the measures recommended for the African dependencies were the introduction of economic, social and political equality; the abolition of conscript labour and pass laws; the limitation of company profits and the removal of restrictions on civil liberties with the exception of censorship of matters of strategic importance.

For the (British) West Indies, the booklet demanded the transfer of power "from the present Crown Colony bureaucracy to the elected representatives of the people, on the following basis: universal adult suffrage; removal of property qualification for membership of [legislative] Councils; people's control of expenditure." The measures did not amount to a demand for immediate and complete independence but for internal self-rule. Coming from writers inbued at that time with the revolutionary ideology of Marxism-Leninism, the demand for only internal self-government seems surprisingly modest.

A charter for the coloured peoples was proposed at a conference of the L.C.P. held from 21st to 23rd July, 1944.[121] Harold Moody and John Fletcher of the Friends' Service

---

[121] L.C.P. *Fourteenth Annual Report,* March, 1945, p. 11.

Council jointly presided. The chief speakers were H. W. Springer, a former treasurer of the L.C.P. who subsequently became secretary of the Barbados Progressive League and member of the legislative council there; Dr. Malcolm Joseph-Mitchell from Trinidad and member of the L.C.P.; C. W. C. Greenidge, a Barbadian member of the L.C.P.; Peter Abraham from South Africa and member of the I.A.S.B.; John Carter, then secretary of the L.C.P.; Rita Hinden of the Fabian Colonial Bureau; Dr. K. A. Korsah (Gold Coast); Rev. I. Ransome Kuti (Nigeria) and Dr. A. Taylor-Cummings (Sierra Leone). The last three were visiting members of the Royal Commission on Higher Education in West Africa.[122]

At the end of the conference, a charter for the coloured peoples was proposed.[123] There were no fundamental differences between it and the earlier ones suggested by the Fabian Colonial Bureau and that jointly submitted by Nancy Cunard and George Padmore. What is worth noting was its submission to all the diplomatic missions in Britain, many of which promised to give it a sympathetic consideration.[124] His Majesty's Government, through the colonial secretary, stated in a reply dated 31st August that they were "not convinced that substitution of a uniform 'Charter' in place of the policy of individual treatment would help the present steady progress."[125]

Exiles in the United States also attempted to apply the principles of the Atlantic Charter to the African world. Among them was the Nigerian from Igboland, Akweke Abyssinia Nwafor Orizu. Since "Abyssinia" is not an Igbo word, the appelation was probably adopted during the Italian invasion as a gesture of support for the beleaguered Ethiopians. Educated at Columbia University (New York) where he obtained a master's degree in Government and Public Law, he

[122] *ibid.*
[123] *ibid.*
[124] *ibid.*
[125] *ibid.*

wrote a book entitled *Without Bitterness; Western Nations in Post-War Africa* published in New York in 1944. Where Padmore and Moody sought reforms with self-determination as the ultimate goal, Orizu demanded immediate autonomy. Africa, he declared, "is indignant with European imperialism, as it has been, as it is, and as some planners still want it to be."[126] By warning the metropolitan powers that Africans wished "to be free now and forever" he anticipated Kwame Nkrumah.

A careful study of the indigenous African political systems led Orizu to reject the imperialist propaganda that Africans were inexperienced in the art of government and therefore incapable of ruling themselves. But his admiration of the African past was far from nostalgic. He was forward-looking enough to realise that in order to survive in the post-war era, Africa must undergo a process of modernisation. The new Africa would strive for economic independence, avoid the mistakes of the industrial West, show goodwill towards the rest of mankind, and above all

> advocate the true democracy — democracy without imperialism, without unequal treaties, without unfair exploitation, without mental slavery and without a racial superiority complex.[127]

The year Nwafor Orizu's book appeared also witnessed the submission of a memorandum on university education by the L.C.P. to the visiting Royal Commission on Higher Education in West Africa. It was a document combining most of the educational ideas of Edward Blyden, J. B. A. Horton and Casely Hayford. More important than this, it reflected the cultural ideas of the Pan-Africanists. In character and purpose, the L.C.P.'s concept of higher education resembled those advocated in the second half of the nineteenth century by

---

[126] *Without Bitterness: Western Nations in Post-War Africa* (New York: Creative Age Press, 1944), p. xiv.
[127] *ibid.,* p. 19.

Horton and Blyden and that of Casely Hayford outlined early in the twentieth century in his book *Ethiopia Unbound* (London, 1911). The L.C.P. desired that the primary aim of training should be "for leadership, and for service to and love of country."[128] As much as possible, institutions of learning should be "mainly manned by Africans, whose objectives would be to bring out the very best possible in the life of the country and thus make West Africa an example to the whole of Africa."[129] Such institutions "while profiting by the experience gained in education in Britain, America and Russia [sic], should nevertheless evolve curricula of their own, calculated to meet the specific needs of the area to be served."[130] In such curricula, ample provision should be made for things which were characteristically African. "Every effort must be assiduously made to avoid merely Europeanising the African or to train him only 'to undertake the routine duties and less responsible work of the fully qualified European Officer."[131]

In recommending that university education should be free, the L.C.P. anticipated developments in Nkrumah's Ghana. Like Blyden, the L.C.P. emphasised the importance of languages. English must be taught in all schools and the multiplicity of African languages reduced to a few workable number of basic languages. Africans should be proficient in at least two. Production of literature in basic African languages should be actively supported by government and philanthropic bodies. Finally, the memorandum urged that the African must be encouraged to be truly himself. Implicit in this concluding plea is the now familiar concept of the "African Personality."

More important as a landmark in the Pan-African move-

[128] *News Notes* (February, 1944), pp. 73-74; L.C.P. *Thirteenth Annual Report* (March, 1944).
[129] *ibid.*
[130] *ibid.*
[131] *ibid.*

ment than the L.C.P.'s memorandum on university education was the formation in Manchester the same year (1944) of the Pan-African Federation mainly due to the initiative of the I.A.S.B. The new organisation was a merger of some exile and colonial nationalist movements in Britain and Africa. Among the constituent pressure groups were: the African Union (Glasgow); the Friends of African Freedom Society (Gold Coast); the I.A.S.B.; the Kimuyu Central Association (Kenya); the Negro Association (Manchester); the United Committee of Coloured and Coloured People's Association (Cardiff); the W.A.S.U. and the West African Youth League.[132] The reader will observe that the L.C.P. is conspicuously absent from the list. Whatever may be the reasons for this exclusion, they do not seem to include conflict of objectives as is evident from the rest of the chapter. Each member organisation was allowed to maintain its separate existence and to retain its local autonomy but required to adhere strictly to the basic aims of the P.A.F. These were: to secure equality of civil rights and independence for African peoples (and other subject races); to "promote the well-being and unity of African peoples and peoples of African descent throughout the world" and to co-operate with peoples who share the aspirations of men of African blood.[133]

The P.A.F. planned the establishment of institutes for the study of African history and culture, the publication of works by and about Africans and "the convening of national and international conferences in order to further its aims and objects."[134] Manchester (58 Oxford Road) was chosen as headquarters because Dr. Peter Milliard and T. Ras Makonnen, the chairman and the general-secretary respectively of the group, were based there. Other officers included E. A. Cowan of the Negro Welfare Centre (assistant secretary) and J. E. Taylor, also of the Negro Welfare Centre (treasurer).

---

[132] George Padmore, *Pan-Africanism or Communism?*, p. 149.
[133] *ibid.*
[134] *ibid.*

Following his arrival from the United States in June, 1945, Francis Kwame Nkrumah was made the regional secretary.

The aspirations of the P.A.F. were re-affirmed and elaborated in an open letter of September, 1945 to Clement Attlee who, as a result of the victory of the Labour Party in the first post-war parliamentary election held in July was now Prime Minister of Britain.[135] The victory of the Labour Party, it was claimed, was an event for which they as colonials had hoped and worked. At last the time had arrived for "Comrade Attlee" and his government to "give the Socialist answer to the Tory imperialism of Mr. Churchill's 'What we have we hold.'" It would be dishonest to condemn only the imperialism of Germany, Japan and Italy; all imperialisms were bad. The P.A.F. as a "responsible body representing vast sections of African and colonial thought, demands for the colonial peoples the immediate right to self-determination" and the following reforms: the speedy implementation of the educational reforms suggested in the West Indies reports on higher education;[136] the publication of the West Indian Royal Commissions' Report "suppressed since 1940;"[137] the removal of the colour bar, of disabilities based on race and all restrictions on civil liberties. The Labour Government was also urged to re-affirm "its determination to keep race-ridden South Africa out of the Protectorates (Bechuanaland, Basutoland and Swaziland." It was suggested that the Colonial Office should summon a conference of the African and other colonial leaders to discuss their problems. Such a conference, in the opinion of the P.A.F., would serve to usher in a period of co-operation and partnership, as against domination; it

[135] There are minor differences between the text of the open letter as published in leaflet form by the P.A.F. probably in October, 1945 and as extensively reproduced by George Padmore in his *Pan-Africanism or Communism?*, pp. 156-8. In this study, the earlier leaflet version has been used. Earlier in July the W.A.S.U. had sent a similar letter to Harold Laski, Chairman of the Labour Party, *Wasu Magazine,* (March, 1946), p. 42.

[136] *Cmd. 6655,* 1945.

[137] See pp. 166-69.

"would be a great stride towards the Century of the Common Man." A conference of some leaders of the people of African descent was held in Manchester the following month but it was called not by the Colonial Office but by the P.A.F.

The recognition of the P.A.F. as an effective platform for opposition to colonial rule can be seen from the tendency of West Indians and Africans to cable details of labour disputes to the secretary of the organisation.[138] The P.A.F. would then either organise a public demonstration or send a deputation to the colonial secretary or both. Thus, on the receipt in 1945 of a report on a general strike in Nigeria, the secretary of the P.A.F. got in touch with the component unions and various action committees were set up.[139] In London, Kwame Nkrumah, the regional secretary of the P.A.F. summoned a public meeting which took place in Conway Hall.[140] Resolutions were adopted expressing solidarity with the Nigerian workers and condemning the colonial administration. Donations were collected in aid of the strikers.[141]

Meanwhile, during the first half of 1945 the I.A.S.B. put out five pamphlets, namely: *Kenya: Land of Conflict; African Empires and Civilizations; The Negro in the Caribbean; The White Man's Duty* and *The Voice of Coloured Labour.*[142] The publications were edited by George Padmore with T. R. Makonnen, Jomo Kenyatta, Wallace Johnson, C. L. R. James and Peter Abrahams as advisory editors. The first pamphlet was written by Jomo Kenyatta. A survey of life and government in pre-colonial Kenyan society and the alienation of most

---

[138] E. B. Ndem, "Negro Immigrants in Manchester: An Analysis of Social Relations within and between the Various Coloured Groups and of their Relations to the White Community," unpublished M.A. thesis, London University, 1954, p. 119.

[139] *ibid.*

[140] *ibid.*

[141] *ibid.*

[142] George Padmore, *Pan-Africanism or Communism?*, p. 150, erroneously attributes the pamphlets to the P.A.F.

of the natives' lands to white settlers led Kenyatta to the conclusion that indigenous Kenyans under colonial rule were oppressed, exploited and deprived of civil liberties. He stressed that Africans would never be satisfied until they enjoyed full self-government, economic and social security which could be achieved in a non-imperialist social order.[143]

The author of *African Empires and Civilizations* was a French historian, Raymond Michelet, who originally wrote it for Nancy Cunard's well-known anthology, *Negro*, from where it was reprinted by the I.A.S.B. The booklet, thirty-nine pages long, may be divided into three broad sections. The first part summarises the main historical facts concerning the Western Sudanese Empires of Ghana, Mali and Songhay. The second section examines various pre-colonial polities in Central and South Africa, notably the kingdoms of Asande, Loanga and Monomotapa (Mwene Mtapa). The third section of the pamphlet quotes freely from Leo Frobenius[144] and Maurice Delafosse[145] to illustrate the high level of civilisation and artistic achievement reached in some of these political systems. Anticipating the conclusions of recent research, Michelet argued that before the European intervention, Africans had formed powerful states comparable to those of contemporary Europe. The African states "developed along far-reaching lines of unsuspected stability, whose civilisation, laws, customs and economic administration were perfectly balanced, and in which above all, the mode of life was simplified to an extent unknown to the white world."

In an editorial note, Padmore warmly commended the

[143] Jomo Kenyatta, *Kenya, Land of Conflict* (London: Mercury Books, 1945), p. 23.

[144] *The Voice of Africa. Being an Account of the Travels of the German Inner African Exploration Expedition in the Years 1910-1912,* transl. by Rudolf Blind (London, 1913). For a recent scholarly analysis of the methods and observations of Frobenius as against his general ideas see J. M. Ita, "Frobenius in West African History," *Journal of African History* Vol. XIII, No. 4 (1972), pp. 673-688.

[145] *Les Negres* (Rieder); see also *Les Nors de l'Afrique* (Paris, 1922).

booklet as a refutation of the slanderous description of Africans as "savages without a past." He hoped that now that Africans stood on the threshold of a new day, they would take pride in the social achievements of their ancestors and "build their future collectivistic society on more lasting foundations, to the benefit not only of themselves but all humanity." This deployment of historical evidence using the best scholarly work then available was much more original than it now sounds.

The Negro in the Caribbean was contributed by Eric Williams, who later became Prime Minister of Trinidad and Tobago. It discussed the early economic system of the West Indies in its historical relation to slavery showing the effects of sugar upon the entire social and political structure in the islands. He had worked out much of this argument in *Capitalism and Slavery,*[146] a major work of historical scholarship.

The White Man's Duty, jointly written by George Padmore and Nancy Cunard, was an enlarged edition of the earlier one published in 1943.[147] The last pamphlet published in 1945 by the I.A.S.B. was *The Voice of Coloured Labour*. It contained the speeches and reports of the African and West Indian delegates to the World Federation of Trade Unions Conference held in London in February the same year.

Most of the above I.A.S.B. publications were sympathetically reviewed in such periodicals as *Empire*, organ of the Fabian Colonial Bureau, *International Affairs* (Journal of the Royal Institute of International Affairs)[148] and *The Times Literary Supplement*. For instance, *The Negro in the Caribbean; African Empires and Civilisations; Kenya: Land of Conflict* were all reviewed in *The Times Literary Supplement* for 2 June, 1945. In its review of *African Empires and Civilizations, Empire* remarked that it was "a melancholy comment

---

[146] (Chapel Hill: University of North Carolina Press, 1945).
[147] See pp. 201-202.
[148] (October. 1945).

on the parochial outlook of many Europeans that, despite the years of sociological study sympathetic to local cultures, such a pamphlet should still be necessary."[149] Reviews of the I.A.S.B. publications in such respectable journals not only helped to publicise the grievances and aspirations of the exiles but were also a measure of the growing impact of their activities on enlightened opinion in Britain. These publications helped to prepare the ground for the historic Manchester Pan-African Congress, the subject of the following chapter.

[149] (May-June, 1945). For further reviews see *The Tribune* (London) (18 March, 1945).

CHAPTER 4

THE MANCHESTER CONGRESS AND ITS AFTERMATH

Early in 1944 Harold Moody and Amy Jacques Garvey separately approached DuBois on the necessity for a post-war Pan-African meeting.[1] The three, together with Paul Robeson announced in April the same year their readiness to assist in convening a "Pan-African Congress to be held in London as soon after the war as possible."[2] Eventually, they lost the initiative to the P.A.F. who not only changed the venue but also arranged every aspect of the conference.

The idea of a convocation in Manchester was first mooted during a Conference of the World Federation of Trade Unions which met in London in February, 1945. To this conference came representatives of black colonial labour from Africa and the Caribbean. Seizing the opportunity, the P.A.F. invited the colonial delegation to a discussion in Manchester at which the necessity for another Pan-African Congress was considered. A provisional agenda was drawn up. "The delegates took it back to their countries and discussed it with their people."[3] Most of the colonial organisations approved the agenda with minor amendments pledging themselves to send delegates.

Exploiting this enthusiasm, the P.A.F. timed the proposed congress to coincide with the second conference of the W.F.T.U. to be held in Paris from 25 September to 9 October

[1] Imanuel Geiss, *op. cit.,* p. 737.
[2] *ibid.*
[3] P.A.F. Press Release, No. 4 (1945), p. 2.

that year.[4] Associations too poor to send delegates "gave mandates to the natives of the territories concerned who were travelling to Paris to attend the World Federation of Trade Unions Conference."[5] Some organizations which did not send delegates to the W.F.T.U. conference mandated individuals already in Britain to represent them.[6]

The task of making the necessary arrangements fell on a special committee comprised of Dr. Peter Milliard (chairman); George Padmore and Kwame Nkrumah (joint political secretaries); Jomo Kenyatta (assistant secretary) and Peter Abrahams (publicity secretary).[7]

Though officially opened on 15 October by the Lord Mayor of Manchester, Alderman Jackson, the Manchester Pan-African meeting was jointly presided over by W. E. B. DuBois and Peter Milliard, president of the P.A.F. The Charlton Town Hall where the conference took place was decorated with the flags of Ethiopia, Haiti and Liberia. Taking part, as in the previous Pan-African meetings, were students, men and women from varied walks of life with a sprinkling of fraternal delegates and observers. But unlike the preceding Pan-African congress, Africa was for the first time adequately represented. Many of these Africans were soon to become important in one capacity or the other in their own countries. Notable among the Nigerian participants were Obafemi Awolowo who subsequently became a premier of Western Nigeria; H. O. Davies, later to be a chairman of Nigeria's state-sponsored newspapers and Jaja Nwachuku, Nigeria's Foreign Minister in the Balewa Administration. The poet, Dr.

---

[4] P.A.F. Press Release, No. 4 (1945), p. 2 (in *G.C.A.R. P.S. Papers,* Acc. No. 77/64, Correspondence File No. 5); George Padmore, *Pan-Africanism or Communism?,* p. 155. The date of the meeting summoned by the P.A.F. is given by the Press Release as February and by Padmore as March. February should be preferred in view of the fact that Padmore wrote nearly eleven years after the event.

[5] George Padmore, *Pan-Africanism or Communism?,* p. 155.

[6] *ibid.,* p. 156.

[7] *ibid.,* p. 155.

Raphael Armattoe, Dr. Hastings Banda and Garba Jahumpa represented Togoland, Nyasaland (now Malawi) and Gambia, respectively. Garba Jahumpa later became Minister of Agriculture and Natural Resources in the Government of Gambia. Also in attendance were Jomo Kenyatta, I. T. A. Wallace Johnson and the South African novelist, Peter Abrahams. The Gold Coast contingent included Kwame Nkrumah, J. S. Annan, Kankam Boadu, E. Duplan and Ako Adjei all of whom served in the Nkrumah Administration;[8] the historian, J. C. de Graft Johnson as well as Joe Appiah and Dr. Karankyi Taylor, both of whom subsequently became bitter opponents of the Nkrumah Government.

All the constituent societies of the P.A.F. were represented.[9] Of the eighteen colonial trade unions and the twenty-five cultural and political organisations represented, the following may be mentioned: the Federal Worker's Trade Union, Trinidad and Tobago; the Workers' Association, Bermuda; St. Kitts-Nevis Trades and Labour Union; the Trade Union Congress, Sierra Leone; the National Council of Nigeria and the Cameroons; the Aborigines' Rights Protection Society, Gold Coast; the National Council of Gambia; the Progressive League, Liberia; the African National Congress, South Africa; the Progressive League, Barbados; the People's National Party, Jamaica; the Labour Party, Grenada; the African Development Association, British Guiana; the Universal Negro Improvement Association, Jamaica and the Negro Welfare and Cultural Association, Trinidad and Tobago.[10] Fraternal delegates include those from the Federation of Indian organisations in Britain and the Independent Labour Party of Britain.

[8] J. S. Annan served as Secretary of Defence; E. Duplan was a key figure in the Bureau of African Affairs, Accra while Ako Adjei filled the post of Foreign Minister but soon quarrelled with Nkrumah.

[9] The L.C.P. sent delegates.

[10] For a full list of the delegates that attended the Manchester meeting see George Padmore, ed., *History of the Pan-African Congress*, 2nd ed. (London: Susan Tulley. 1963), pp. 71-74.

The impressive list of trade unions, political parties and cultural organisations represented naturally leads one to regard the conference as the most representative in the series. But in reality, it was not. What was gained from the participation, for the first time, of Gambia and the adherents of Garveyism was offset by the non-representation of Haiti, the French Caribbean, the French Negro Africa, Ethiopia, Portuguese Africa and the Belgian Congo. There were no delegates from Arab North Africa which for all practical purposes still remained outside the pale of the Pan-African movement. And apart from W. E. B. DuBois, Black America was similarly unrepresented.

If the Manchester meeting could scarcely be said to be more representative than any of the preceding pan-African congresses, the character of its representation differed from the earlier ones in some respects. For the first time, the African participants came not as individuals, as hitherto had been the case, but as accredited delegates from organisations. Equally worth noting is the fact that either in terms of sheer number of delegates or organisations participating, Africa was for the first time adequately represented.

Bitter condemnations of the colonial system marked the proceedings of the congress for two main reasons. One was due to the preponderance of professional politicians and trade unionists imbued with socialist ideas. The other reason lay in the fact that the conference took place at a time when the incompatibility between foreign domination and the principles of the Atlantic Charter had everywhere become glaringly self-evident. Discussions centred on the familiar issues of racial discrimination, the shortcomings of the social, economic and constitutional policies of the metropolitan powers and independence as the ultimate objective. Specifically, the following formed the topics of debate; "The Colour Problem in Britain"; "Imperialism in North and West Africa"; "Oppression in South Africa": "The East African Picture":

"Ethiopia and the Black Republics" and "The Problem in the Caribbean."

The first day of the conference was devoted to an examination of "The Colour Problem in Britain."[11] The main reports were delivered by the Gold Coaster Edwin J. Duplan and E. Aki-Emi of the Negro Welfare Centre, Liverpool and the Coloured Workers' Association, London respectively. They complained mainly of discrimination in employment. Supporting statements were made by Peter Abrahams of the I.A.S.B. and the Nigerian F. O. B. Blaize, a W.A.S.U. delegate.

"Imperialism in North and West Africa" was discussed in the first session of the second day of the meeting. The principal *rapporteur* was Kwame Nkrumah, joint political secretary of the congress. He outlined the political and economic trends in these regions blaming colonialism as one of the major causes of wars. At the same time he called for a strong and vigorous action to eradicate it. Nkrumah's statement was supplemented by a number of reports notably from J. S. Annan, secretary of the Gold Coast Railway Civil Servants' and Technical Workers' Union; Wallace Johnson, secretary of the Sierra Leone Youth League; Soyemi Coker of the Nigerian Trade Union Congress; J. Appiah and Kankam Boadu of the W.A.S.U.; J. Downes Thomas of the Bathurst Citizen's Committee (Gambia); Magnus Williams representing the National Council of Nigeria and the Cameroons and M. O. Davies of the Nigerian Youth Movement.

Special attention was given to the South and Central African problems with Marko Hlubi and Peter Abrahams, a representative of the South African National Congress, as the principal speakers. The former opened the debate with an examination of the social, economic and political disabilities

---

[11] Details of the proceedings of the conference are published in George Padmore, ed., *Colonial and ... Coloured Unity: A Programme of Action* (Manchester: Pan-African Service, Ltd., 1947), pp. 27-54. See also P.A.F. Press Release, Nos. 5, 7-11 (1945) (In *G.C.A.R.P.S. Papers*, Acc. 77/64, Correspondence File No. 5).

suffered by the coloured people in the Union of South Africa. South Africa's native policy, he explained, was based on the segregation of Africans while discrimination underlay all legislation. Though the Africans were denied the vote, they were forced to pay poll and hut taxes whether they were employed or not. Those who went to the towns to work were herded in "allocations" which were nothing more than ghettoes. These conditions could not be changed, for Africans had no union recognised by the employers. Furthermore, the Riotous Assembly Act made protest meetings illegal. Concluding, Marko Hlubi appealed to African descendants elsewhere to help their "brothers" in South Africa to break the bonds which shackled them to the white Herrenvolk.

Peter Abrahams, the other principal speaker, continued the enumeration of the grievances of the indigenous population of South Africa. Attention was drawn to the Pass Laws which everywhere in the Union hedged the Africans in. In addition to the poll and hut tax receipts which served as passes, there were ten others which the Africans were obliged to carry at one time or another. Passes were needed to leave the reserve to go to town, to travel on the railway, to seek employment, to visit another location, to stay out after the nine o'clock curfew hour. The African was also obliged to obtain a pass to live within a municipal location to carry on trade. If he was a teacher or preacher, he had to secure a special pass to show that he was exempted from carrying all the others.

Jomo Kenyatta acted as the official reporter on "The East African Picture." His statement covered six territories, namely: Kenya, Somaliland, Uganda, Tanganyika (now Tanzania), Nyasaland (now Malawi) and the Rhodesias. The East African peoples, he explained, fell into three divisions: farmers, cattle rearers and hunters. "Each group had its own territories, which it considered its own property and on which it could move as it pleased, cultivating here today and there tomorrow, building its villages here and there as it wanted, or hunting as it wished. Many of these people lived happily and contented."[12]

The advent of white settlers and the consequent allocation of the natives' land to them had changed the picture. In a supporting statement, Garba Jahumpa of the Trades Union Council of Gambia, urged the conference "to demand, first and foremost, the complete freedom of our South African brothers." He believed that the duty of the conference delegates was "to learn about all our peoples from all over the world, and if we went back to our different countries and remained dormant, the Congress will have been a failure."[13] The Congress should resolve to establish somewhere in the world a central council which would keep in touch with the whole of the African world and developments there.

A report of "Ethiopia and the Black Republics" was given by T. R. Makonnen, secretary of the P.A.F. He accused Britain of planning to join Ogaden Province, a section of ancient Ethiopia, to British and Italian Somaliland in order to enlarge the British Empire.[14] As compensation the British Government, he alleged, was prepared to return to Ethiopia part of Eritrea, which formed an integral part of Ethiopia before it was grabbed by Italy. Supporting Makonnen, Peter Abrahams reiterated that there were only three states in the world run and controlled by black men. They were Haiti, Liberia and Ethiopia. It was important that Africans and their descendants should be most vigilant in the interests of these three states.

The main reports of the West Indian territories were delivered by George Padmore and Ken Hill of the People's National Party, Jamaica. Padmore traced the history of the West Indies from the arrival of Columbus there late in the fifteenth century to the Emancipation Act of 1833. He said that the West Indies could briefly be described as the "sugar section of British imperialism, for in the West Indies you have a

12 *ibid.*, p. 40.
13 *ibid.*, p. 42.
14 *ibid.*, p. 44.

Government of sugar for sugar by sugar."[15] In his statement, Ken Hill assured the conference that the West Indians had never forgotten their racial origins and that they looked upon Mother Africa with pride. They pledged themselves to work for her redemption and support the fight of African peoples for complete freedom and independence. A supplementary statement from Claude Lushington, representing the West Indian National Party, declared self-government as the object of his party. He was convinced that as long as the West Indians remained under alien domination they would continue to be exploited by absentee owners. "Let us govern ourselves, if even badly at first rather than be well governed by others," he concluded.[16] This concluding remark is significant as suggesting the probable source of Kwame Nkrumah's well-known subsequent declaration that independence in danger was preferable to foreign subjugation.

After five days of discussion, the conference adopted far-reaching resolutions which may be examined under the headings of specific and general demands.[17] Immediate independence was demanded for British and French West Africa, the British Sudan, the French North African colonies of Algeria, Tunisia and Morocco as well as the Italian dependency of Lybia. Comprehensive constitutional, economic and social reform were urged for British Central and East Africa, the French Congo, the Belgian Congo, the British West Indies and British Guiana (now Guyana). These reforms, to be implemented at once, included the enfranchisement of every native adult, the removal of restrictions upon civil rights, the abolition of all racial and discriminatory laws, the revision of the civil and criminal codes as well as the system of taxation,

[15] *ibid.*, p. 46.

[16] *ibid.*, p. 48.

[17] The resolutions are published in George Padmore, ed., *Colonial and ... Coloured Unity: A Programme of Action* (Manchester: Pan-African Service, 1947), pp. 55-67. The "Resolution to U.N.O. on South West Africa," *ibid.*, pp. 64-65 was not adopted at the Manchester Conference but later in 1946. See *News Letter* (December, 1946), pp. 40-41.

the re-allocation of land especially in East and Central Africa, the establishment of new industries and the development of the existing ones. Also demanded were the "introduction of all forms of modern social legislation in existence in metropolitan areas, e.g., old-age pensions, family allowances, national health and unemployment insurances" and compulsory free education at elementary and secondary school levels.

The resolutions supported the demand of Egypt for "the removal of British armed forces," regarded the "struggle of our brothers in South Africa as an integral part of the common struggle for national liberation throughout Africa," and opposed the South African request for the incorporation, into the Union, of the High Commissioned Territories of Bechuanaland, Basutoland and Swaziland on the ground that the natives concerned did not wish such a transfer.

The governments and peoples of Ethiopia, Liberia and Haiti were assured that any manifestation of imperialist encroachment which threatened their independence would be resisted. At the same time, the metropolitan powers were informed that these states symbolized the political hopes and aspirations of African peoples still under imperialist domination. The Congress supported in the interest of justice and economic geography the claims of the Somalis and Eritreans to be returned to their Motherland (i.e., Ethiopia) instead of being parcelled out to foreign powers. It also demanded the withdrawal of the British Military Administration from Ethiopian soil and the extension by the United Nations Relief Organisation to the Abyssinians the same aid as was being afforded to the other victims of aggression.

The Congress identified itself with the heroic struggles of the thirteen million people of African descent in the United States in their fight to secure the rights of full citizenship, political, economic, and social. Africans and peoples of African descent throughout the world would continue to support their Afro-American "brothers" in their fight for their rights by intelligent organized planning, legal contention and political pressure. The successful realisation of the political, economic and social aspirations of the Afro-Americans was bound up with the emancipation of all African peoples, as well as other dependent peoples and the working class everywhere.

The other part of the resolutions — the general demands — consisted of a declaration to the colonial peoples and a challenge to the imperial powers to honour the principles of the Atlantic Charter. In their "Declaration to the Colonial Workers, Farmers and Intellectuals," the delegates expressed their belief in the right of all peoples to govern themselves and control their own destiny. All dependencies must be free from alien control, political and economic. The struggle for political power by the colonial peoples was the "first step towards, and the necessary prerequisite to, complete social, economic and political emancipation."

Concluding, the declaration called on the workers and farmers of the Colonies to organize effectively. Colonial workers must be in the front battle against Imperialism. "Your weapons — the Strike and the Boycott — are invincible."

The Congress ended its deliberations by inviting the metropolitan governments to implement the principles of the Atlantic Charter in their dependencies. Africans and their descendants were determined to be free and desired "the right to earn a decent living; the right to express our thoughts and emotions, to adopt and create forms of beauty." They were not ashamed to have been an age-long patient people. But they were unwilling "to starve any longer while doing the world's drudgery, in order to support by their poverty and ignorance a false aristocracy and a discredited imperialism." And if the western world showed itself still determined to rule mankind by force, then Africans, as a last resort, might have to appeal to force in order to achieve self-determination even if force destroyed them and the world. That the metropolitan powers might not timidly hand over freedom on a platter of gold was for the first time in the history of the pan-African movement recognised. This recognition meant a shift from the earlier strategy of peaceful and constitutional opposition to one of active resistance and "positive action."

The Manchester Pan-African Congress truly marks a turning point in the history of the Pan-African movement. The turning point consists neither in the unequivocal manner in which the delegates expressed their desire for independence nor in the hostile tone in which the desire was voiced. As we have seen in the preceding chapter, unequivocal demands for freedom and harsh criticisms derived further impetus from the Atlantic Charter, the temporary collapse of the British empire in the Far East and the anti-colonial utterances of several of the leading American citizens of the day, notably, Wendell Willkie.

There was therefore nothing new or revolutionary in the militancy and resolutions of the delegates to the Manchester meeting. Hence, Arthur Creech Jones, the first post-war Labour Colonial Secretary, could say that it "did not require the impetus of the [Manchester] Pan-African Congress or the demand for Indian freedom to induce the Labour Ministers at the Colonial Office in 1945 to drive ahead with political, social and economic changes in the colonies."[18]

It was the strategy rather than the resolutions adopted at this meeting that made it a turning point in the history of the Pan-African movement. Before the Manchester meeting, Pan-Africanism was, in the main, a protest movement of middle-class Afro-American intellectuals resident outside Africa and in which little or nothing of real interest to the African and West Indian masses had been said. Not surprisingly, it received practically no support from the nationalist organisations in Africa and the masses there and in the Caribbean.

The Manchester Congress reversed this situation. The old belief that the struggle for freedom could be fought and won in

---

[18] *The Guardian* (London) (3 September, 1963), p. 8.

Europe was laid aside. Henceforward, the struggle must be conducted in the homelands as the Indians were already doing. Though DuBois was present and active, the new approach reflected the socialist influence of George Padmore and Kwame Nkrumah. The African and the West Indian workers as represented by their trade unions and political parties became associated, for the first time, with the Pan-African movement. The winning of popular support for the movement constituted only one aspect of the new strategy. Another aspect consisted in the call upon the intellectuals and the masses to join forces in the campaign for political emancipation.

In this new strategy, the African trade unions subsequently played a significant role. Imanuel Geiss has aptly described them as "the labour-wing of the nationalist movement" and shown how by strikes, mass demonstrations and boycotts they played a considerable part.[19] But in attributing the militancy that marked the post-war activities of these trade unions to a new impetus to industrialisation engendered by the War, he missed the point. The explanation for both the militancy and the deep involvement of the trade unions in the postwar African nationalist movements lies more in the newly acquired nationalist ideas of the returned soldiers and the Manchester deliberations than in any other factor. Was it not at this gathering that the trade unions were told that they "must be in the front of the battle against imperialism?" The recognition that freedom has to be fought for, the decision to shift the battle front to African soil and enlist the support of the masses as well as the adoption of a strategy of "positive action," all these ushered in a new phase in the history of the Pan-African movement. From now on the ideals which had been formulated in America and Europe would begin to be heard increasingly in Africa herself as African liberation movements grew from strength to strength.

[19] "Some Remarks on the Development of African Trade Unions," *The Journal of the Historical Society of Nigeria* Vol. 3, No. 2 (December, 1965), p. 367.

To give effect to the programme drawn up, the Congress charged the executive of the L.C.P. to take steps to "publicise the resolutions and other directives adopted by the delegates, and to establish suitable machinery through which advice and assistance could be extended to the organisations represented in the Congress."[20] Consequently, the P.A.F. set up a working committee with DuBois and Kwame Nkrumah as president and secretary-general respectively.[21] At a meeting of the committee held in London, it was decided that the headquarters of the Pan-African Congress should be established in London "to act as a kind of clearing house for the various political movements that would take shape in the colonies."[22] In a letter to the Gold Coast A.R.P.S., Nkrumah announced that an international secretariat had been set up in London to maintain contact between all colonial organizations.[23] Nkrumah further explained that all the organisations represented at the Manchester meeting were expected to affiliate to the P.A.F. stressing that affiliation would not involve the surrender of local autonomy.[24]

While arrangements were being made to establish in London the proposed headquarters of the Pan-African Congress, some West Africans approached Nkrumah on the necessity to form a West African National Secretariat (W.A.N.S.).[25] Among the West Africans were Wallace Johnson, G. Ashie-Nikoi who represented the Gold Coast A.R.P.S. and the Gold Coast Farmers' Association at the Manchester Conference[26] and Kojo Botsio who subsequently served in the Nkrumah Administration. The W.A.N.S. was

[20] George Padmore, *Pan-African or Communism?*, p. 172.
[21] K. Nkrumah, *Ghana: The Autobiography of Kwame Nkrumah* (Edinburgh: Thomas Nelson and Sons, 1961), p. 45.
[22] *ibid.*
[23] Nkrumah to J. P. Allottey-Hammond, 25 November, 1945 (in *G.C.A.R.P.S. papers*, Acc. No. 77/64. Correspondence File No. 5).
[24] *ibid.*
[25] Kwame Nkrumah, *Ghana*, p. 45.
[26] *ibid.* George Padmore, ed., *Colonial and... Coloured*

eventually established in London at a meeting held on 14 December, 1945.[27] Nkrumah was appointed secretary assisted by the Nigerian, Bankole Akpata. The objects of the organisation were:

> 1. To maintain contact with, co-ordinate, educate and supply general information on current matters to the various political bodies, trade unions, farmers, educational, cultural and other progressive organisations in West Africa with a view to realizing a West African Front for a United West African National Independence.

> 2. To serve as clearing house for informations [*sic*] on matters affecting the destiny of West Africa; and to educate the peoples and the working class in particular, of the imperialist countries concerning the problems of West Africa.

> 3. To foster the spirit of national unity and solidarity among the various territories of West Africa for the purposes of combating the menace of artificial territorial divisions now in existence.

> 4. To work for unity and harmony among all West Africans who stand against imperialism.

> 5. To publish a series of pamphlets on West African affairs to be known as the West African National Secretariat series, and a monthly paper, THE NEW AFRICAN, to be published in London.[28]

There seems to be no evidence that the proposed W.A.N.S. pamphlets were published. But in March, 1946, the maiden issue of *The New African* appeared with the sub-title "The Voice of the Awakened African" and the motto "For Unity and Absolute Independence." Eight months later, publication

---

[27] Kwame Nkrumah to Allottey-Hammond, 8 February, 1946 *(G.C.A.R.P.S. Papers,* Acc. No. 78/64, Correspondence File No. 6).
[28] *ibid.*

of the magazine ceased owing to financial difficulties of the W.A.N.S.[29]

The W.A.N.S. found a substantial measure of acceptance in West Africa where by the end of March, 1946 the organisations supporting the Secretariat included the Gold Coast A.R.P.S., the Farmers' Committee of the Gold Coast and Nigeria, the Trade Union Congress of Sierra Leone and the West African Youth League, Sierra Leone branch.[30] In Britain, the W.A.N.S. received even greater support among the exiles and during the one and a half years beginning in February, 1946 the pan-African initiative seemed to have passed over to it.

At a meeting of Africans held in London on 27 March, 1946 and summoned by the W.A.N.S., a resolution was adopted for immediate transmission to the United Nations then meeting in New York.[31] The exiles were quick to see the new possibilities offered by the U.N. which, unlike the defunct League of Nations, was not dominated by the colonial powers. The resolution expressed dissatisfaction with the United Nations Organization for excluding from direct representation millions of "freedom-loving" peoples of Africa and other parts of the colonial world.[32] The Trusteeship Council of the U. N. was invited "to take such steps as may affect the speedy realisation of complete independence for the peoples of the colonies."[33]

In the summer of 1946, the W.A.N.S. and the W.A.S.U. jointly summoned a meeting held in London from 30 August to 1 September and attended by representatives of British and French West Africa. French West Africa was represented by Sourous Apithy and Leopold Senghor, both of whom were at

[29] Nkrumah to Allottey-Hammond, 29 September, 1947 (*G.C.A.R.P.S. Papers*, Acc. No. 78/64, Correspondence File No. 6).

[30] Nkrumah to Allottey-Hammond, 8 February, 1946; Allottey-Hammond to Nkrumah, 14 March, 1946 (*G.C.A.R.P.S. Papers*, Acc. No. 78/64, Correspondence File No. 6).

[31] *The New African* (May, 1946), p. 23.

[32] *ibid.*

[33] *ibid.*

that time members of the French National Assembly.[34] The theme of the conference was "Unity and Independence of All West Africa"; the purpose "to discuss the present political, economic and social conditions in West Africa, and to determine in that light a plan for creating a united and independent West Africa."[35] The conference unanimously called for the creation of an All-West African National Congress in the belief that united and independent West Africa could, and would act as the lever with which the entire African continent would be liberated for all time from foreign domination and exploitation.[36] In calling for an All-West African National Congress, the conference attempted, but unsuccessfully, to revive, with a broader basis, the National Congress of British West Africa which soon collapsed after the death of J. E. Casely Hayford, one of its founders.[37]

In November, 1946 representatives of the W.A.N.S., the P.A.F., the L.C.P. and the Transvaal Council of Non-European Trade Unions despatched a resolution to the United Nations Trusteeship Council.[38]

The resolution urged the Trusteeship Council to reject South Africa's demand to incorporate the mandated territory of South West Africa. The Council was further asked to take over the administration of the mandate and to require of the Union of South Africa an undertaking to respect and abide by the principle of the United Nations Charter in the treatment of all peoples within its jurisdiction on pain of expulsion from membership of the United Nations Organization.[39] An investigation of the social, economic and political conditions of the coloured community in the Union was demanded. The

[34] Kwame Nkrumah, *op. cit.,* p. 47.

[35] *Wasu Magazine,* Vol. XII, No. 3 (Summer, 1947), pp. 13-15.

[36] *ibid.*

[37] *ibid.*

[38] *News Letter* (December, 1946), pp. 40-41. The resolutions were also published in George Padmore, ed., *Colonial and ... Coloured Unity* (Manchester: Pan-African Service, 1947), pp. 64-66.

[39] *ibid.,* p. 64.

resolution emphasised that the policy pursued by the South African Government towards its subjects of non-European origin was "a direct negation of the principles of racial tolerance, justice and freedom."

Since the year 1920, when the Union became the mandatory of South West Africa, the native policy of the Union had steadily deteriorated. The passage in 1936 of the Native Franchise Act, the Native Land Act and the Urban Areas Act deprived the native of the Cape Province

> of the right to buy, hire or occupy land wherever they chose and confined them to restricted areas; the right to be on the Common Voters Roll, their representation being limited to three appointed European members in a House of Assembly consisting of one hundred and fifty-three members; their right to sell their labour where they chose by restricting their movements.[40]

There was little doubt that in its attitude to the territory of South West Africa, the Union Government had assumed a position unbecoming of a trustee and true of a conqueror bent upon territorial aggrandisement and the spoliation and humiliation of the vanquished.[41] Such a Government, the resolution argued, could not reasonably be entrusted with the care of subject and helpless peoples. The racial policy of that Government was a direct affront to the avowed determination of the United Nations to re-affirm faith in fundamental human rights, in the dignity and worth of the human being, in the equal rights of men and women of nations large and small.[42] The resolution admitted that Africans were not the only victims of this racialism for the Indians, about a quarter of a million in number, suffered a similar discriminatory treat-

---

[40] *ibid.,* p. 65.
[41] *ibid.*
[42] *ibid.,* pp. 65-66.

ment. Concluding, the resolution demanded justice and social equality for the Indian community in South Africa.[43]

In addition to sponsoring resolutions and conferences on matters considered to be of crucial importance to peoples of African descent, the W.A.N.S. attempted to stimulate opposition to colonial rule in West Africa. As early as June, 1946, Nkrumah had despatched one hundred copies each of the March, April and May issues of *The New African* to the Gold Coast A.R.P.S. and presumably to the other West African organisations which had expressed support for the objects of the W.A.N.S.[44] The P.A.F. also made a similar effort to quicken the pace in the colonies of the campaign against imperialism when in January, 1947 it launched *Pan-Africa*, a monthly journal of African life, history and thought. It was edited by T. R. Makonnen, assisted by Dinah Stock.

Unlike *The New African*, the *Pan-Africa* had an impressive staff of associate and contributing editors from different parts of the British Empire and the world. In June the list of such contributors included David Talbot about whom little or nothing is known (Ethiopia); Kwame Nkrumah and Samson Morris, from Grenada who in 1950 became the secretary of the L.C.P. (England);[45] H. W. Springer, a former treasurer of the L.C.P. who returned to Barbados to become secretary of the Progressive League and member of the Legislative Council there (Barbados); W. Esuman-Gwira Sekyi, a well-known Gold Coast lawyer and one time secretary of the Gold Coast A.R.P.S. (Gold Coast); Magnus Williams, a Nigerian politician who represented Nnamdi Azikiwe and the National Council of Nigeria and the Cameroons at the Manchester Congress (Nigeria); Yagoub Osman who later became Sudan's ambassador to Moscow (Sudan); Jomo Kenyatta, later

[43] *ibid.,* p. 66.
[44] Nkrumah to Allottey-Hammond, 11 June, 1946 (*G.C.A.R.P.S. Papers,* Acc. No. 78/64, Correspondence File No. 6).
[45] *League of Coloured Peoples' Review* (January, 1951).

president of Kenya.[46] The *Pan-Africa* excited alarm in official quarters and was banned by East African colonial governments as "seditious."[47]

Earlier in January, 1946 the I.A.S.B. had started a monthly with the title *Colonial Parliamentary Bulletin*. Edited by Padmore, the *Bulletin* was devoted entirely to questions, discussions and debates in the British Parliament concerning colonial and dependent peoples. For instance the March-April (1946) issue reproduced parliamentary questions and answers on West, East and South Africa, the West Indies, the Middle East as well as South East Asia. To overseas readers interested in imperial affairs, the *Bulletin* offered a unique opportunity of following the way the Labour Government was tackling colonial administration in the British Empire.

The *Bulletin* was supplemented by books penned by a number of the exiles. Their aim was to further expose the evils of foreign domination and to speed up the African revolution. One entitled *My Africa* appeared in New York in 1946 and was produced by Mbonu Ojike, a Nigerian and graduate of the University of Chicago. The first part of the book is autobiographical, the rest a clear exposition of African customs and traditions. Like Edward W. Blyden, Orishatuke Faduma and Mojola Agbebi, Ojike opposed the de-Africanising policy of the European colonial officials and Christian missionaries. Ojike's pride in African culture is evident from the following excerpt:

> Let each girl, of each color, be proud of what she is, she cannot be another. It is ridiculous and degrading to invent chemicals and urge ones face to sear its skin and become lighter or darker.
>
> For the African to seek modernisation in shameful foreign names is equally disgraceful. His language is one

---

[46] *Pan-Africa* (June, 1947).
[47] George Padmore, *Pan-Africanism or Communism?*, p. 174.

vital mode of expressing his culture and remaining honorably African. Christian missionaries and not Christianity have no one else to blame for this uncultural practice. A man can be as good as anyone else intellectually, financially, politically and religiously whether he is called James or Ikoli or Churchill or Stalin.[48]

Not surprisingly he urged Africans to boycott what was boycottable in foreign culture, an exhortation that earned him in his own country the nickname "Boycott King."

Of the exiles' publications that appeared after the Manchester Conference, none aroused as much controversy as George Padmore's *How Russia Transformed Her Colonial Empire.* Published late in 1946 and written with the help of Dorothy Pizer, the work was a comparative study of Soviet methods of solving colonial and racial minorities problems with British and other western metropolitan administrations in Africa and Asia. The book was widely reviewed in the British press and even in places as far afield as India,[49] Jamaica[50] and Nigeria.[51] It met a mixed reception among the British reviewers. F. A. Ridley, a member of the Independent Labour Party, commended it as an important book, which could become a classic on the colonial question.[52] But *The Times Literary Supplement* considered it unbalanced accusing Padmore of writing with unqualified admiration for the Soviet scheme of things.[53]

Another publication which admired the Marxist-Leninist attitude to the colonial problem was a booklet by Kwame Nkrumah entitled *Towards Colonial Freedom* and published in London in 1947. Nkrumah rejected the imperial doctrines of "civilising mission" and "trusteeship."[54] Imperialism was

[48] Mbonu Ojike, *My Africa* (New York: John Day, 1948), p. 108.

[49] *A Nationalist Review of Indian Affairs* (January, 1947).

[50] *Public Opinion* (11 January, 1947); (3 May, 1947).

[51] *West African Pilot* (Lagos) (5 May, 1947).

[52] *The Socialist Leader* (14 December, 1946).

[53] (11 January, 1947).

[54] *Towards Colonial Freedom* (London: Panaf Books, 1947), p. 1.

denounced as calculated exploitation[55] and the teachings of Marx and Lenin upheld as "the most searching and penetrating analysis of economic imperialism."[56]

Meanwhile the controversy over the merits and demerits of Padmore's new book continued. It was in the midst of this debate that Harold Moody, who had been leader of the L.C.P. since its inception in 1931, suddenly died. With the death of Moody in 1947, the presidency of L.C.P. was assumed by the famous West Indian cricketeer, Learie Constantine, with Dr. Malcolm Joseph-Mitchell, an economist from Trinidad, as general secretary.

New leaders also appeared in the W.A.S.U.; of these, many of whom were soon to become important in their countries, the following may be named: Ako Adjei, K. Boadu, Kojo Botsio, all of whom later served in the Nkrumah Administration; Dennis C. Osadebay who was later made a premier of Mid-Western Nigeria; Okoi Arikpo, later Nigeria's Commissioner for Foreign Affairs and Albert Margai, who subsequently become a prime minister of Sierra Leone. The role some of these young nationalists were soon to play in West African politics was foreshadowed by the keen interest they showed in, and the assistance they gave to, the National Council of Nigeria and the Cameroons (N.C.N.C.) delegation which arrived in London on 10 July, 1947.

The purpose of the N.C.N.C. mission was to present a memorandum to the new Colonial Secretary, Arthur Creech Jones, setting out the grievances of the Nigerian people with particular reference to the Richards Constitution introduced in 1945.[57] The members of the delegation included Nnamdi Azikiwe, editor of a daily, the *West African Pilot*; Mallam Bukar Dipcharima who later joined the Northern People's

---

[55] *ibid.,* pp. 1, 11.

[56] *ibid.,* p. 11.

[57] For the provisions of the Richards Constitution, see James Coleman, *Nigeria: Background to Nationalism* (Berkeley and Los Angeles: University of California Press, 1958), pp. 271-95.

Congress (Nigeria) and became a member of Balewa's Administration and Mrs. Ransome Kuti, wife of Reverend Kuti who was a member of the Commission on Higher Education in West Africa appointed in 1944.[58] The W.A.S.U. not only gave a reception in honour of the delegates but also "sponsored for them a public meeting at the Conway Hall and in co-operation with other [exile] organisations, another at Euston Hall."[59] George Padmore himself served as press secretary to the mission.[60] Such were the links established between the delegation and the exiles that before the mission returned to Nigeria early in August, Nnamdi Azikiwe endorsed the decision of the Manchester Congress and the W.A.N.S. to work for "immediate self-government and the realization of a United West African Federation."[61]

A few months after the departure of the N.C.N.C. mission, Kwame Nkrumah was offered the general secretaryship of the United Gold Coast Convention, formed on 4 August, 1947.[62] On the advice of the W.A.N.S., Nkrumah accepted the offer and on 14 November he left London for the Gold Coast.[63]

The year 1948 witnessed an intensification of the political consciousness of the members of the W.A.S.U. in particular, largely as a result of the labour unrest which broke out in the Gold Coast early that year. European traders were boycotted while ex-servicemen demanded some compensation for fighting the Empire's wars. Demonstrations by ex-servicemen culminated in disturbances in several major cities including Accra and were put down with loss of life. Some political leaders were arrested, among them, Kwame Nkrumah. On 29 February the W.A.S.U. despatched resolutions of protest to the British Prime Minister, Clement Attlee, Governor Creasy

[58] See Chapter 3.
[59] *Wasu Magazine* Vol. XII, No. 5 (Summer, 1948), p. 37.
[60] George Padmore, *Pan-Africanism or Communism?*, pp. 174-75.
[61] *ibid.,* p. 175.
[62] Dennis Austin, *Politics in Ghana, 1946-1960* (London: Oxford University Press, 1964), p. 54.
[63] *ibid.*

of the Gold Coast and the secretary-general of the United Nations.[64] At the same time a "patriotic message" was sent to Agyeman Prempeh 11, the Ashantchene of Ashanti.[65] Three days later, the W.A.S.U., the W.A.N.S. and the Gold Coast Students' Union sent a joint deputation to the Colonial Office in further protest.[66] In Manchester, the African Students' Union formed there in 1946 with the Nigerian, Eyo Bassey Ndem as secretary, held a public protest meeting in the Charlton Town Hall.[67] Ndem attended the Manchester Conference as the delegate of the Calabar Improvement League.[68]

In the Summer, 1948 issue of their organ, the W.A.S.U. called upon the British Government to "take a brave and statesmanlike decision to free the rest of her 'Colonial Empire.' " It was this keynote of independence for the colonial empire, particularly in Africa, that marked the activities of the exiles for the rest of 1948. This keynote is well illustrated in "The African's Prayer" adapted by the W.A.S.U.:

> Our Country, which art on Earth,
>> Honoured be thy Name;
>> Thy Freedom come, Thy work be done
>> Abroad, as it is done at home.

[64] *Wasu* Vol. XII, No. 5 (Summer, 1948), p. 399.

[65] *ibid.*

[66] *ibid.*

[67] E. B. Ndem, "Negro Immigrants in Manchester: An Analysis of Social Relations Within and Between the Various Coloured Groups and of Their Relations to the White Community," unpublished M.A. thesis, London University, 1954, p. 99. Ndem who was secretary of the African Students' Union from 1946 to 1948 does not give the date of the meeting or the names of any of the participants. The public meeting is the only activity of the A.S.U. during 1946-48 discussed. But he explains that "It [A.S.U.] has a wide and all embracing objective viz. political, social and literary interests. Aside from political activities which occupy its attention more than anything else, it provides a forum for debates, lectures and all matters of educational interest."

[68] George Padmore, ed., *Colonial and ... Coloured Unity* (Manchester: Pan-African Service, 1947), p. 71.

[69] Vol. XII, No. 5, p. 3.

Give us each day the vision clear
  And forgive us our foolishness,
  As we forgive them that daily try to fool us.

And lead us not into submission,
  But deliver us from trickery.
  For thine will be Freedom,
  Due Power, and due glory,
  For ever and ever — Amen.[70]

This concern for the destiny of the African peoples led Lord Milverton (lately Sir A. Richards) to accuse Ladipo Solanke of aiming to make W.A.S.U. first and foremost a political organisation for the promotion of certain political aims.[71] Milverton's fears might have been partly prompted by the way in which branches of the W.A.S.U. in West Africa attracted both the intelligentsia and traditional rulers and the fact that members of the parent union, upon returning home, invariably entered politics. It was significant that the principal organisers of the United Gold Coast Convention on 4 August, 1947 were J. W. de Graft Johnson, R. S. Blay, J. B. Danquah and Ako Adjei, some of them pioneer and all of them former executive members of the W.A.S.U.[72] It was also significant that the Convention invited Kwame Nkrumah, a vice-president of the W.A.S.U. in 1946 to become its first secretary.[73]

With the return of Kwame Nkrumah to the Gold Coast and the development of national consciousness in the four British West African territories, interest in a West African Federation, which, since the time of Edward W. Blyden, had been a chief objective of some West African intellectuals, began to decline. There emerged in London such organisations

---

[70] *ibid.,* p. 4.
[71] *West Africa* (2 October, 1948), p. 1004.
[72] Dennis Austin, *op. cit.,* pp. 52-53.
[73] *ibid.,* p. 54.

with a national basis as the Nigerian Union, the Gold Coast Students' Union, the Sierra Leone Students' Union, and the Gambia Union. These unions maintained a considerable attitude ot independence towards one another and to the W.A.S.U., directing most of their attention to problems concerning the corresponding country. The L.C.P. also began to decline shortly after 1947 when its founder-leader Harold Moody died. The association maintained a precarious existence for another four years after which it finally collapsed. Nor did the P.A.F. fare any better than the L.C.P. and the W.A.S.U. after the departure of Jomo Kenyatta and Kwame Nkrumah. The departure of these two men seemed to have robbed the P.A.F. of much of its former impetus and dynamism. The last issues of *Pan-Africa* and the *Colonial Parliamentary Bulletin* appeared in 1948 and for over a decade there was not a common pan-African journal based in Europe. Indeed, during the decade after the Manchester gathering, national self-government became the most urgent question in African politics.

This preoccupation is aptly illustrated by *Aids to African Autonomy. A Review of Education and Politics in the Gold Coast* contributed by S. D. Cudjoe, a Gold Coast medical practitioner trained at Edinburgh University and the Royal College of Physicians and Surgeons. Though published in London in 1949 and reprinted the next year, that is, some six years before Padmore's famous *Pan-Africanism and Communism?* the booklet is scarcely mentioned even by serious scholars. Yet the author's ideas are no less revolutionary than Padmore's, his concern for the fortunes of Africa and the Africans equally passionate, his style probably more sophisticated and elegant. For these reasons Cudjoe's tract receives extensive coverage here.

The author addressed the volume to those educated men and women of Africa directly or indirectly involved in politics who might be under the mistaken impression that individual achievements would "establish the respect we desire for our race as a whole, while we remain a subject people."[74] Castigating the methods and impact of European missionary enterprise, he regretted that the missionaries themselves seemed to lack adequate educational values by which they could select what was good in African culture. "They undermined the whole of the African framework, because they could neither understand nor appreciate it. Though they tried hard to make the Africans ashamed of their past, yet their new converts were unwilling to dissociate themselves from ties which had given their people a measure of security for generations.[75] The attempt to uproot what was essentially African and introduce another entirely western in outlook produced receptive converts who could not differentiate between humility and humiliation, because the freedom of doubt and question had been denied them.[76]

As a group, Cudjoe went on, the Gospel preachers neglected to challenge the rightness of the European conquest even though they knew that the Empire was built and sustained by force of arms to serve the interest of the invaders. He deplored the readiness with which the missionaries resorted to charitable collections in the metropolitan country when it was clearly the duty of imperial administrations to provide adequately for African education.

Turning to the methods of missionary education, the Pan-Africanist remarked that the missionary schools did not adapt their textbooks to the environment of African life, thus Cudjoe contended that if her ideas of good conditions under the influence of civilisation included a capitalist economy as

[74] S. D. Cudjoe, *Aids to African Autonomy. A Review of Education and Politics in the Gold Coast* (London: the College Press, 1950), Preface.
[75] *ibid.,* p. 3.
[76] *ibid.,* p. 4.

making it difficult for the African children to grasp the new knowledge. The difficulties arose not only from the meaning of foreign words but also from the whole train of associations those words possessed in their country of origin. Similarly, books translated into the local languages retained an almost literal rendering of thought patterns which the African mind found alien.

Cudjoe's attacks on the metropolitan powers and their African collaborators were equally biting. Foreign domination was a fact progressive Africans ought to be ashamed of. "The condition of African progress is not foreign rule, but emancipation in the widest possible sense."[77] Where a government failed to translate its avowed belief in freedom and equality into practice, it was the duty of the people to take steps to secure those rights.[78] Educated Africans must initiate an exchange of views with the masses immediately in order to "create that psychological period of incubation so necessary for the inauguration of concerted action. Nothing could be more positive than their visionary grasp of those things which will be needed to recreate a virile and united Africa, or their determination to harness all the basic elements of nationalism, which are already there in the tribal consciousness."[79]

Cudjoe regretted that while every nation in the world fought a civil war or staged a revolution as a step towards unity, imperial historians have made such antecedents appear barbarious only in the case of non-European peoples, and thus succeeded in presenting European domination of Africa as an instrument for peace.[80] Margery Perham was rebuked for pleading with Europeans not to consider the black man inferior until he had been placed in really good conditions

[77] *ibid.*, p. 20.
[78] *ibid.*, p. 19.
[79] *ibid.*, p. 20.
[80] *ibid.*, p. 22.

under the influence of civilisation for at least 500 years.[81] It is a great wonder that she postpones for 500 years a decision which is so glaringly self-evident."[82]

The author condemned the seizure of African territories as fundamentally unjust stressing that none of the British African possessions belonged to the Crown either by natural right or by the willing sanction of African traditional law.[83] Those who defended the subjection of Africans on the ground of native misrule were reminded of the insistence of E. D. Morel[84] that the mis-government of modern European politicians had "brought Europe to a state of misery and wretchedness unequalled in the history of the world."[85] In Morel's opinion the chief forces destroying European civilisation whether in Europe itself, Africa, Asia or the United States lay precisely in a limited conception of liberty. The imperial powers would jeopardise world peace again if they insisted on maintaining the pre-war conditions in their dependences. Colonial and world justice must rest on enlightened majority decisions, not might.[86] He agreed with Bertrand Russell that there was "no hope for the world unless power can be tamed and brought into the service, not of this or that group of fanatical tyrants, but of the whole human race, white, yellow or black, for science has made it inevitable that all must live or all must die."[87]

Finally, Cudjoe warned that neither the Empire nor the Commonwealth would survive for long unless

---

[81] *ibid.,* p. 24.

[82] *ibid.*

[83] *ibid.,* p. 28.

[84] *The Black Man's Burden. The White Man in Africa from the Fifteenth Century to World War I* (New York and London, 1920), reprinted in 1969 by Monthly Review Press, New York.

[85] Quoted in S. D. Cudjoe, *Aids to African Autonomy,* p. 28.

[86] *ibid.,* p. 41.

[87] Bertrand Russell, *Power: A New Social Analysis* (London: George Allen and Unwinn, 1938).

all are free. This is the noble death for the more efficiently the Empire maintains the bondage of Africa, the more it poisons itself in the process of inevitable suicide.[88]

As a case for the immediate removal of the foreign yoke, Cudjoe's tract is persuasive and may be compared with Tom Paine's *Common Sense*. Underlying the Gold Coaster's argument are the political doctrines that there are no people unfit for liberty or incapable of creating a democracy of their own; that self-determination was not a prize to be awarded to Africans only after they had attained a prescribed maturity and that no real progress was possible without freedom from the start.

To what extent Cudjoe's pamphlet influenced the exiles and events in the fatherland is difficult to say. But it is certain that Padmore read the fuller manuscript from which the volume was extracted.[89] Given the nationality of the author and Padmore's special relation with Nkrumah, we may assume that Nkrumah must have seen it and perhaps showed it to the other leaders of the Gold Coast liberation movement. The work was also known in W.A.S.U. circles and the appointment of the author to the union's Board of Directors in the early fifties may have been a gesture of appreciation.[90]

All the same, the desire to end colonial bondage was not universal in Africa and the Caribbean during the immediate post-war years. Such French-speaking African politicans as Leopold Sedar Senghor of Senegal preferred greater participation in the political process within the French Union to self-government. Despite its Communist orientation, even the *Rassemblement Democratique Africain,* led by Felix Houphouet-Boigny from the Ivory Coast and formed in 1946 by prominent African politicians to fight the elections to the French National Assembly, clashed with the colonial author-

---

[88] S. D. Cudjoe, *Aids to African Autonomy,* p. 42.

[89] *ibid.,* Acknowledgements.

[90] *West Africa* (28 August, 1954), p. 808.

ities not for demanding independence but because they were pressing for further social, political and economic reforms. It was significant that the disturbances which swept over Madagascar in March, 1947 were blamed on the *Mouvement Democratique de Renovation Malgache* because the party "had asked for more freedom within the French Union." [91]

As time passed French-speaking Africans became increasingly dissatisfied with an arrangement which treated them as Frenchmen. "They now wished to be recognised for what they were, and not to be patronised."[92] In July, 1952 a military *coup d'etat*, spearheaded by General Neguib and Colonel Gamel Abdel Nasser, overthrew the regime of King Farouk who had become a stooge of the British Government. The same year witnessed the outbreak of the Mau Mau movement, a desperate attempt by a desperate people to change a system of economic and social injustice that had been a marked feature of Kenyan history.[93] Two years later the Algerians launched the *Front de Liberation National* in revolt against the French overlords.

Then came the Bandung Conference of 1955 at which Africans and Asians affirmed their solidarity in their effort to dislodge imperialism. They even went further to formulate methods whereby unity among the independent nations of Africa and Asia could be quickened. For the Africans, the conference proved to be of great psychological and political significance. It was the first time, at least in modern history, that Africans spoke as equal participants in an international forum on issues concerning the continent as a whole and its relations with the world at large. After Bandung the pressures for change grew stronger everywhere.

[91] Guy de Lusignan, *French-Speaking Africa Since Independence* (London: Pall Mall Press, 1969), p. 12.

[92] *ibid.*, p. 11.

[93] B. A. Ogot and J. A. Kieran, ed., *Zamani: A Survey of East African History* (Kenya: East African Publishing House and Longmans, 1968), p. 283.

Men like the medical doctor, R. N. Duchein of Liberia realised that self-government represented only a means to the ultimate Pan-African aims of political unity, cultural emancipation and economic independence. To keep the wider aspirations afloat, he launched a society in 1954 in Liberia styled the Pan-African Unification Organisation. Its members were Africans drawn from various colonies who found common ground in the idea of African unity. With the intensification of the struggle for self-determination, some members went back to their respective countries thereby weakening the association. In 1957 Duchein published a document, *The Pan-African Manifesto,* in Accra. His purpose was to revive interest in continental unity.

The Liberian stressed that his group harboured goodwill towards all the races. Nonetheless he attributed the relative backwardness of Africa to European intrusion and condemned "all attempts at adopting new ways brought by another race claiming to be superior."[94] In his view, "everything African which is not inconsistent with modern science and with the progress of Africa must be considered superior and maintained to be improved in the line of African tradition. We believe in an African Personality."[95]

Of the reasons he advanced why Africans must unite, two may be mentioned. First, because "foreign races have determined to take Africa for themselves for ever."[96] Second, without a powerful nation capable of defending "ourselves, we are doomed to disappear as a race or live in insignificance like the Indians of the Americans."[97] To ensure African unity and survival, Duchein advocated the formation of a Pan-African Federation extending over the whole of Africa south of the Sahara "where Africans will rule themselves and enjoy fully in

[94] R. N. Duchein, *The Pan-African Manifesto* (Accra: Guinea Press, 1957), p. 12.
[95] *ibid.*
[96] *ibid.,* p. 9.
[97] *ibid.*

liberty, respected, the inalienable rights of man."[98] It should be noted that the proposed Federation embraced African descendants "scattered abroad who want to come back to their motherland and integrate in African life."[99] By also including Egypt in the United States of Africa he envisaged, "because of the great civilisation our forefathers built there,"[100] Duchein foreshadowed the bringing of Arab North Africa into the mainstream of Pan-Africanism in 1958.

Concluding, Dr. Duchein warned that no nation would welcome the emergence of a strong Africa capable of plying an important role in world affairs. "Most will dread it, while a few which pretend to be friends of Africa wish a free Africa checkered into a multitude of small nations constantly at loggerheads with one another, so as to have a better chance to exploit them."[101]

These arguments and other sentiments were later used by Nkrumah who probably read the manifesto for it was published in Accra. As if in response to Duchein's appeal for a continental outlook there emerged in March, 1958 the Committee of African Organizations with headquarters at 200 Gower Street, London.

The C.A.O. started as a federation of African students unions in England. Subsequently, membership was extended to student bodies in other parts of Europe as well as the United States, Canada, the Soviet Union and Eastern Europe. The aim of the C.A.O. was "unity for Africa and freedom for all African countries."[102] Its organ was called *United Africa* of which a Ghanaian student, Mr. Antwi Akuako, was one of the editors. Prominent members of the organization included Mr. Simon Kapwepwe, who later became Zambia's Foreign

[98] *ibid.*
[99] *ibid.,* p. 12.
[100] *ibid.*
[101] *ibid.*
[102] Kwesi Armah, *Africa's Golden Road* (London: Heinemann, 1965), p. 8.

Minister, Mr. Oliver Tambo of the African National Congress of South Africa, William Abrahams, a well-known Ghanaian Professor of Philosophy and associate of Kwame Nkrumah and Oscar Kambona who later served in Julius Nyerere's Administration as Minister of Foreign Affairs.[103]

Under the auspices of the C.A.O., such important African leaders as Kwame Nkrumah, Jomo Kenyatta, Milton Obote, Chief Albert Luthuli, Mr. Kenneth Kaunda, Dr. Hastings Banda, Nnamdi Azikiwe and the West Indian lawyer, Mr. David Pitt, gave public lectures.[104] In January, 1959, after his release from detention in connexion with the Mau Mau Affair, Jomo Kenyatta led a delegation of the Kenya African National Union to London for constitutional talks. While in London, he addressed a public meeting organised by the C.A.O. at the Africa Unity House.[105] His topic was: "African Freedom and Unity." He paid a warm tribute to Kwame Nkrumah saying that the independence of Ghana marked the end of the European domination of Africa.

Indeed, the emancipation of Ghana served to pave the way for closer co-operation among African peoples. Between 1958 and 1963 African leaders began to meet at frequent intervals. Some of these meetings were conferences of states already independent. Others were non-governmental gatherings of leaders of independence movements and trade unions.

[103] *ibid.*
[104] *ibid.*, p. 9.
[105] *ibid.*, p. 10.

CHAPTER 5

ATTEMPTS AT CLOSER UNION AND THE EMERGENCE OF THE O.A.U.

The impact of the Bandung conference, the Loi-Cadre of 1956 conceding internal autonomy to the French overseas territories, the independence of Morocco and Tunisia the same year followed by that of Ghana the next as well as promises of freedom for other British possessions, all served to pave the way for closer co-operation among African peoples. Was it not in 1957 that Kwame Nkrumah, the Prime Minister of Ghana, told the world that the independence of his country would be meaningless unless it was linked with the total liberation of the continent of Africa? No wonder he invited George Padmore and DuBois to the new nation.

While the independence celebrations were still going on, Nkrumah announced his intention of summoning a meeting of the self-governing states of Africa which actually met in Accra from 15 to 22 April, 1958.[1] Eight countries were represented, namely: Egypt, Ethiopia, Ghana, Liberia, Libya, Morocco, Sudan and Tunisia. Of these, five were from North Africa. South Africa declined the invitation to attend unless other "responsible powers" came.

In his opening speech, the Ghanaian Prime Minister said: "We, the delegates of this conference, in promoting our foreign relations, must endeavour to seek the friendship of all and the emnity of none. We stand for international peace and security in conformity with the United Nations Charter. This will enable us to assert our own African personality and to develop

[1] *West Africa* (26 April, 1958), p. 387.

according to our ways of life, our own customs, traditions and cultures. "[2]

Wide ranging resolutions were adopted on political, economic, social and cultural matters.[3] The participating governments resolved to preserve the unity of purpose and action being forged as well as "the fundamental unity of outlook on foreign policy so that a distinctive African personality will play its part in co-operation with other peace-loving nations to further the cause of peace." They agreed to avoid any action that might endanger their freedom of interests and to resort to direct negotiations to settle differences among themselves and if necessary to conciliation or mediation by other free African states. They affirmed the right of African peoples to run their own affairs promising direct assistance to the Algerian revolutionaries and the opponents of apartheid in South Africa. The delegates recognised the need to increase trade by improving communications between their countries and encouraging the investment of foreign capital and skills "provided they do not compromise the independence, sovereignty and territorial integrity of our state."

Anticipating many subsequent attempts at economic co-operation, the conference recommended the establishment of a Joint Economic Research Commission. Among other functions, the Commission was intended to explore the possibility of co-ordinating the economic planning in each state towards the achievement of an all-African economic co-operation; to make proposals by which independent African nations could receive foreign capital, employ foreign experts and encourage co-operation with other countries without destroying their unity or compromising their sovereign status. The Commission was also expected to examine the possibility of holding economic conferences and creating an

[2] Quoted in Teshome Adera, *Nationalist Leaders and African Unity* (Addis Ababa: Berhanena Selam Printing Press, 1963), p. 147.

[3] *West Africa* (10 May, 1958), p. 449. For a full text of the Resolutions, see Colin Legum, *Pan-Africanism: A Short Political Guide* (New York: Frederick A. Praeger, 1962), Appendix 4.

African common market and to ensure the establishment of equitable social and economic policies which would provide national prosperity and social security for all citizens.

Turning to relations between the races, the delegates condemned discrimination in all its forms and made elaborate recommendations for the improvement of cultural relations among the African peoples. Reciprocal visits of artists as well as annual inter-African sports meetings and youth festivals were approved. They decided to facilitate the exchange of teachers, professors, students and educational material. The revision of history and geography textbooks and syllabi used in schools was recommended "with the view to removing any incorrect information due to colonial and other foreign influences." Periodic and ad hoc conferences of African educators, scientists, men of letters and journalists were also proposed. Also recommended was research on African culture and civilization as well as the establishment of African publishing firms whose main function would be to introduce Africa's culture, civilization and developments to the world and to the various African countries.

Finally the participating governments set up a machinery for future consultation by ordering their permanent representatives at the United Nations to co-ordinate all matters of common concern; to take any steps necessary to implement conference decisions, and to make preparatory arrangements for future conferences. It was agreed that Heads of the independent African states should meet at least once every two years and that meetings of Foreign or other Ministers should be held from time to time "to study and deal with particular problems of common concern to the African state." April 15, the date of the meeting, was declared "African Freedom Day" to be observed every year.

The Accra Conference of 1958 was the first time that African co-operation was discussed at a governmental level and the first time that African governments had in concert called on the colonial authorities to apply the principle of self-determination to their African possessions. Commenting on the gathering the well-known English journalist, Colin Legum declared, quite rightly, that "the Accra Conference has opened a new chapter in the history of Africa, and in the relations between Africa and Europe."[4]

In December the same year (1958) an All-African Peoples' Conference (AAPC) was convened in Accra by Nkrumah in his capacity as chairman of the Ghana Convention Peoples' Party.[5] The arrangements were, however, made by a preparatory committee composed of representatives of Ghana, Nigeria, Egypt, Somaliland and Morocco. It was a meeting of African leaders from territories still under foreign domination. Two hundred delegates representing sixty-two nationalist organisations attended. Notable participants included Dr. Felix Moumie, leader of the Union of the Peoples of the Cameroons; Mr. Ntau Mkhehle of the Basutoland Congress Party; and M. Robert Holden from Angola. The N.C.N.C. contingent was led by Mr. N. S. McEwen who, with the Ghanaian trade unionist, Mr. John Tettegah, was elected Joint Secretary to the Conference. Also present were Dr. Horace Bond, a former President of Lincoln University (United States) and Dr. Marguerite Cartwright, an Afro-American author and journalist.[6] Among the fraternal delegates and observers may be mentioned a party of six Soviet writers led by the distinguished Russian Historian, Professor Potekin. Both Mr. Nikita Khruschev and Mr. Chou En-Lai sent greetings. Only two of Africa's major parties — the Northern People's Party of Northern Nigeria and the R.D.A. were not represented though conference organisers said they had been invited.[7]

Mr. Tom Mboya, member of the Kenya Legislative Council and Secretary-General of the Kenya Council of

[4] *The Listener* (1 May, 1958), p. 722.

[5] *West Africa* (29 November, 1958), p. 1143; (6 December, 1958), p. 1167; (13 December, 1958), p. 1191.

[6] *West Africa* (29 November, 1958), p. 1143.

[7] *West Africa* (13 December, 1958), p. 1191.

Labour, took the chair. Opening the conference, Nkrumah declared this to be the decade of African independence. He affirmed that the independence of Ghana would be meaningless unless it was linked up with the total emancipation of the continent. The delegates were urged to achieve first "the political kingdom: all else would follow." They were warned that imperialism could arise from regions outside Europe.[8] Accra was not an extension of Europe or any other continent.

In his address, the chairman contrasted the gathering with the Berlin Conference seventy-two years ago when foreign powers partitioned the continent. Africans were tired of being governed by other people and wanted everywhere to control their own destiny. Referring to the Cold War, he appealed to the big powers not to involve Africa, stressing, "we will not tolerate interference from any country, and I mean any."[9]

An address entitled "The Future of Africa" by DuBois, now 91 years of age and unwell, was given on his behalf by his wife. Among other things, the veteran Pan-Africanist said: "If Africa unites, it will be because each part, each nation, each tribe gives up a part of the heritage for the good of the whole. That is what union means; that is what Pan-Africa means."[10] Concluding he told the audience that they had nothing to lose but their chains; they had a continent to recover, freedom and human dignity to regain.[11]

At the end of their deliberations, the delegates announced that they had formed a permanent organisation with headquarters and secretariat in Accra. The purpose of the new institution was to:

> Promote understanding and unity among peoples of Africa;
>
> Accelerate the end of imperialism and colonialism;

[8] *ibid.*

[9] *ibid.*

[10] For a full text of the Address see W. E. B. DuBois, *The World and Africa: An Inquiry into the Part Which Africa Has Played in World History*, enlarged ed., (New York: International Publishers, 1965), pp. 305-310.

[11] *ibid.*, p. 310.

> Mobilise world opinion against denial to Africans of
> political and fundamental human rights;
> Develop feeling of one community to assist the
> emergence of a United States of Africa.[12]

Membership was opened to all African national political
organisations and national federations of labour that subscribed to the aspirations of the gathering.

The enthusiasm generated among participants returning to
their own countries influenced subsequent developments a
great deal. Among the obscure delegates was the Congolese,
Patrice Lumumba, who went back to his native Belgian Congo
to address a mass meeting in Leopoldville. This rally and other
activities of his helped to precipitate Belgium's decision to end
colonial rule in the country. At a seminar on contemporary
Africa held at Northwestern University (United States) in
1951, a high-ranking Belgian colonial administrator believed
that Belgium would remain in the Congo for another seventy-
five years.[13] But in 1960 alone, seventeen African territories
including the Belgian Congo, won their freedom.

Two weeks before the AAPC of 1958, shortly after Guinea
had won her independence outside the French Community as
re-organised by General de Gaulle, Nkrumah and the
Guinean President Sékou Touré announced the decision of
their two countries to constitute themselves as the nucleus of a
union of West African States.[14] They had been inspired "by the
example of the 13 American colonies, the tendencies of the
countries of Europe, Asia and Middle East to organise in a
rational manner, and the declaration of the Accra Conference."[15]

Ghana also agreed, subject to parliamentary approval, to
lend Guinea $10 million to stabilise the economy and provide
administrative and technical aid. Guinea needed the money

---

[12] *West Africa* (20 December, 1958), p. 1215.
[13] Hans Kohn and Wallace Sokolsky, eds., *African Nationalism in the Twentieth Century* (New York: Van Nostrand Company, 1965), p. 8.
[14] *West Africa* (29 November, 1958), p. 1143.
[15] *ibid.*

badly to prevent total collapse after France's withdrawal of her civil servants and equipment credits in retaliation against Guinea's refusal to remain in the French Community.

On his return to Conakry, the capital of Guinea, Sékou Touré claimed that his visit had blazed a trail for African independence and solidarity which he hoped would be translated "into a common co-operation and action in all fields to realise rapidly a United States of Africa."[16]

Accordingly, measures were taken in the following months to bring about closer co-operation, notably the exchange of resident-ministers who would attend cabinet meetings in the country to which they were accredited. On 1st May, 1959, Sékou Touré and Nkrumah further stated that the Union was open to all independent African nations. The member states would "decide in common what portion of sovereignty shall be surrendered to the Union in the full interest of the African community."[17] There would be a union flag with red, gold and green strips, an anthem and a motto. Each member country or federation was allowed to retain its local national flag, anthem and motto. "Independence and Unity" was declared as the motto of the Union whose general policy would be to build up a free and prosperous African community and its main objective "will be to help our African brothers subjected to domination with a view to ending their state of dependence, widening and consolidating with them a Union of Independent African States."[18] There would be Union citizenship and no visas would be needed to travel from one member territory to another.

Heads of State in the Union would determine common policy on matters of defence, but each constituent country would have its own army. Provision was made for an Economic Council charged with the task of formulating general economic policy and setting up a Union Bank capable of

[16] *ibid.*
[17] *West Africa* (9 May, 1959), p. 447.
[18] *ibid.*

issuing and backing the currencies of the members of the Union.[19] Finally, to bring Africans closer together, the Union would take measures to co-ordinate historical research, the teaching of languages and cultural activities designed to promote the harmonious development of African civilisations."[20]

The use of the term "Union" as opposed to federation seemed to have alarmed President William Tubman of Liberia who now took the initiative of inviting Nkrumah and Touré to a conference at Sanniquellie, a small Liberian village. The, meeting produced the Sanniquellie Declaration of 19 July, 1959.[21]

George Padmore attended in his capacity as Nkrumah's Adviser on African Affairs. The three governments agreed to speed up the revolutionary movement and bring about "unity, co-operation, harmony, coherence and mutual understanding" in Africa.[22] After reviewing the two communiques on the Ghana-Guinea Union as well as Tubman's proposals for an "Associated States of Africa," they proposed nine principles for consideration at the Second Conference of Independent African States to be held in Ethiopia the next year.

Among the principles were: that the organisation would be called "Community of Independent African States" with "Independence and Unity" as its motto; the inherent right of Africans to self-determination; no member of the community should interfere in the domestic affairs of the other; the extermination of colonialism; the right of dependent territories to join the community after obtaining their freedom and the creation of an Economic Council, a Culture Council and a Scientific and Research Council.[23]

In a separate communique, Tubman, Touré and Nkrumah

[19] *ibid.*
[20] *ibid.*
[21] *West Africa* (15 August, 1959), p. 60.
[22] *ibid.*
[23] *ibid.*

demanded pre-independence elections in French Cameroons to be conducted under the supervision of the U.N. The reference is to Felix Moumie who was now in exile, his party (UPC) having been banned. They supported the inclusion of the Algerian Question on the agenda of the forthcoming session of the U.N. General Assembly and condemned apartheid. South West Africa, later Namibia, was considered to be a Trust Territory over which the U.N. could not relinquish responsibility. France came under severe attack for testing atomic devices in the Sahara. African culture was seen "as one of the essential elements of the struggle against colonialism." Finally, the three governments agreed to make the rehabilitation and diffusion of African culture an imperative national duty.[24]

The Sanniquellie Declaration represented a compromise between the radical provisions of the Ghana-Guinea Union and Tubman's views of African solidarity. On the one hand, Nkrumah and Touré spoke for radical Pan-Africanists bent on rapid decolonisation and speedy unification of the fatherland. On the other, Tubman stood for those who, though no less committed to African emancipation and unity, preferred a cautious and gradual approach. "The revolutionary core made the compromise, and would do so again later, because of the urgent priority it gave to liberation issues."[25]

This polarization of the Pan-African movement also found expression at the All-African Peoples' Conference of Tunis which met six months later, from 25 to 30 January, 1960. About 180 delegates from 30 African territories attended it. In addition to violent anticolonial resolutions, the participants recommended the establishment of an organization to co-ordinate the aid and solidarity of all the independent countries

---

[24] *ibid.*
[25] Immanuel Wallerstein, *Africa, The Politics of Unity: An Analysis of a Contemporary Social Movement* (London: Pall Mall Press, 1968), p. 38.

and the sending of African volunteers to fight in Algeria.[26] Ghana's proposals for political union were rejected. But proposals for an African common market, bank and technical research institute were approved. Also adopted were resolutions for closer economic and cultural co-operation. Differences of opinion occurred over the question of international affiliation by African trade unions. While the Tunisians and Nigerians, supported by central and east Africans, desired to maintain their existing connexions, Morocco, Ghana, Guinea and the UPC pressed for the severance of all trade union ties with international bodies. It was eventually agreed to refer the matter to a foundation conference of African trade unions planned for May of that year. Eventually it was resolved that the All-African Trade Unions Federation should not affiliate to any of the international bodies but that each local union could have the right to decide its own international relations.[27]

The division into two camps, the radical and the conservative, was confirmed at the Addis Ababa Congress of the African nations, which took place from 14 to 26 June, 1960. More than 250 delegates and observers from 20 African territories, eleven of them already independent, were present.[28] The Algerian Provisional Government, then in exile, also participated. In his inaugural speech, the Ethiopian Emperor, Haile Selassie, emphasised that the fate of Africa was no longer determined by foreigners. The traditions of Berlin and Algeciras, together with the entire system of colonialism, were being eliminated from the continent. Though Africans now had their destiny in their own hands, they must never slacken in their determination "never to allow new forms of colonialism, whatever their guise may be, to take hold of any of us, in threat to the hard-won independence and, indeed to the

[26] For full text of the Resolution see Colin Legum, *op. cit.*, pp. 236-247.

[27] A foundation conference of the All-African Trade Unions Federation did not take place in May, 1961 as originally planned in May, 1960.

[28] *Second Conference of Independent African States, Addis Ababa, 14-26 June, 1970* (Addis Ababa: Government of Ethiopia Publication, 1960), p. 1.

stability and peace of the world."[29] African leaders, the Emperor went on, "must, in self-abnegation press forward the economic, political and spiritual welfare of their peoples in the interest, not merely of national gain but of that transcendent continental unity which alone can bring to a close the era of colonialism and Balkanization."[30]

His Excellency, Mr. Ato Yiema Deressa, the Ethiopian Foreign Minister and Chairman of the Conference, reviewed with satisfaction some practical applications of the resolutions passed at the Accra meeting. An Economic Commission for Africa had been launched, Ethiopia had made available 200 scholarships for African students to attend Ethiopian educational institutions and several profitable consultations had taken place, among them, "the Conference in Monrovia last year[31] to which Liberia, made so statesmenlike a contribution, and the recent conference in Accra on the matter of Atomic Tests in the Sahara."[32] Guinea, Togoland and Cameroons which achieved self-government during the intervening two years received a warm welcome. So too were the participants from Nigeria, Congo and Somaliland, then on the verge of securing their own freedom. Africans must hold themselves in readiness to resist "every attempt by foreign interests to influence or compromise the independence of emerging states and by a solid front, deny to those interests the attainment of their selfish goals."[33]

To maintain solidarity, the chairman urged African peoples to avoid every occasion for dissension among themselves and refrain from meddling in the domestic affairs of their brothers and neighbours. "Every form of propaganda, whether by press, by radio, or by word of mouth as between African

[29] *ibid.,* p. 27.
[30] *ibid.*
[31] The reference is to the African Foreign Ministers' Conference of August 1959. For details see *West Africa* (15 August, 1959), p. 609.
[32] *Second Conference of Independent African States,* p. 28.
[33] *ibid.,* p. 30.

States and peoples should be absolutely excluded."[34] Africans must never allow divided counsel to guide them whether at the United Nations or elsewhere. There were no reasons, the chairman concluded, "why our unity and brotherhood should not only provide the settlement of all internal differences, but also ensure that no action can be taken on the international scene except that it be with mutual consent and with full understanding."[35]

In an indirect reference to Nkumah's attempt to persuade the Ewe ethnic group in Togoland to join their kith and kin in Ghana, Mr. J. Rudolph Grimes, Head of the Liberian Delegation, thought that a way of avoiding friction and balkanization was to accept the present boundaries of African countries. With the Sanniquellie Declaration in mind, he said that Liberia has proposed a program of West African Regional Co-operation while at the same time advocating consultation for a larger African Organization in which regional efforts can be united under the title "Community of Independent African States."[36] He expressed the hope that preliminary discussions would be started during the conference "for the summoning of a conference at a time and place to be agreed upon at the earliest possible time to develop the charter of this Organization."[37]

Recommending the Sanniquellie Declaration for adoption, Mr. Ako Adjei of the Ghana delegation claimed that

> The unity, which the three leaders discussed and agreed upon, was intended to be a real political unity of independent African States, and not merely a system of economic co-operation. The three leaders signed a joint declaration in which they proclaimed to the whole world

[34] *ibid.*
[35] *ibid.*
[36] *ibid.*, p. 33.
[37] *ibid.*

the principles upon which the Union of African States shall be based.[38]

Adjei suggested that a committee of experts be appointed to work out the details of the proposed Union. The committee might consist of ministers, diplomats and economists and some of the subjects to be considered might include the formation of a Customs Union, the removal of trade barriers and the establishment of an African Development Fund.[39] In the words of the Ghanaian delegate, "the problems confronting our peoples in Africa today are so important and so vital to our very existence, that we cannot afford to dissipate our energies in fruitless argument and academic polemical debate."[40] The conference was assured that the provisions of the Ghana Constitution included the readiness of the people of Ghana to surrender their sovereignty in whole or in part in the interest of a Union of African States.[41]

Though Mr. Yusuf Mataima Sule, representing Nigeria, agreed that Pan-Africanism was the only solution to all "our problems in Africa," he dismissed the idea of a union then as premature preferring Tubman's approach through functional co-operation.[42] Mr. Sule placed the first priority on breaking all artificial economic, cultural and social barriers. All these must be done before political unification. He weakened his otherwise reasoned argument when he resorted to personal attack. Ghana's demand for immediate union, he told the gathering, was merely a device to make Nkrumah ruler of the entire continent. In the Nigerian's opinion, "individual ambition and greed for power may spoil everything; it will spoil the good work we have done and ruin the good work we are capable of doing in the future."[43] Mr. Sule believed that the Conference of

[38] *ibid.,* p. 42.
[39] *ibid.,* p. 43.
[40] *ibid.*
[41] *ibid.,* p. 42.
[42] *ibid.,* pp. 66-67.
[43] *ibid.,* p. 67.

Independent African States was the most effective mechanism for considering African problems and fostering African unity. He saw the development of the Conference of the Independent African States into a permanent organisation with a secretariat centred in Africa and a regular schedule of meetings as a step towards strengthening existing ties between African nations, encouraging co-operation and consultation in matters of common concern.[44] The permanent organisation would also be a centre of information on virtually every question affecting the interest and welfare of the continent. For administrative purposes, it should also be divided into several sections, including foreign commerce.

These suggestions were endorsed by the gathering who now requested the President of the Conference to ask Heads of African States to initiate consultation through diplomatic channels with a view to promoting African unity and to consider the matter at their next meeting in 1962.[45] That the Sanniquellie Declaration had been rejected was clear.

Not daunted, President Nkrumah, repeated the demand for a Union of African States in a speech on African Affairs given at the Ghana National Assembly on 8 August, six weeks after the Addis Ababa Conference.[46] "Political freedom is essential in order to win economic freedom, but political freedom is meaningless unless it is of a nature which enables the country which has obtained it to maintain its economic freedom."[47] The African struggle for liberty and unity must begin with political union. A loose confederation of economic co-operation was time-wasting. Only a political union would ensure uniformity in their foreign policy "projecting the African personality and presenting Africa as a force important to be reckoned with."[48]

[44] *ibid.,* p. 70.

[45] For a text of the Resolution see *ibid.*, pp. 101-108.

[46] Kwame Nkrumah, *Africa's Challenge: A Time of Danger and of Hope* (Accra: Government of Ghana Publication, 1960).

[47] *ibid.,* p. 9.

[48] *ibid.*

The President harmed his cause and made more enemies when he proceeded to denounce the supporters of a loose economic co-operation as imperialist protagonists and puppet leaders bent on blocking the path to African unity.[49] Political union, he emphasised, meant a common foreign policy and defence policy, as well as rapid, social, economic and industrial developments. The economic resources of Africa were immense and staggering. It was only through unity that those resources could be utilised for the progress of the continent and for the happiness of mankind. He saw three alternatives open to African states: "firstly, to unite and save our continent; secondly, to disunite and disintegrate; or thirdly, to sell out" to foreign powers.[50]

The Ghanaian leader also reviewed events in the Congo which regained independence only four days after the Addis Ababa Conference. The violence, anti-white feeling and sectionalism that accompanied the proclamation of freedom were seen as the inevitable consequence of eighty years of colonial subjection. Nkrumah was convinced that prompt action by the African nations would prevent complete disintegration, if not advertise African solidarity.

As prime minister, Lumumba left no one in doubt about his endorsement of Nkrumah's approach to African unity and views on economic independence. "We have absolutely no intention," he declared,

> of letting ourselves to be guided by any ideology whatsoever. We have our own ideology, a strong, noble ideology which is the affirmation of the African personality ...
>
> Government policy will be none other than that of the people. It is the people who dictate our actions, and we

[49] *ibid.*
[50] *ibid.*, p. 1.

operate according to the interests and aspirations of the people. Independence is the beginning of a real struggle.[51]

Though such pronouncements naturally alarmed the European multinational company, *Union Miniere du Haute Katanga,* the Congolese themselves lacked unity contrary to the implication of the prime minister's speeches. While his party, the *Movement National Congolais,* stood for a unitary state, the *Parti Solidaire Africain* led by Antoine Gizenga as well as Albert Kolonji's Kasai faction of the MNC wanted a federation. The supporters of a federal system found a spokesman in Joseph Kasavubu, leader of the Abako Party. In order not to delay independence, Lumumba agreed to form a coalition government conceding the presidency to Kasavubu.

But men like Weise Tshombe had different ideas. Under his leadership, the *Confederation de Associations Ethniques du Katanga* better known as *Conakat,* tried to secede within a few weeks of independence. Grasping the opportunity, *Union Miniere* offered assistance to the rebel regime, much to the chagrin of the African peoples. Thus, Lumumba's efforts to crush the secession became a symbol of African unification and resistance to neo-colonialism. His death, in mysterious circumstances, while the Katanga Crisis was still raging, made him a martyr of Pan-Africanism.

Indeed, it would be mistaken to suppose that the Congo Question had no adverse effects on the large problem of African unity. With the intervention of the big powers, the crisis acquired Cold War dimensions. Hopes of an early settlement vanished. The more a quick solution faded into the background, the louder Nkrumah's plea for an African Union grew. Overcome by impatience, he resorted to invectives which merely served to harden the suspicion of the gradualists. By

[51] Quoted in Wilfred Cartey and Martin Kilson, ed., *The African Reader: Independent Africa* (New York: Random House, 1970), pp. 87-89.

October, 1960 when Nigeria attained self-rule, division had become rivalry.

Actually in the same month, a meeting of twelve states *d'expression francaise* was summoned by Felix Houphouet-Boigny in Abidjan to discuss their attitude to the Franco-Algerian dispute. "The need for such an initiative had become urgent in view of their approaching application for membership of the United Nations."[52] At a second conference which took place in Brazzaville from 15 to 19 December, they decided to form a more permanent association. This decision was implemented at a third meeting in Dakar held the following month. Out of these conferences grew a bloc known as the Brazzaville Group. Among the member states were Congo (Brazzaville), Ivory Coast, Senegal, Mauritania, Cameroon and Madagascar. Togoland, Guinea and Mali as well as the French-speaking countries of North Africa were excluded.

The Brazzaville Declaration, issued on 19 December, 1960,[53] upheld the sovereignty of Mauritania, whose admission to the United Nations was vetoed by the Soviet Union. All "African States anxious for liberty and dignity of Africa, and anxious to avoid cold war on our continent," were exhorted to secure the admission of Mauritania. Fearing that the Franco-Algerian conflict might degenerate into a world crisis, in which Africa would bear the cost, the Brazzaville Powers resolved to ask France firmly to conclude the war in Algeria in 1961, and after frank negotiations to apply honestly the principle of self-determination.[54] The super-powers were accused of seeking to recolonize Congo (Leopoldville) either directly or indirectly through the intermediary of certain Asiatic and African States.[55] A solution to the problem could only be found

[52] Colin Legum, *Pan-Africanism*, p. 50.
[53] For a text of the Declaration, see Colin Legum, *Pan-Africanism*, Appendix 13.
[54] *ibid.*, p. 180.
[55] *ibid.*

at a Round Table Conference which would group together the representatives of every party without exception.[56]

While opposing political union in the sense of integrated institutions, the Brazzaville Powers agreed to appoint a commission with a view to establishing a plan of African and Madagascan economic co-operation on such matters as monetary and credit problems, crop price stabilisation, the harmonisation of the different national development plans and guarantees to private investment.[57] The commission was intended to consider the creation of an Afro-Malagasy Investment Bank as well as the "problems posed by the adhesion, to come or already achieved, of Members States of the Conference to various organisations of the European Community as well as to the various international organisations of a financial and economic character, in the hope of safeguarding their emergent national economies."[58]

The deliberate exclusion of certain African territories from the Brazzaville bloc created a dangerous precedent driving progressives and moderates further apart. In January, 1961, King Mohammed V of Morocco summoned a meeting in Casablanca to which selected African countries and Ceylon — a strange member — were invited. The ostensible reason for calling the meeting was the Congo situation. For some time, African states in support of Lumumba had felt the need to co-ordinate their efforts. Since they had become a minority in the African Group at the United Nations, they were anxious to regain their influence. None the less, a more compelling motive that drove King Muhammed to summon the conference was the apparent isolation of Morocco following the rejection of her claim to Mauritania by the United Nations General Assembly the previous month. Because of their support for Mauritania, the Brazzaville Group received no invitation. Apart from the King, Presidents Nasser, Nkrumah,

[56] *ibid.*
[57] *ibid.*, p. 181.
[58] *ibid.*, p. 182.

Sékou Touré and Modibo Keita of Mali attended. The Algerian Provisional Government was represented by its Prime Minister, Mr. Ferhat Abbas, Libya by her Foreign Minister and Ceylon by her Ambassador to Cairo.

Five major subjects dominated the proceedings, namely: Mauritania, Congo, Israel, a Union of African States and a constitutional framework for the Casablanca Powers.

Before the congress, Ghana, Libya and the Algerian Provisional Administration did not recognise Morocco's claim that Mauritania formed part of her territory. Hence, Ghana supported Mauritania's application to become a member of the United Nations. But for the sake of solidarity, the three governments changed their policy.

The debate on the Congo problem was reduced to an argument between Ghana and the rest. In the end, only Ghana refused to withdraw her troops from the United Nations Command in the Congo. With the same vehemence, Ghana opposed the attempt to give direct military assistance to Antone Gizenga's Stanleyville Regime on the ground that such aid was logistically impossible. The debate on Israel occasioned little disagreement probably because the Ghanaian delegates were unwilling to isolate themselves on yet another issue.

At the end of the deliberations, the Conference approved an African Charter setting out the aims of its signatories: freedom, unity, non-alignment, de-colonisation and co-operation among African nations.[59] To further these ends, the delegates agreed to form an "African Consultative Assembly, as soon as conditions permit, composed of the representatives of every African State, having a permanent seat and holding periodical sessions."[60] A Joint African High Command was proposed. Its functions would be to ensure the common

[59] For a text of the charter see Colin Legum, *Pan-Africanism*, Appendix 15.

[60] *ibid.*, p. 187.

defence of Africa in case of aggression against any part of this continent.[61] The Charter also provided for several committees, among them: the African Political Committee consisting of Heads of States, the African Economic Committee comprising Ministers of Economic Affairs and the African Cultural Committee made up of Ministers of Education. A liaison committee would be created to ensure co-operation between the various bodies.

By supporting the claim of Algeria to self-determination and denying the same right to Mauritania, the participants put themselves in a situation that was both ridiculous and untenable. Predictably, Israel was denounced as an "imperialist base."

The broad principles outlined in the Charter were incorporated in the Protocol of the African Charter signed at a meeting of Foreign Ministers in Cairo held from 30 April to 5 May, 1961.[62] Libya and Ceylon did not take part. The Foreign Ministers also approved the establishment of a secretariat at Bamako, the capital of Mali, with a Moroccan as secretary-general.

At two subsequent meetings of the Economic Committee, agreement was reached on proposals for an African Common Market, payments, customs union, a development bank, planning council, joint air and shipping lines and a telegraph union. In August, 1961 the Cultural and Defence Committees met in Tangier and Cairo respectively. At the latter gathering, it was decided to set up an African Military High Command.

Just as the Brazzaville Congress helped to precipitate the Casablanca convocation, so the latter helped to spark off the Monrovia meeting of May, 1961. Altogether, twenty African states sent delegates including sixteen Heads of State. Among the participating governments were those of the

---

[61] *ibid.*, p. 188.
[62] For details of the Protocol see *ibid.*, Appendix 16.

Brazzaville bloc. Two of the original sponsors, Guinea and Mali, changed their mind at the last moment due to pressure from Ghana. Morocco and Egypt, the fourth and fifth Casablanca Powers, were also unrepresented. Sudan withdrew her acceptance a few days before the meeting because Mauritania had been invited. Congo (Leopoldville) received no invitation because of the desire to avoid controversy with the Casablanca States over credentials. Thus, although the Monrovia Congress was so far the largest single gathering of African leaders, it was actually less representative than the preceding Casablanca meeting. With the exception of Tunisia, North Africa was unrepresented.

In the absence of men like Nkrumah and Nasser, it was easy for the otherwise soft-spoken and gentle Prime Minister of Nigeria, Sir Tafawa Balewa, to emerge as the dominating figure. So pervasive was his influence that he was able to steer the discussion clear of controversial issues, finally maneuvering the conference into accepting a gradual and functional approach to African unity; such vexed issues as the repeated tests of atomic devices in the Sahara by Franco and the Ethiopia-Somalia border dispute were swept under the carpet so as to create a facade of unanimity. The anti-colonial and anti-apartheid resolutions were made to lose much of their force by the failure of the delegates to recognise the Algerian Provisional Government. On the Congo question, they condemned assassinations as a means of securing political power. The principles of absolute equality, inviolability of African frontiers and non-interference (not applicable to colonial territories) in each other's affairs were affirmed. Deep regret was expressed at the absence of the Casablanca nations who it was hoped would be present at subsequent conferences.

The delegates appointed a commission to meet in Dakar, the capital of Senegal, within three months to consider machinery for economic, technical, scientific and educational co-operation and to submit recommendations to a later congress in Lagos.[63]

Accordingly, the members of the commission from nineteen of the twenty Monrovia Powers (Ethiopia sent no experts) assembled in Dakar in July, 1961. They drew up sixteen recommendations for approval at the next meeting of Heads of State in Lagos. Among the recommendations were proposals for regional customs unions, progressive harmonisation of external tariffs, a development fund, payments union and improved communications.

Though the Monrovia decisions were not fundamentally different from the provisions of the Casablanca African Charter, the Ghanaian press denounced the delegates as imperialist agents. Liberia, the host country, was described as being "in the economic-mess pot with her split, deformed and distorted personality."[64] President Tubman himself was called upon to admit that he was "an American first, African second."[65]

Infuriated by the tactless fulminations of Ghanaian journalists, the *West African Pilot,* a Nigerian daily, descended to the same level of abusive language. The newspaper recalled that Ghana was supposed to be united with Guinea: yet both countries possessed neither a common parliament nor a common currency. Echoing Mr. Yusuf Maitama Sule's accusation at the Addis Ababa Conference of June, 1960, the paper claimed that Nkrumah's real aim was to swallow up little Togo and chew off parts of Ivory Coast. The campaign for an African parliament and an Africa without boundaries was described as a cloak to conceal his aims.[66]

Politicians joined in the press war. In a press statement on

---

[63] For resolutions of the Monrovia Conference see Colin Legum, *op. cit.,* Appendix 17.

[64] Quoted in Colin Legum, *Pan-Africanism,* p. 54.

[65] *ibid.*

[66] *West African Pilot* (18 May, 1961), editorial.

African Affairs issued on 28 June, 1961,[67] Chief Obafemi Awolowo, Leader of the Opposition in Nigeria, advocated the division of the continent into zones as a first practical step towards the emergence of an All-Africa political union. In each zone, there would be functional co-operation on economic, political and cultural matters culminating in a zonal political union. Unsure of his facts the Nigerian politician ruled out political unification on a continental scale because, according to him, Africa lacked the "racial, cultural and linguistic homogeneity of the U.S.A., the centuries-old cultural and national unity of China and (to a great extent) of India, and the ideological orientation and cohesion of Russia [*sic*]."[68] Awolowo went on to urge the immediate formation of an Organisation for African Community on the model of the American Confederation. His solution combined functional co-operation at the confederal level and political unification at the regional or zonal level.

In an article published in *Foreign Affairs* for October, 1961, President Sylvanus E. Olympio of Togoland commended the Monrovia Conference for opening the way to international co-operation while preserving the national sovereignty of African states. He was convinced that few serious governments would be willing to relinquish their hard-won seats in international councils, seats which permitted them to be heard and which granted them the moral security provided by access to world opinion. Furthermore, experience showed that "in building a house one starts with a foundation, not a roof."[69]

In an earlier article also published in *Foreign Affairs,* Leopold Senghor had similarly warned that a United States of Africa was "not something to be brought into being overnight."[70] The history of the United States, Soviet Union and Germany proved that "a federation is really possible only

[67] Reprinted in extenso in Colin Legum, *op. cit.,* Appendix 24.
[68] *ibid.,* p. 269.
[69] *Foreign Affairs* Vol. 40 No. 1 (October, 1961), p. 51.
[70] *Foreign Affairs* Vol. 39, No. 2 (January, 1961), p. 243.

between states that are at equal economic levels and have equal political maturity."[71] Disapproving of the call at the Tunis All-African Peoples' Conference for an African Common Market, he contended that African economies were more than complementary as if the same situation was not true of the members of the European Common Market. It was paradoxical, he went on,

> that at the very time some of the newly independent African states pretend to champion African unity they quarrel about frontiers and claim pieces of neighbouring territories, support emigres and phantom governments at great expense, see Fifth Columns everywhere.[72]

By a strange coincidence, the emergence of the East African Common Services Organisation later in the year seemed to vindicate the practicability of the views of Senghor, Olympio and Awolowo. Actually, the East Africa Common Services Organisation grew out of the East Africa High Commission set up by the British authorities in 1948. From October, 1961 to August, 1962 rivalry among African peoples and organisations continued unabated. Two African trade unions, the All-African Trade Union Federation and the African Trade Union Confederation competed for recognition. The one received the support of the Casablanca Powers, the other that of the Monrovia bloc.

Side by side with the squabbles between the various groupings went national disputes between some of the African states themselves. These disputes had the effect of heightening the tension within the movement for African unity. We have already noted Morocco's claim that Mauritania constituted part of her territory. The Moroccans also had a frontier dispute with the Algerians which resulted in warfare. Similarly,

---

[71] *ibid.*, p. 240.
[72] *ibid.*, p. 244.

218

Ethiopia, Kenya and Somalia quarrelled over their borders. Cameroon accused Guinea of harbouring Felix Moumie, then in exile, his UPC Party having been banned, and Nigeria of interferring in a plebiscite which led to the incorporation of Northern Cameroon in Nigeria.

Tunisia blamed Egypt for an attempt to assassinate President Habib Bourgibah. The Ewe problem ensured continued enmity between Togoland and Ghana. "Many fellow nationalists resented the impression that Nkrumah was staking a claim to lead the whole continent, particularly when his diplomacy seemed to be interfering in their internal affairs and considerable groups of their younger generation looked to him as their militant inspiration."[73]

Five days before the resumed Monrovia conference in Lagos on 25 January, 1962, Nkrumah made a statement on certain aspects of African unity before the Ghana National Assembly. Without mentioning Awolowo, Olympio and Senghor by name, he rejected their arguments against continental union. He remained convinced that

> local associations, regional commonwealth and territorial groupings will be just another form of balkanisation, unless they are conceived within the framework of a large union based on the model of the United States of America or the Union of Soviet Socialist Republics. When the first thirteen states in the North American continent tried to promote the idea of a United States of America, this was ridiculed as an empty dream which was vigorously resisted by many. And who would have thought that seventy-five different nationalities at various levels of economic, social and political development in Russia [*sic*] could have been welded into the mighty force which the Soviet [Union] has become within this comparatively short space of time. I believe that Russia even began with three states.

[73] John Hatch, *A History of Postwar Africa* (New York and Washington, 1965), p. 400.

Nkrumah might have added that in the case of America, confederation or loose association nearly led to total collapse within the first decade of independence. It was the failure of a confederal system that prompted the Philadelphia Convention (1787) which gave birth to the United States of America. Concluding his speech, President Nkrumah said: "Our survival depends upon the political unity of Africa. The forces that unite us are far greater than the difficulties which divide us at present."

As the opening day of the Lagos Conference approached, Africans and observers elsewhere hoped that the Casablanca Group would attend so that their mutual hostility might at least be diminished. However, the exclusion of the Algerian Provisional Government by the sponsors angered the Casablanca Powers. Consequently, they boycotted the meetings. Libya and Tunisia also refused to attend for the same reason; their absence was offset by the presence of two newcomers, Tanganyika and Congo (Leopoldville). Altogether no less than seventeen Heads of State or Government came. Despite the impressive number of countries participating, not a single North African nation sent delegates.

Welcoming the gathering, Governor-General Nnamdi Azikiwe deplored the absence of the Casablanca Powers and tried to make up for the unrepresentative nature of the Congress by emphasising the combined population of the Monrovia Group estimated at 133.1 million as against 53.1 for the Casablanca bloc.

Apparently displeased by Azikiwe's divisive arithmetic, Emperor Haile Selassie made it clear that Ethiopia belonged to "one group only — the African group." The emperor pointed out that a close and careful analysis of the policies adopted by the African nations on a wider range of questions emphasised, not the differences among them, but the large number of views which they shared in common.[74] He therefore lamented the

[74] Haile Selassie's Speech is given in extenso in Vincent Bakpetu Thompson, *op. cit.,* p. 175.

exclusion of the Algerian Provisional Government whose absence had caused a number of other nations whose representatives should be seated in these halls to decline invitations extended to them.[75] Ethiopia, the Emperor stated unequivocally, is committed to the principle of political unity among African States — "indeed, we believe that we all are, and that we differ only in our assessment of the speed with which the most desirable of goals can be attained."[76] The task before Pan-Africanists was to devise the means whereby this basic agreement might be most rapidly advanced. "The furtherance of political unity, then, would be a fundamental objective of the Organisation of African States."[77]

The Dakar recommendations of the commission appointed at Monrovia as well as proposals for a functional approach to African unity submitted by Nigeria, Liberia and Ethiopia were examined.[78] At the end of the discussion, the conference accepted in principle a draft charter for a permanent Inter-African and Malagasy Organisation which was confirmed four months later, with a few amendments, at a meeting of Foreign Ministers also held in Lagos.

According to the Charter, the purpose of the permanent body was to promote a better life for the peoples of Africa and Malagasy by enlisting the efforts of member states through cooperative and joint actions.[79] The document enshrined the principles of sovereign equality of member nations irrespective of their wealth, size and population; non-interference in the domestic affairs of member states; respect for the territorial integrity of each country; peaceful settlement of all disputes; unqualified condemnation of any subservient activity on the

---

[75] *ibid.*
[76] *ibid.*
[77] *ibid.*
[78] *West African Pilot* (26 January, 1962).
[79] For a full text of the proposed Charter of the Inter-African and Malagasy States Organisation see Remi Fani-Kayode, *Blackism* (Lagos and London: V. Cooper and Partners, 1965), Appendix I.

part of neighbouring or other states; the constant promotion of cooperation in the fields of economics, health, nutrition, education and culture and dedication to the total emancipation of the remaining colonies in Africa.[80] Membership of the Organization was open to every independent state in Africa and Malagasy under indigenous African rule. There were provisions for an Assembly of Heads of States and Governments, a Council of Ministers and a General Secretariat as well as specialised agencies.[81] Finally, the gathering adopted the Dakar recommendations.

A careful examination of the provisions of the Charter and the resolutions shows that Emperor Haile Selassie was right when he remarked that not much difference existed between the programmes of the various Pan-African groupings. Though the resolutions derived from the principle of functional approach, subsequent events demonstrated that this opening address had paved the way for the reconciliation of the two major groupings: Casablanca and Monrovia.

At their Addis Ababa meeting held the following month, in February, 1962, the Pan-African Freedom Movement for East, Central and Southern Africa pledged "to establish a Federation of the component states of PAFMECA as a first real and logical step toward the full realisation of total African political unity and as the best method of speeding up the liberation of Africa."[82]

A communique — of May the same year — issued after consultations between Sékou Touré and Leopold Senghor at Labe in Guinea announced the decision of the two leaders to increase their joint efforts to bring together the Monrovia and Casablanca camps. On 28 June, Sékou Touré and Haile Selassie conferred at Asmara in Ethiopia. Events in Algeria

---

[80] *ibid.,* p. 76.

[81] *ibid.,* pp. 77, 80-81.

[82] *The Fourth PAFMECA Conference Held in Addis Ababa February 2nd to 10th, 1962. (Speeches and Statements),* (Publication of the Africa Department of the Foreign Office, Addis Ababa, Ethiopia, [n.d.]), p. 81.

and Congo (Leopoldville), both of which had been major points of disagreement between the radicals and the moderates, came to the aid of African unity. On 1 July, 1962 Algeria became independent. At the same time, a new administration controlled neither by Antoine Gizenga nor Tshombe, emerged in Congo (Leopoldville). Hence, a meeting of the Casablanca Heads of State at Cairo in June was able to support a proposal by Guinea for a continental conference.

During a visit to Conakry in August, Houphouet-Boigny said that he agreed with the necessity of bringing the two groups together as soon as possible to discuss African unity. In the same month, President Modibo Keita of Mali, visiting the Ivory Coast, expressed the hope that in a few months time, there would be nothing fundamental separating the two blocs. And in October Houphouet-Boigny, Modibo Keita and Sékou Touré met in Komodougou in Guinea to exchange views on African and international problems. It is important to note that the three presidents had not met together since 1958.

The same universal desire of an end to the Casablanca-Monrovia conflict was abundantly reflected in the exertions of the London-based Committee of African Organizations. As soon as it became known that a congress of African states was being planned for May, 1963 in Ethiopia, the CAO summoned a meeting of the All-African Students of Europe which took place in Friends House, London from 17 to 19 April. A four-point resolution was unanimously passed for transmission to all Heads of African States and Governments:

1. The Youth of Africa expect the leaders of Africa meeting at Addis Ababa to perform one clear and honest duty — the duty to unite all the States of Africa.
2. To this end, they should as individuals sink all their personal differences and as groups should disband the Casablanca, the Monrovia and the Brazzaville Groups, so-called.
3. They should draw up a charter of African Unity to which all the States should subscribe.

4. The Addis Ababa Conference should give a name to
the Union and appoint a secretariat as well as the seat of
its operations.[83]

In addition, the participants drew up a Manifesto also sent
to all the African leaders.[84] Among other things, the students
called for a Pan-African News Agency, a Pan-African Radio
and Television Service, a Pan-African Army under a joint
High Command and an African Common Market.[85] They
urged the inclusion of African history, music, culture, and
languages in the syllabi of African universities.[86]

On 22 May, 1963 the Casablanca and Monrovia factions
assembled in the Ethiopian capital of Addis Ababa where they
agreed on a compromise formula for achieving African unity.
With the exception of Morocco and Togoland, all the thirty-
two sovereign nations were represented by their Heads of State
or Government. Mr. Kwesi Armah, a member of the CAO was
also present. A notable absentee was President Olympio of
Togo who was assassinated four months before the conference.

Haile Selassie's welcome address struck the keynotes of
compromise and unity which pervaded the proceedings. It was
the duty and privilege of the delegates to rouse the slumbering
giant of Africa, not to the nationalism of Europe of the
nineteenth century, not to regional consciousness, but to the
vision of a single African brotherhood bending its united
efforts towards the achievement of a greater and nobler goal.[87]
The emperor warned that while they agreed that the ultimate
destiny of this continent lay in political union, they must at the

---

[83] Kwesi Armah, *Africa's Golden Road* (London: Heinemann, 1965),
p. 26.

[84] For a text of the Manifesto see *ibid.*, Appendix III.

[85] *ibid.*, pp. 284-85.

[86] *ibid.*, p. 285.

[87] A full text of the Emperor Haile Selassie's Welcome Address is printed
in *Addis Ababa Summit, 1963* (Publication of the Ministry of Information,
Addis Ababa, Ethiopia) and the *Journal of Modern Studies* Vol. 1, No. 3
(September, 1963), pp. 281-291.

same time recognize that the obstacles to be overcome in its achievement were many and quite formidable.[88]

The emperor's counsel of caution and gradualism did not prevent Nkrumah from using the occasion to re-state the case for immediate political unification. His argument may be summarized as follows. Africa is a rich continent but her mineral and natural resources are unevenly distributed. So long as the African states remain separate political units, most of them will not only be poor but will have little or no prospect of escaping poverty because most of them depend on the sale abroad of primary products. As far as one can see into the future, the terms of trade will move against them. Furthermore, as population increases and technological improvement is applied to the land, the number of the landless will multiply. African governments will then not only be unable to do more for their own people than the colonial regimes and all "the resentment which overthrew colonialism will be mobilised against us."

The only sensible solution is to develop heavy industry at the same pace as agriculture, but this can only be done on a continent-wide scale. Unless great industrial complexes are established in Africa — which can only be done in a United Africa — African peasants will find themselves at the mercy of foreign cash crop markets and African governments will face the same unrest which dislodged the imperialists. Unless the African farmer is assured of a fair market, education and mechanisation and even capital for development are no use to him. If African states fail to establish great industrial complexes, what have the urban workers and the peasants gained from political independence?

> Unite we must. Without necessarily sacrificing our sovereignties, big or small, we can here and now forge a political union based on Defence, Foreign Affairs and Diplomacy, and a Common Citizenship, an African

[88] *ibid.*

> Currency, an African Monetary Zone an African Central Bank. We must unite in order to achieve the full liberation of our continent. We need a Common Defence System with an African High Command to ensure the stability and security of Africa.[89]

Though pragmatic and persuasive, Nkrumah's argument failed to produce a positive response. Only a handful of the participants, notably Mr. Milton Obote, the Prime Minister of Uganda, supported him. Having previously antagonised most African leaders through his dynamic, excessive zeal and indiscreet pronouncements, Nkrumah was hardly the best advocate of his case. Was he not accused of meddling in the internal affairs of Nigeria and the Cameroon and even of instigating the assassination of a fellow African president, Sylvanus Olympio? No wonder the conference applauded President Ahidjo's (Cameroon) suggestion that the summit should condemn the subversion of one African nation by another.

Thus hatred of a single personality and his administration was allowed to overshadow a question of fundamental importance. The result was that the delegates rejected immediate political unity opting for consultation and functional co-operation.

A Charter institutionalizing the movement for African unity was adopted and subsequently ratified by the participating governments.[90] Under the Charter, a permanent body named the Organisation of African Unity has been launched with the following aims:

> (a) to promote the unity and solidarity of the African States;

---

[89] *Addis Ababa Summit* (1963), p. 47.
[90] For provisions of the O.A.U. Charter see Appendix.

226

(b) to co-ordinate and intensify their co-operation and efforts;

(c) to achieve a better life for the peoples of Africa;

(d) to defend their sovereignty, their territorial integrity and independence;

(e) to eradicate all forms of colonialism from Africa; and

(f) to promote international co-operation, having due regard to the Charter of the United Nations and the Universal Declaration of Human Rights.

The O.A.U Charter enshrines the principles of the sovereign equality of all member countries, peaceful settlement of disputes, noninterference in the domestic affairs of States and non-alignment.

An Assembly of Heads of State and Government is the supreme organ. The Heads or their duly accredited representatives meet annually to discuss matters of common concern to Africans. It also interprets the Charter and can amend it. Two-thirds of the total membership constitute a quorum at any meeting of the Assembly.

A Council of Ministers is the subordinate executive body to the Assembly of States and Governments. It is made up of Foreign Ministers or any other ministers appointed by member nations.

A General Secretariat is the third principal institution of the Organisation. Headed by an administrative Secretary-General, it implements decisions of the Assembly and the Council of Ministers.

Another major organ is the Commission of Mediation, Conciliation and Arbitration. In addition are five specialised commissions, namely: Economic and Social Commission; Education and Cultural Commission; Health, Sanitation and Nutrition Commission; Defence Commission, and Scientific, Technical and Research Commission.

Commenting on the inauguration of the O.A.U., Mr. Cyril

Falls, a former Chichele Professor of the History of War at Oxford, wrote:

> By far the most significant event of the recent past is, however, the conference at Addis Ababa. Africa has achieved "Summit" at a time when Europe and North America are merely hoping for one and by no means sure they will get it. It will certainly take a long time before, if ever, she reaches a general alliance such as N.A.T.O. or that dominated by the Soviet Union, but she has taken a long and sensational step on the road. Even a year ago it would have needed a very bold and percipient prophet to imagine anything of the kind.[91]

At the first meeting of the O.A.U. Council of Ministers at Dakar in August, 1963, Addis Ababa was chosen as the permanent headquarters of the organisation. The first regular session of the Assembly of Heads of State and Government took place in Cairo from 1 to 21 July, 1964. Then followed the second regular summit in Accra in October, 1965. Relations with Britain and the right of the O.A.U. to intervene in Rhodesia by force if necessary dominated the discussion. The leaders demanded the release of all political prisoners in the territory, the abolition of all repressive and discriminatory laws as well as the convening of a new constitutional conference representing all parties. They also considered the recognition of the Rhodesian government in exile and the extending to it of financial, military and moral assistance.[92]

Events between 1965 and 1973 made the O.A.U. appear impotent if not purposeless. It increasingly came under fire over questions with which it has been most closely identified in the popular mind: the struggle against white minority rule and colonialism. The decision to break diplomatic relations with British over her apparent connivance at the unilaterial decla-

---

[91] *The Illustrated London News* (15 June, 1963), p. 919.
[92] *OAU Perspective; Third Regular Assembly 1966* (Publication of the Ministry of Information, Addis Ababa, Ethiopia), p. 7.

ration of independence by the white minority in Rhodesia proved a humiliating farce. Only a handful of the African states, notably Tanzania, Ghana and Egypt, obeyed the call. The O.A.U. proved equally powerless in the face of the activities of foreign mercenaries in Congo (Leopoldville), now Zaire. Nor was the Organisation able to bring the long and bloody Nigeria-Biafra Civil War to an end. The Portuguese still clung to their African colonies of Angola, Mozambique and Guinea (Bissau), albeit with increasingly difficulty. Apartheid remained the order of the day in South Africa which also maintained its illegal hegemony over South West Africa (Namibia). When Sékou Touré asked for help to ward off a Portuguese-backed attack on Guinea in November, 1970, it took the O.A.U. two weeks to meet in Lagos to consider the situation. General Yakubu Gowon, who came to power in Nigeria as a result of a military coup, must have spoken on behalf of millions of Africans when he told the conference that "a situation cannot seriously be regarded as an emergency if it has to wait two weeks for a solution."[93] Shortly afterwards, the General called for the setting up of an African High Command without further delay. He made the demand at the O.A.U. Summit of June, 1972 held in the Moroccan city of Rabat.

This growing disenchantment with the O.A.U.'s functional approach to African unity found expression in the warm tributes paid to Kwame Nkrumah on the occasion of his death in exile in 1972. Like Nigeria's Tafawa Balewa, he too had been overthrown in a military take-over. Sentiments of disillusion were also expressed in the following year when the first decade of the O.A.U. was commemorated. A former Nigerian diplomat and editor-in-chief of *AFRICA* magazine, Mr. Raphael C. Uwechue, remarked angrily:

> Now a new orientation is necessary to close the yawning credibility gap between what we have proclaimed for ten

[93] *African Development* (May, 1973), p. 29. See also *Daily Mail* (Freetown) (30 Nov., 1920), p. 8

years and what we have actually done in that period. Our organisation is the victim of an out-dated charter which, by stressing *states* rather than the *African people,* places self-defeating emphasis on our illogical inheritance from our colonial past.[94]

The present structure and powers of the O.A.U. Secretariat, he believed, were simply unsuited to the kind of functions it was intended to perform. If the organisation was to earn the respect of millions of Africans, the Secretariat must be revitalised and given a freer hand to regulate inter-state matters. The founding fathers were probably right in limiting the powers of the Secretary-General at the time the O.A.U. was launched. Their caution over what was then a new venture was understandable. "But that was ten years ago. Africa has since come of age. Her needs have changed."[95] Another African political commentator dismissed the organisation "as a mutual admiration club, a trade union of heads of state and governments that is forever 'vigorously condemning' and 'expressing deep concern,' but showing little ability or willingness to do anything else."[96]

Perhaps it is too early to attempt a serious assessment of the O.A.U. On the historical scale, a decade is an extremely short time. Furthermore, we do not as yet have access to all the documents, including confidential files, of the organisation. Even then, most of what are regarded as the failures of the organisation have either been over-simplified or exaggerated. Portugal's decision in 1974 to decolonise, which the critics did not foresee, was due in large measure to the O.A.U.'s anti-colonial resolutions and assistance to freedom movements. In that year, Portugal not only recognised the right of Guinea (Bissau) to self-determination but also promised to withdraw

---

[94] *Africa* (An International Business, Economic and Political Monthly), (May, 1973), editorial.

[95] *ibid.*

[96] *African Development* (May, 1973), p. 29.

from the remaining enclaves of Mozambique and Angola by 1976.

Without the O.A.U.'s innumerable resolutions "expressing deep concern" on minority administrations in Southern Africa, the rest of the world would probably have set aside the United Nations' sanctions on Rhodesia and recognised the rebel regime just as Western Europe ignored the League of Nations' embargo on Italy during the Italo-Ethiopian conflict in the 1930s. If the O.A.U. states failed to break diplomatic relations with Britian over Rhodesia's unilateral declaration of independence, it was mainly because the economic arrangements between them and England made such a move suicidal. As members of the Sterling Area, their currencies were issued and backed by the Bank of England.

Nor was it possible for the O.A.U. to intervene in the Nigerian Civil War in a meaningful way. The problem, by no means easy, was how to reconcile two rights. On the one hand was human suffering and tragedy. On the other, the organisation's principles of respect for the territorial integrity of member countries and non-interference in their domestic affairs. These principles bound the hands and the feet of the organisation so far as the issue was concerned. Opponents of balkanisation further argued that if Biafra was allowed to secede from the Nigerian Federation, the other African states would disintegrate into their component units. Admittedly the argument was fallacious for societies do not disintegrate simply because the constitutional arrangements in a neighbouring community have proved unworkable. It is also true, as Julius Nyerere who approved of Biafra's secession maintained, that man-made values do not belong to a higher order than human beings.[97]

---

[97] Four member states of the O.A.U. actually recognized Biafra as a sovereign nation namely: Tanzania, Zambia, Ivory Coast, and Gabon; Haiti also accorded recognition. The secession eventually collapsed in January, 1970. For further details see Frederick Forsyth, *The Biafra Story* (Harmondsworth: Penguin, 1969).

In these respects, the O.A.U. Charter appears imperfect. However these defects do not alter the fact that the member states had already pledged themselves to operate the Charter as ratified four years before the crisis. To condemn the O.A.U. for observing its rules is to miss the point. The point is to discover unwholesome principles and persuade the organisation to delete them from its Charter. Surely, there is no perfect constitution anywhere in the world.

CHAPTER 6

CONCLUSION: PAN-AFRICANISM AND BLACK POWER AFTER 1963

The general exclusion of the representatives of the African descendants in the United States, Caribbean and Brazil from the deliberations of the O.A.U. leaves one to wonder whether any connexion still exists between post-1963 Black Power Movement and what one may style continental Pan-Africanism. They are themselves divided on the issue. As recently as July, 1964, the Afro-American civil rights leader, Malcolm X (his real name was Malcolm Little) told an O.A.U summit:

> We in America, are your host brothers and sisters, and I am only to remind you that our problems are your problems. As the African-Americans "awaken" today, we find ourselves in a strange land that has rejected us, and, like the prodigal son, we are turning to our elder brothers for help. We pray our pleas will not fall upon deaf ears ....

> Your problems will never be fully solved until and unless ours are solved. You will never be fully respected unless we are also respected. You will never be recognized as free human beings until and unless we are also recognized and treated as human beings.[1]

A similar plea was made a decade later (1973) by Calvin Lockhart, the film actor from the Bahamas and of "Cotton

---

[1] George Breitman, ed., *Malcolm X Speaks; Selected Speeches and Statements* (New York: Grove Press, 1966), pp. 73-75, *passim*.

Comes to Harlem" fame. For many black exiles, he pointed out, Africa was and would remain an important ancestral base from which, from time to time, they could draw inspiration and strength today. He went on:

> one of the major psychological problems of Africa is that while he can always say "I have a *country*," he cannot really say "I have a *home*". This is very often his dilema. He needs a home — an original point of reference. I think that all Black people in the world should have dual citizenship and that of whatever other country they now live in.[2]

On the other hand black American observers like Tony Thomas and Nathan Hare think that success in the struggle on American soil is a prerequisite for the liberation and unification of Africa itself.[3] According to Hare:

> The struggle in America is paramount — not only because Black people (Africans) around the world look to us for leadership. It is also because America, the world's number one imperialist, is an octopus, with tentacles choking other nations all over the world. Though it may be desirable and useful to chop off a tentacle here and there, including its strongest and most destructive tentacles in our Africa, the most lasting and devastating damage will be done in the heart of the octopus.[4]

In the view of the Nigerian publicist and ex-diplomat, Mr. Raphael C. Uwechue, there is an urgent need to develop and sustain a dynamic link between Africans and their descendants

[2] *Africa* (An International Business, Economic and Political Quarterly), No. 27 (November, 1973), p. 15.
[3] See for e.g. Tony Thomas and Robert Allen, *Two Views on Pan-Africanism* (New York: Pathfinder Press, 1972), pp. 14-21.
[4] Nathan Hare, "Wherever We Are," *Black Scholar* (March, 1971), pp. 34-35.

abroad for the mutual benefit of both parties. He laments that the Organisation of African Unity, with its interest riveted on African *states* instead of African *peoples,* avoids the matter altogether.[5] We are reminded that these exiles number some 100 million, that is, approximately a quarter of Africa's present population. Among them are to be found, especially in the U.S.A., the largest concentration of highly trained black manpower in the world: scientists, scholars, soldiers and professional men and women of all descriptions.

Several African heads of state have also expressed concern about the predicament of their kith and kin in exile, for instance, President J. K. Nyerere told the Das es Salaam pan-African gathering of 1974 that "as long as black people anywhere continue to be oppressed on the grounds of their colour, black people everywhere will stand together in opposition to that oppression in future as in the past."

All the same it will be misleading to think that the views of Nyerere and Uwechue represent the policy of the O.A.U. on the matter. Until that body begins to treat the disabilities of the diaspora as its own problems by initiating concrete measures, it is reasonable to assume that our political leaders are also undecided as to whether the African exiles should remain abroad or return to their ancestral continent.

[5] *Africa* (November, 1973), editorial. See also his editorial in *Africa* (July, 1976).

APPENDIX

THE CHARTER OF THE ORGANIZATION OF AFRICAN UNITY

We, the Heads of African States and Governments assembled in the City of Addis Ababa, Ethiopia;

CONVINCED that it is the inalienable right of all people to control their own destiny;

CONSCIOUS of the fact that freedom, equality, justice and dignity are essential objectives for the achievement of the legitimate aspirations of the African peoples;

CONSCIOUS of our responsibility to harness the natural and human resources of our continent for the total advancement of our peoples in spheres of human endeavour;

INSPIRED by a common determination to promote understanding among our peoples and co-operation among our States in response to the larger aspirations of our peoples for brotherhood and solidarity, in a larger unity transcending ethnic and national differences;

CONVINCED that, in order to translate this determination into a dynamic force in the cause of human progress, conditions for peace and security must be established and maintained;

DETERMINED to safeguard and consolidate the hard-won independence as well as the sovereignty and territorial integrity of our States, and to fight against neo-colonialism in all its forms;

DEDICATED to the general progress of Africa;

PERSUADED that the Charter of the United Nations and the Universal Declaration of Human Rights, to the principles of which we reaffirm our adherence, provide a solid foundation for peaceful and positive co-operation among states;

DESIROUS that all African States should henceforth unite so that the welfare and well-being of their peoples can be assured;

RESOLVED to reinforce the links between our states by establishing and strengthening common institutions;
HAVE agreed to the present Charter.

ESTABLISHMENT

Article I

1. The High Contracting Parties do by the present Charter establish an Organization to be known as the ORGANIZATION OF AFRICAN UNITY.
2. The Organization shall include the Continental African States, Madagascar and other Islands surrounding Africa.

PURPOSES

Article II

1. The Organization shall have the following purposes:
    a. to promote the unity and solidarity of the African States;
    b. to co-ordinate and intensify their co-operation and efforts to achieve a better life for the people of Africa;
    c. to defend their sovereignty, their territorial integrity and independence;
    d. to eradicate all forms of colonialism from Africa; and
    e. to promote international co-operation, having due regard to the Charter of the United Nations and the Universal Declaration of Human Rights.
2. To these ends, the Member States shall co-ordinate and harmonize their general policies, especially in the following fields:
    a. political and diplomatic co-operation;
    b. economic co-operation, including transport and communications;
    c. educational and cultural co-operation;
    d. health, sanitation, and nutritional co-operation;
    e. scientific and technical co-operation; and
    f. co-operation for defence and security.

PRINCIPLES

Article III

The Member States, in pursuit of the purposes stated in Article II, solemnly affirm and declare their adherence to the following principles:

1. the sovereign equality of all Member States;
2. non-interference in the internal affairs of States;
3. respect for the sovereignty and territorial integrity of each State and for its inalienable right to independent existence;
4. peaceful settlement of disputes by negotiation, mediation, conciliation or arbitration;
5. unreserved condemnation, in all its forms, of political assassination as well as of subversive activities on the part of neighbouring States or any other State;
6. absolute dedication to the total emancipation of the African territories which are still dependent;
7. affirmation of a policy of non-alignment with regard to all blocks.

MEMBERSHIP

Article IV

Each independent sovereign African State shall be entitled to become a Member of the Organization.

RIGHTS AND DUTIES OF MEMBER STATES

Article V

All Member States shall enjoy rights and have equal duties.

Article VI

The Member States pledge themselves to observe scrupulously the principles enumerated in Article III of the present Charter.

INSTITUTIONS

Article VII

The Organization shall accomplish its purposes through the following principal institutions:

1. the Assembly of Heads of State and Government;
2. the Council of Ministers;
3. the General Secretariat;
4. the Commission of Mediation, Conciliation and Arbitration.

THE ASSEMBLY OF HEADS OF STATE AND GOVERNMENT

Article VIII

The Assembly of Heads of State and Government shall be the supreme organ of the Organization. It shall, subject to the provisions of this Charter, discuss matters of common concern to Africa with a view to co-ordinating and harmonizing the general policy of the Organization. It may in addition review the structure, functions and acts of all the organs and any specialized agencies which may be created in accordance with the present Charter.

Article IX

The Assembly shall be composed of the Heads of State and Government or their duly accredited representatives and it shall meet at least once a year. At the request of any Member State and on approval by a two-thirds majority of the Member States, the Assembly shall meet in extraordinary session.

Article X

1. Each Member State shall have one vote.
2. All resolutions shall be determined by a two-thirds majority of the Members of the Organization.
3. Questions of procedure shall require a simple majority. Whether or not a question is one of the procedure shall be determined by a simple majority of all Member States of the Organization.
4. Two-thirds of the total membership of the Organization shall form a quorum at any meeting of the Assembly.

Article XI

The Assembly shall have the power to determine its own rules of procedure.

THE COUNCIL OF MINISTERS

Article XII

1. The Council of Ministers shall consist of Foreign Ministers or such other Ministers as are designated by the Governments of Member States.
2. The Council of Ministers shall meet at least twice a year. When requested by any Member State and approved by two-thirds of all Member States, it shall meet in extraordinary session.

Article XIII

1. The Council of Ministers shall be responsible to the Assembly of Heads of State and Government. It shall be entrusted with the responsibility of preparing conferences of the Assembly.
2. It shall take cognizance of any matter referred to it by the Assembly. It shall be entrusted with the implementation of the decisions of the Assembly of Heads of State and Government. It shall co-ordinate inter-African co-operation in accordance with the instructions of the Assembly and in conformity with Article II (2) of the present Charter.

Article XIV

1. Each Member State shall have one vote.
2. All resolutions shall be determined by a simple majority of the members of the Council of Ministers.
3. Two-thirds of the total membership of the Council of Ministers shall form a quorum for any meeting of the Council.

Article XV

The Council shall have the power to determine its own rules of procedure.

GENERAL SECRETARIAT

Article XVI

There shall be an Administrative Secretary-General of the Organization, who shall be appointed by the Assembly of Heads of State and Government. The Administrative Secretary-General shall direct the affairs of the Secretariat.

Article XVII

There shall be one or more Assistant Secretaries-General of the Organization, who shall be appointed by the Assembly of Heads of State and Government.

Article XVIII

The functions and conditions of services of the Secretary-General, of the Assistant Secretaries-General and other employees of the Secretariat shall be governed by the provisions of this Charter and the regulations approved by the Assembly of Heads of State and Government.

1. In the performance of their duties the Administrative Secretary-General and the staff shall not seek or receive instructions from any government or from any other authority external to the Organization. They shall refrain from any action which might reflect on their position as international officials responsible to the Organization.
2. Each member of the Organization undertakes to respect the exclusive character of the responsibilities of the Administrative Secretary-General and the Staff and not to seek to influence them in the discharge of their responsibilities.

COMMISSION OF MEDIATION, CONCILIATION AND ARBITRATION

Article XIX

Member States pledge to settle all disputes among themselves by peaceful means and, to this end, to decide to establish a Commission of Mediation, Conciliation and Arbitration, the composition of which and conditions of service shall be defined by a separate Protocol to be approved by the Assembly of Heads of State and Government. Said Protocol shall be regarded as forming an integral part of the present Charter.

SPECIALIZED COMMISSION

Article XX

The Assembly shall establish such Specialized Commissions as it may deem necessary, including the following:
1. Economic and Social Commission;
2. Educational and Cultural Commission;
3. Health, Sanitation and Nutrition Commission;
4. Defence Commission;
5. Scientific, Technical and Research Commission.

Article XXI

Each Specialized Commission referred to in Article XX shall be composed of the Ministers concerned or other Ministers or Plenipotentiaries designated by the Government of the Member States.

Article XXII

The functions of the Specialized Commissions shall be carried out in accordance with the provisions of the present Charter and of the regulations approved by the Council of Ministers.

THE BUDGET

Article XXIII

The budget of the Organization prepared by the Administrative Secretary-General shall be approved by the Council of Ministers. The budget shall be provided by contributions from Member States in accordance with the scale of assessment of the United Nations; provided, however, that no Member State shall be assessed an amount exceeding twenty percent of the yearly regular budget of the Organization. The Member States agree to pay their respective contribution regularly.

SIGNATURE AND RATIFICATION OF CHARTER

Article XXIV

1. This Charter shall be open for signature to all independent sovereign African States and shall be ratified by the signatory States in accordance with their respective constitutional processes.
2. The original instrument, done if possible in African languages, in English and French, all texts being equally authentic, shall be deposited with the Government of Ethiopia which shall transit certified copies thereof to all independent sovereign African States.
3. Instruments of ratification shall be deposited with the Government of Ethiopia, which shall notify all signatories of each such deposit.

ENTRY INTO FORCE

Article XXV

This Charter shall enter into force immediately upon receipt by the Government of Ethiopia of the instruments of ratification from two-thirds of the signatory States.

REGISTRATION OF THE CHARTER

Article XXVI

This Charter shall, after due ratification, be registered with the Secretariat of the United Nations through the Government of Ethiopia in conformity with Article 102 of the Charter of the United Nations.

INTERPRETATION OF THE CHARTER

Article XXVII

Any question which may arise concerning the interpretation of this Charter shall be decided by a vote of two-thirds of the Assembly of Heads of State and Government of the Organization.

ADHESION AND ACCESSION

1. Any independent sovereign African State may at any time notify the Administrative Secretary-General of its intention to adhere or accede to this Charter.
2. The Administrative Secretary-General shall, on receipt of such notification, communicate a copy of it to all the Member States. Admission shall be decided by a simple majority of the Member States. The decision of each Member State shall be transmitted to the Administrative Secretary-General, who shall, upon receipts of the required number of votes, communicate the decision to the State concerned.

MISCELLANEOUS

Article XXIX

The working languages of the Organization and all its institutions shall be, if possible, African languages, (or, if not, then) English and French.

Article XXX

The Administrative Secretary-General may accept on behalf of the Organization gifts, bequests and other donations made to the Organization, provided that this is approved by the Council of Ministers.

Article XXXI

The Council of Ministers shall decide on the privileges and immunities to be accorded to the personnel of the Secretariat in the respective territories of the Member States.

CESSATION OF MEMBERSHIP

Article XXXII

Any State which desires to renounce its membership shall forward a written notification to the Administrative Secretary-General. At the end of one year from the date of such notification, if not withdrawn, the Charter shall cease to apply with respect to the renouncing State, which shall thereby cease to belong to the Organization.

AMENDMENT OF THE CHARTER

Article XXXIII

This Charter may be amended or revised if any Member State makes a written request to the Administrative Secretary-General to this effect; provided, however, that the proposed amendment is not submitted to the Assembly for consideration until all the Member States have been duly notified of it and a period of one year has elapsed.

Such an amendment shall not be effective unless approved by at least two-thirds of all the Member States.

IN FAITH WHEREOF, We, the Heads of African State and Government, have signed this Charter.

Done in the City of Addis Ababa, Ethiopia, this 25th day of May, 1963.

Algeria	*President Ben Bella*
Burundi	*King Mwambutsa*
Cameroon	*President Ahmadou Ahidjo*
Central African Republic	*President David Dacko*
Chad	*President Francois Tombalbaye*
Congo (Brazzaville)	*President Fulbert Youlou*
Congo (Kinshasa)	*President Joseph Kasavubu*
Dahomey	*President Hubert Maga*
Ethiopia	*Emperor Haile Selassie*
Gabon	*President Leon M'ba*
Ghana	*President Kwame Nkrumah*
Guinea	*President Sékou Touré*
Ivory Coast	*President Felix Houphouet-Boigny*
Liberia	*President William V. S. Tubman*
Libya	*King Idris I*

Malagasy Republic	*President Philibert Tsiranana*
Mali	*President Modibo Keita*
Mauritania	*President Makhtar Ould Daddah*
Niger	*President Hamani Diori*
Nigeria	*Prime Minister Alhaji Sir Abubakar Tafawa Balewa*
Rwanda	*Foreign Minister Callixte Habamenshi*
Senegal	*President Leopold Seda Senghor*
Sierra Leone	*Prime Minister Sir Milton Margai*
Somalia	*President Abdullah Osman*
Sudan	*President Ibrahim Abboud*
Tanganyika	*President Julius Nyerere*
Tunisia	*President Habib Bourguba*
Uganda	*Prime Minister Milton Obote*
United Arab Republic	*President Gamal Abdel Nasser*
Upper Volta	*President Maurice Yameogo*

BIBLIOGRAPHY

PRIMARY MATERIAL
MANUSCRIPT

1. *Bridgeman Collection* (in owner's possession). The Papers contain some correspondance, but thin, from the West African Student's Union and Marcus Garvey; newspaper cuttings on the Italo-Ethiopian crisis; some publications of the West African Students' Union and Marcus Garvey's Universal Negro Improvement Association and African Communities League. The Papers also contain some early numbers of *The Negro Worker* edited by George Padmore and a substantial amount of material on the League Against Imperialism.
2. *C.O. 554/49* (Public Record Office, London). Contains material relating to the National Congress of British West Africa.
3. *C.O. 554/50* (Public Record Office, London). Contains material relating to the National Congress of British West Africa.
4. *C.O. 554/51* (Public Record Office, London). Contains material relating to the National Congress of British West Africa.
5. *Gold Coast A.R.P.S. Papers* (Cape Coast Archives, Ghana). They are probably the richest single source on the 1945 Manchester Pan-African Conference and the activities of the West African National Secretariat. They also contain some correspondance from the West African Students' Union, the Negro Welfare Association, The International African Service Bureau and the Pan-African Federation. *The Sekyi Papers* form an integral part of the *Gold Coast A.R.P.S. Papers.*
6. *F.O. 403/363* (Public Record Office, London). Memorandum by Dr. Blyden on the Liberian situation communicated to the British Foreign Office on 24 May, 1905.
7. *Moral Papers* (London School of Economics). Miscellaneous

correspondence F.9/B. They include a few letters from Dr. E. W. Blyden.

8. *Moorland Collection* (Howard University Library, Washington D.C.) contains some publications of the U.N.I.A.; letters of Booker T. Washington relating to Pan-Africanism; material on DuBois' Pan-African interests and a copy of Dr. R. N. Duchein's *The Pan-African Manifesto.*

9. *Booker T. Washington Papers* (Library of Congress, Washington D.C.) contains several letters from Henry Sylvester Williams in connexion with the activities of the African Association (London) and the Pan-African Conference 1900. It also contains a few letters from Marcus Garvey concerning the U.N.I.A.

10. *Wallace Johnson Collection* (Institute of African Studies, Legon, Ghana). The collection is in the form of a thirty-page typescript. It comprises, in the main, some details about the personal life of Wallace Johnson; Wallace Johnson's comments — surprisingly sketchy — on the N.C.B.W.A., the Negro Welfare Association (London), P.A.F. as well as a substantial amount of material on the West African Youth League and the attitude of the League to the Italo-Ethiopian Crisis.

11. *Schomburg Collection* (New York City Library). Contains quite a number of letters by Dr. Mojola Agbebi as well as his *Inaugural Sermon* of 21 December, 1902; John Edward Bruce Papers; Alexander Crummell Papers; an almost complete file of the I.A.S.B.'s *International African Opinion*; Mbonu Ojike's *My Africa*; some publications and tracts of Benito Sylvain; *The Crisis,* organ of the N.A.A.C.P.; *Without Bitterness: Western Nations in Post-War Africa* by A. A. Nwafor Orizu; Alexander Walter's autobiography, *My Life and Work* as well as many tracts by Dr. Edward W. Blyden including *Liberia's Offering: Being Addresses, Sermons, etc.*

PRINTED MATERIAL

12. *The African Repository* (Journal of the American Colonization Society), Vol. I-LXVIII, March, 1825 - January, 1892, Washington D.C. (Fourah Bay College, University of Sierra Leone). Contains most of the tracts of Dr. Edward W. Blyden.

13. *Publications of the Abyssinia Association* (Bridgeman Collection)
   (a) *Nemesis,* London, 1939.

(b) *Memorandum on the Policy of His Majesty's Government toward Ethiopia,* London, 1941.

14. *British Official Publications* (London University Library, Senate House)
    (a) *West Indian Royal Commission 1938-1939: Recommendations, Cmd. 6174,* 1940.
    (b) *Statement of Policy on Colonial Development and Welfare, Cmd. 6175,* 1940.
    (c) *West Indian Royal Commission Report, Cmd. 6607,* 1945.
    (d) *Report of the Commission on Higher Education in the Colonies, Cmd. 6647,* 1945.
    (e) *The Colonial Empire (1939-1947), Cmd. 7167,* 1947.
    (f) *Parliamentary Debates,* 1929-1948.

15. *Publications of the International African Service Bureau*
    (a) *International African Opinion* (George Padmore Research Library, Accra). Vol. 1, No. 1, July 1938 - Vol. 1, No. 5, November, 1938.
    (b) *Pamphlets* (George Padmore, Research Library, Accra; British Museum).
        (i) Levis, W. Arthur. *The West Indies Today.* London, 1938.
        (ii) Padmore, George. *Hands Off the Protectorates.* London, 1938.
        (iii) Cunard, N. and G. Padmore. *The White Man's Duty.* London, 1943.
        (iv) Kenyatta, Jomo. *Kenya, Land of Conflict.* London, 1945.
        (v) Williams, Eric. *The Negro in the Caribbean.* London, 1945.
        (vi) Michelet, R. *African Empires and Civilizations.* London, 1945.
        (vii) Padmore, George, ed. *The Voice of Coloured Labour.* London, 1945.
        (viii) Cunard, N. and G. Padmore. *The White Man's Duty* enlarged ed. London, 1945.
    (c) *Colonial Parliamentary Bulletin* (British Museum) Vol. 1, No. 3, March-April, 1946 - Vol. III, No. 6, September, 1948.

16. *Publications of the League Against Imperialism* (Bridgeman Collection)

(a) *The Anti-Imperialist Review,* Vol. 1, No. 1, September-October, 1931.

(b) *Abyssinia,* London, 1935.

17. *Publications of the League of Coloured Peoples.*
Mostly in the British Museum. Copies of many of them as well as useful newspaper cuttings are also in the possession of Dr. Christine Moody.

(a) *The Keys,* July, 1933-September, 1939. Continued as *News Notes,* No. 1, October, 1939. Continued as *L.C.P. Letter* No. 2, November, 1939 - No. 6, March, 1940. Continued as *News Letter,* No. 7, April, 1940 - No. 104, December, 1948.

(b) Buyton, Charles R. *Impressions of Liberia, Nov. 1934: A Report to the League of Coloured Peoples.* London: League of Coloured Peoples Publication, [n.d].

(c) *Annual Reports*
(i) *Seventh Annual Report,* March, 1938; Previous annual reports were printed in *The Keys.*
(ii) *Eighth Annual Report,* March, 1939.
(iii) *Ninth Annual Report,* March, 1940.
(iv) *Tenth Annual Report,* April, 1941.
(v) *Eleventh Annual Report,* March, 1942.
(vi) *Twelfth Annual Report,* March, 1943.
(vii) *Thirteenth Annual Report,* March, 1944.
(viii) *Fourteenth Annual Report,* March, 1945.
(ix) *Fifteenth Annual Report,* March, 1946.

(d) *Papers and Correspondence Relating to Appointments in the Colonial Service.* Published in *The Keys.*

18. *Publications of the League of Nations* (British Museum)
(a) *International Commission of Enquiry in Liberia* (Official No. C.658 M. 272. 1930 VI), Geneva, 1930.
(b) *Dispute between Ethiopia and Italy, Request by the Ethiopian Government* (Official No. C. 230 (1). M. 114 (1). 1935 VII), Geneva, 1935.
(c) *Dispute between Ethiopia and Italy. Memorandum by the Italian Government on the situation in Ethiopia* (Official No. C. 340. 171 1935 VII), Geneva, 1935.

19. *Publication of the National Association for the Advancement of Coloured People* (George Padmore Research Library, Accra); *The Crisis,* 1918-1934 (Microfilm).

20. *Publication of the Pan-African Association,* London (British Museum).
    The Pan-African Vol. 1, No. 1 (October, 1901).

21. *Publications of the Pan-African Federation.* The publications are widely dispersed in Cape Coast Archives, Ghana; George Padmore Research Library, Accra; Rhodes House Library, Oxford; the National Library of Scotland, Edinburgh and the British Museum. The largest concentrations are in the George Padmore Research Library, Accra and the British Museum.
    (a) *Pan-African Congress: Declaration and Resolutions adopted at the Fifth Pan-African Congress at Manchester, England,* October 13-21, 1949.
    (b) Open Letter to Clement Attlee (British Prime Minister), September, 1945. Printed as a leaflet.
    (c) *Pan-African,* Vol. 1, No. 1 (January, 1947); Vol. 11, No. 4 (April, 1948).
    (d) Padmore, George, ed. *Colonial and ... Coloured Unity: A Programme of Action.* Manchester: Pan-African Service, Ltd., 1947.

22. *Publications of the Universal Negro Improvement Association and African Communities League:*
    (a) *Petition of the Universal Negro Improvement Association and African Communities League to the League of Nations,* New York, 1922.
    (b) *Renewal of Petition of the Negro Universal Improvement Association and African Communities League to the League of Nations,* London, 1928.
    (c) "The Case of the Negro for International Racial Adjustment, Before the English People." Speech delivered by Marcus Garvey, Royal Albert Hall, London, England, on Wednesday, June 6, 1928. London: Poets' and Painters' Press, 1968.

23. *Publication of the West African National Secretariat.* Cape Coast Archives, Ghana.
    The New African Vol. 1, No. 1, (March, 1946); Vol. 1, No. 3 (May, 1946).

24. *Publications of the West African Student's Union* (British Museum):
   (a) *Wasu* (WASU MAGAZINE), No. 1 (March, 1926); Vol. XII, No. 3, (1947).
   (b) *United West Africa (Or Africa) at the Bar of the Family of Nations,* London, 1927. (Also available at National Library of Scotland, Edinburgh).
   (c) *The Truth About Aggrey House: An Exposure of the Government Plan for the Control of African Students in Great Britain.* London, 1934.
   (d) Annual Reports (published in *Wasu*):
      (i) *The Annual Report up to the Year Ended 31st December 1938.*
      (ii) *The Annual Report up to the Year Ended 31st December 1939.*
      (iii) *The Annual Report and Audited Accounts for the Year Ended 31st December 1940.*
      (iv) *W.A.S.U. Annual Report and Audited Accounts for the Year Ended 31st December 1941.*
      (v) *W.A.S.U. Annual Report and Audited Accounts for the Year Ended 31st December 1942.*
      (vi) *W.A.S.U. Annual Report and Audited Accounts for the Year Ended 31st December 1943.*

25. *Publications of the Government of Ethiopia:*
   (a) *Second Conference of Independent African States,* Addis Ababa, 14-26 June, 1960, Addis Ababa, 1960.
   (b) *The Fourth PAFMECA Conference Held in Addis Ababa February 2nd to 10th 1962* (Speeches and Statements). Addis Ababa, n.d.
   (c) *Addis Ababa Summit, 1963.*
   (d) *OAU Perspective. Third Regular Assembly.* Addis Ababa, 1966.

26. *Articles:*

Azikiwe, Nnamdi. "Realities of African Unity." *African Forum* Vol. 1, No 1 (Summer, 1965).

DuBois, W.E.B. "Pan-Africanism." *Voice of Africa* (June, 1961).

Greg, W. R. "Dr. Arnold." *Westminister Review* Vol. XXXIX, No. 1 (January, 1843).

Kenyatta, Jomo. "African Socialism and African Unity." *African Forum* Vol. 1, No. 1 (Summer, 1965).

Logan, Rayford. "The Historical Aspects of Pan-Africanism: A Personal Chronicle." *African Forum* Vol. 1, No. 1 (Summer, 1965).

Nyerere, Julius. "The Nature and Requirements of African Unity." *African Forum* Vol. 1, No. 1 (Summer, 1965).

————. "A United States of Africa." *The Journal of Modern African Studies* Vol. 1, No. 1 (1963).

Olympio, Sylvanus. "African Problems and the Cold War." *Foreign Affairs* (October, 1961).

Padmore, George. A collection (4 vols.) of most of George Padmore's articles is available at the George Padmore Research Library, Accra.

————. "The Revolt in Haiti." *The Labour Monthly* (June, 1939).

————. "Forced Labour in Africa." *The Labour Monthly* (April, 1931).

————. "Hands Off the Colonies." *The New Leader* (25 January, 1933).

————. "The Struggle for Bread." *The Negro Worker* (June-July, 1933).

————. "Colonial Fascism in the West Indies." *The People* (Trinidad) (21 May, 1938).

————. "A Negro Surveys the Colonial Problem." *The African Morning Post* (Accra) (30-31 January; 1 February, 1939).

————. "The Colonial Question." *Empire* (May, 1939).

————. "Colonials Demand Britain's War Aims." *The New Leader* (15 February, 1941).

?   "Whither the West Indies." *The New Leader* (29 March, 1941).

————. "No Atlantic Charter for Colonies." *The New Leader* (24 January, 1942).

————. "Uncle Sam's Black Ward." *Tribune* (23 October, 1942).

————. "Britain Follows Mussolini." *The New Leader* (17 July, 1943).

————. "Russia and the Colonial Question." *The Socialist Leader* (25 January, 1947).

27. *Contemporary Books and Tracts*
Abrahams, Peter. *Tell Freedom.* London, 1954.

Adams, H. G. *God's Image in Ebony: Being a Series of Biographical Sketches, Facts, Anecdotes, etc. demonstrative of the Mental Powers and Intellectual Capacities of the Negro Race.* London, 1854.

Adera, Teshome. *Nationalist Leaders and African Unity.* Addis Ababa, 1963.

Agbebi, Mojola. *Inaugural Sermon, Delivered at the Celebration of the First Anniversary of the "African Church," Lagos, West Africa, December 21, 1902* (in *Schomburg Collection*).

Ali, Duse Mohamed. *In the Land of the Pharaohs: A Short History of Egypt from the Fall of Ismail to the Assassination of Boutros Pasha.* London, 1911.

Angell, Norman. *The Great Illusion.* London, 1910.

——. *The Fruits of Victory.* London, 1921.

——. *This Have and Have Not Business.* London, 1936.

Aptheker, Herbert, ed. *W.E.B. DuBois, The Correspondence of W.E.B. DuBois: Selections, 1877-1934,* Vol. I. Amherst, Mass.: University of Massachusetts Press, 1973.

Armistead, Wilson. *A Tribute for the Negro: being a vindication of the Moral, Intellectual and Religious Capabilities of the Coloured Portion of Mankind: with Particular reference to the African Race.* Manchester, 1848.

Azikiwe, Nnamdi. *Renascent Africa.* Lagos, 1937.

Blyden, Edward W. For other tracts of E. W. Blyden see the *African Repository*, 1862-1892.

——. *The West African University.* Freetown, 1872.

——. *Christianity, Islam and the Negro Race,* 2nd ed. London, 1888.

——. *African Life and Customs.* London, 1908.

——. *Liberia's Offering: Being Addresses, Sermons, etc.* New York, 1892.

Bowen, J. W. E., ed. *Africa and the American Negro: Addresses and Proceedings of the Congress on Africa.* Atlanta, 1896.

Congress on Africa. *Chicaco Congress on Africa, 1894* by Frederick Perry Noble (in *Schomburg Collection*).

Crummell, Alexander. *The Future of Africa.* New York, 1862.

Cudjoe, S. D. *Aids to African Autonomy.* London: The College Press, 1949.

Cunard, Nancy, ed. *Negro.* London, 1934.

Delaney, Martin R. *The Condition, Elevation, Emigration and Destiny of the Coloured People of the United States Politically Considered.* Philadelphia, 1852.

——. *Official Report of the Niger Valley Exploring Party.* New York and London, 1861.

DuBois, W. E. B. *Dusk of Dawn: An Essay towards an Autobiography of a Race Concept.* New York, 1940.

——. *The Negro.* Home University Library, 1915.

——. *The World and Africa.* New York: International Publishers, 1965 (Contains a full list of the works of DuBois).

Equiano's Travels. Abridged and edited by Paul Edwards. London, 1967.

Ferris, William H. *The African Abroad, Or His Evolution In Western Civilization Tracing His Development Under Caucasian Milieu.* New Haven, 1913.

——. *Alexander Crummel: An Apostle of Negro Culture.* Washington D.C.: American Negro Academy. Occasional Papers No. 20, 1920.

Garvey, Amy Jacques, ed. *Philosophy and Opinions of Marcus Garvey,* 2 vols. New York, 1923/26.

——. *Garvey and Garveyism.* London: Collier-Macmillan, 1970.

Garvey, Marcus. *The Tragedy of White Injustice.* New York, 1927.

Germany Speaks. By 21 leading members of Party and State. With a Preface by Joachim von Ribbentrop, Reich Minister of Foreign Affairs. London, 1938.

Gregoire, H. *An Enquiry concerning the Intellectual and Moral Faculties and Literature of Negroes.* Translated by O. B. Warden. Brooklyn, 1810.

Hailey, Lord. *An African Survey.* Oxford, 1938.

——. *World Thought on the Colonial Question.* Johannesburg, 1946.

Hayford, J. E. Casely. *Ethiopia Unbound, Studies in Race Emancipation.* London, 1911.

Hill, H. C. and Martin Kilson, eds. *American Leaders on Africa from the 1880s to the 1950s.* London, 1969.

Holly, Rev. James Theodore. *A Vindication of the Capacity of the Negro Race for Self-Government and Civilised Progress, As*

Demonstrated by Historical Events of the Hytian Revolution and the Subsequent Acts of that People Since their National Independence. New Haven, Connecticut, 1857.

Horton, J. A. B. *West African Countries and Peoples... A Vindication of the African Race.* Introduction by George Shepperson. Edinburgh: Edinburgh University Press, 1969.

James, C. L. R. *The Black Jacobins.* London, 1938.

———. *A History of Negro Revolt.* London, 1938.

Johnson, J. de Graft. *Towards Nationhood in West Africa.* London, 1928.

Kenyatta, Jomo. *Facing Mount Kenya.* London: Mercury Books, 1938.

Lewis, W. Arthur. *Labour in the West Indies* (Fabian Society Research Series). London 1939.

———. *The West Indies.* London, 1946.

McKay, Claude. *Harlem: Negro Metropolis.* New York: E. P. Dutton and Co., 1940.

Mellon, M. T. *Early American Views on Negro Slavery.* New York: the New American Library, 1969.

Locke, Alaine, ed. *The New Negro.* New York: Atheneum, 1969.

Moody, Harold A. *Youth and Race.* London, 1936.

———. *Christianity and Race Relations.* London, 1943.

———. *Freedom for all Men.* London, 1943.

———. *The Colour Bar.* London, 1945.

Mudgal, H. G. *Marcus Garvey. Is He the True Redeemer of the Negro?* New York City: the African Publication Society, 1932.

Nembhard, L. S. *Trials and Triumphs of Marcus Garvey.* Jamaica, 1940.

Nkrumah, Kwame. *Towards Colonial Freedom.* London: Heinemann, 1962.

———. *Ghana: The Autobiography of Kwame Nkrumah.* Edinburgh: Thomas Nelson and Sons, 1961.

———. *Africa Must Unite.* London: Heinemann, 1963.

———. *Africa's Challenge: A Time of Danger and Hope.* Accra, Government of Ghana publication, 1960.

Ojike, Mbonu. *My Africa.* New York: John Day, 1946.

Orizu, A. A. Nwafor. *Without Bitterness: Western Nations in Post-War Africa.* New York: Creative Age Press, 1944.

Padmore, George. *The Life and Struggles of Negro Toilers.* London, 1931.

——. *How Britain Rules Africa.* London, 1936.

——. *Africa and World Peace.* London, 1937.

——. *How Russia Transformed Her Colonial Empire.* London: Dennis Dobson, 1946.

——. and Dorothy Pizer. *Pan-Africanism or Communism? The Coming Struggle for Africa.* London: Dennis Dobson, 1956.

Spiller, G., ed. *Papers on Inter-Racial Problems Communicated to the First Universal Races Congress held at the University of London, July 26-29, 1911.* London: King and Son, 1911.

Vaughan, D. *Negro Victory: The Life Story of Dr. Harold Moody.* London, 1950.

Walters, Alexander. *My Life and Work,* 2 Vols. New York, 1917.

White, Walter. *A Man Called White: The Autobiography of Walter White.* New York: the Viking Press, 1948.

Willkie, Wendell. *One World.* London: Cassell and Co., 1943.

Woolf, Leonard. *Mandates and Empire.* London, 1928.

——. *Imperialism and Civilization.* London, 1928.

——. *The League and Abyssinia.* London, 1936.

Work, F. E. *Ethiopia: A Pawn in European Diplomacy.* New York, 1935.

28. *Newspapers* (British Museum)

African Morning Post (Accra)

Daily News (London)

Gold Coast Chronicle (Accra)

Lagos Standard

Manchester Guardian

New Leader (London)

Socialist Leader (London)

The Times (London)

29. *Periodicals* (British Museum)

Abyssinia

African Times and Orient Review

Africa (An International Business, Economic and Political Monthly) (Fourah Bay College Library)

African World

Colonial Parliamentary Bulletin (ed. by George Padmore)

Labour Monthly

Lagos Weekly Record
Listener
New Times and Ethiopia News
Peace
Sierra Leone Weekly News
West Africa
Negro Worker (George Padmore Research Library, Accra; Bridgeman Papers)
Voice of Africa (Africana, University of Ghana, Library).

SECONDARY SOURCES

30. *Articles*

Bennett, George. "Pan-Africanism." *International Journal* XVIII/1 (Winter, 1962-63), 91-96.

Drake, St. Clair. "Rise of the Pan-African Movement." *Africa* (Special Report) III/4 (April, 1958), 5-9.

Garigue, P. "The West African Students' Union: A Study in Culture Contact." *Africa,* XXIII (1953), 55-69.

Geiss, I. "Notes on the Development of Pan-Africanism." *Journal of the Historical Society of Nigeria* III/4 (June, 1967), 719-740.

——. "Pan-Africanism." *Journal of Contemporary History* IV/1 (January, 1969), 187-200.

Irele, Abiola. "Negritude or Black Cultural Nationalism." *The Journal of Modern African Studies* III/3 (October, 1965), 321-348.

Isaacs, H. R. "The American Negro and Africa: Some Notes." *Phylon* XX/3 (1959), 219-233.

Pankhurst, Richard. "Ethiopia and Africa: The Historical Aspect." *Ethiopia Observer* III/2 (1964), 155.

Shepperson, George. "Notes on Negro American Influence on the Emergence of African Nationalism." *Journal of African History* I/2 (1960), 299-312.

31. *Books*

Armah, Kwesi. *Africa's Golden Road.* London: Heinemann, 1965.

Asante, S. K. B. *Pan-African Protest West Africa and the Italo-Ehiopian Crisis 1934-1941.* London: Longman, 1977.

Ayandele, E. A. *Holy Johnson: Pioneer of African Nationalism, 1836-1917.* London: Frank Cass and Co., 1970.

Baeta, C. G., ed. *Christianity in Tropical Africa.* London: Oxford University Press, 1968.

Boxer, C. R. *Race Relations in the Portuguese Colonial Empire.* London: Oxford University Press, 1963.

Barraclough, G. *An Introduction to Contemporary History.* London: C. A. Watts and Co., 1964.

Bracey, J. H. Jr. *et al. Black Nationalism in America.* New York: the Bobbs-Merrill Co., 1970.

Broderick, F. L. *W. E. B. DuBois: Negro Leader in Time of Crisis.* Stanford, Cal.: Stanford University Press, 1957.

Buell, R. L. *The Native Problem in Africa,* 2 vols. New York: Macmillan, 1928.

Carr, E. H. *International Relations between the Two World Wars, 1919-1939.* London, 1947.

Cervenka, Z. *The Unfinished Quest for Unity: Africa and the O.A.U.* London: Julian Friedmann Publishers, 1977.

Cohan, D. W. and J. P. Green. *Neither Slave nor Free.* Baltimore and London: Johns Hopkins University Press, 1972.

Cronon, E. D. *Black Moses: The Story of M. Garvey and the Universal Negro Improvement Association.* Madison: University of Wisconsin Press, 1955.

Curtin, P. D. *The Image of Africa.* London: Macmillan, 1965.

Davidson, Basil. *Africa: History of a Continent.* London: Weidenfeld and Nicolson, 1966.

Davis, J. A., ed. *Africa Seen by American Negroes.* Paris: Presence Africaine, 1962.

Decraene, P. *Le Panafricanisme.* Paris, 1959.

Delf, George. *Jomo Kenyatta.* London: Victor Gollancz, 1961.

Diop, Cheik Anta. *The Cultural Unity of Negro Africa.* Paris: Presence Africaine, 1962.

Fishel, L. H. and B. Quarles, eds. *The Negro American: A Documentary History.* Illinois: Scott, Foresman and Co. and William Morrow and Co., 1967.

Franklin, J. E. H. *From Slavery to Freedom.* New York: Alfred A. Knopf, 1948.

Frenkel, M. Y. *Edward Blyden and American Nationalism.* Moscow: Africa Institute, Academy of Sciences, 1972.

Freyre, Gilberto. *The Masters and the Slaves: A Study in Brazilian Civilization.* Translated by Samuel Putnam. New York: Alfred A. Knopf, 1955.

——. *The Racial Factor in Contemporary Politics.* Occasional papers of the Research Unit for the Study of Multi-Racial Societies, University of Sussex, Herts, 1966.

Fyfe, Christopher. *Africanus Horton: West African Scientist and Patriot, 1835-1883.* London: Oxford University Press, 1972.

Hodgkin, Thomas. *Nationalism in Colonial Africa.* London: Frederick Muller, 1956.

Hooker, James. *Black Revolutionary: George Padmore's Path from Communism to Pan-Africanism.* London: Pall Mall Press, 1967.

——. *Henry Sylvester Williams: Imperial Pan-Africanist.* London: Rex Collings, 1975.

Kohn, Hans. *The Idea of Nationalism.* New York: Collier Books, 1967.

Langley, J. Ayodele. *Pan-Africanism and Nationalism in West Africa, 1900-1945: A Study in Ideology and Social Classes.* London: Oxford University Press, 1973.

Legum, Colin. *Pan-Africanism: A Short Political Guide.* New York: Frederick A. Praeger, 1962.

Little, Kenneth. *Negroes in Britain: A Study of Racial Relations in English Society.* London, 1948.

Lowenthal, D. *West Indian Societies.* London: Oxford University Press, 1972.

Lusignan, Guy de. *French Speaking Africa Since Independence.* London: Pall Mall Press, 1969.

Lynch, Hollis R. *Edward Wilmot Blyden: Pan-Negro Patriot, 1832-1912.* London: Oxford University Press, 1967.

Mazrui, Ali A. *Towards a Pax Africana.* London: Weidenfeld and Nicolson, 1967.

——. *Africa's International Relations.* London: Heinemann, 1977.

Moon, P. T. *Imperialism and World Politics.* New York: Macmillan, 1961.

Mathurin, O. C. *Henry Sylvester Williams and the Origins of the Pan-African Movement*. New York: Greenwood press, 1975.

Otite, O., ed. *Themes in African Social and Political Thought*. Enugu: Fourth Dimension Pub., 1978.

Meier, A. and E. Rudwick. *From Plantation to Ghetto*. New York: Hill and Wang, 1976.

Pan-Africanism. A publication of the British Information Services. London, 1962.

Pan-Africanism Reconsidered. Edited by the American Society of African Culture. Berkeley and Los Angeles: University of California Press, 1962.

Redkey, Edwin S. *Black Exodus: Black Nationalist and Back-to-Africa Movements 1890-1910*. New Haven, Conn.: Yale University Press, 1969.

Rodrigues, J. H. *Brazil and Africa*. Berkeley and Los Angeles: University of California Press, 1965.

Rout, Leslie B., Jr. *The African Experience in Spanish America*. London: Oxford University Press, 1976.

Stuckey, S. *The Ideological Origins of Black Nationalism*. Boston: Beacon Press, 1972.

Tannenbaum, F. *Slave and Citizen*. New York: Vintage Press, 1947.

Thompson, V. Bakpetu. *Africa and Unity: The Evolution of Pan-Africanism*. London: Longmans, 1969.

Thorpe, E. E. *The Mind of the Negro: An Intellectual History of Afro-Americans*. Louisiana, 1961.

Thomas, T. and R. Allen. *Two Views on Africanism*. New York: Pathfinder Press, 1972.

Vincent, Theodore. *Black Power and the Garvey Movement*. Berkeley: the Ramparts Press, 1971.

Wauthier, Claude. *The Literature and Thought of Modern Africa*. London: Pall Mall Press, 1966.

Wallerstein, I. *Africa - The Politics of Unity: An Analysis of a Contemporary Social Movement*. London: Pall Mall Press, 1968.

Weisbord, R. G. *Ebony Kinship: Africa, Africans and the Afro-Americans*. London: Greenwood Press, 1973.

32. *Unpublished Dissertations*

Contee, Clarence Garner. "W. E. B. DuBois and African Nationalism, 1914-1945." Ph. D. dissertation, The American University, Washington D.C., 1969.

Desta, Mengiste. "The Evolution of the Pan-African Movement." M. A. thesis, Howard University, 1960.

INDEX

Banda, Hastings, 163, 193
Banneker, Benjamin, 21
Barbour-James, J. A., 84, 106
Bellegarde, M. Dantes, 83, 90
Beton, Isaac, 84, 92
Biafra, 231
Blackman, Peter, 132-33
Blay, R. S., 184
Blundell, Muriel, 119
Blyden, Edward Wilmot, 4, 25, 28, 29-40, 45, 50, 57-64, 65, 67, 70, 97, 153, 180, 185
Boadu, Kankam, 163, 181
Boigny, Felix Houphouet, 189, 211, 223
Bond, Dr. Horace, 198
Boston (U.S.A.), 9
Botsio, Kojo, 173, 181
Brazil, 16, 94
Brazzaville Declaration, 221
Brazzaville Group, 212-13
Bridgeman, Reginald, 102-03
British Emancipation Act, 14
Broadhurst, Robert, 84
Brown, Rev. Henry B., 53
Bruce, John Edward, 60, 65, 67, 73
Bureh, Bai, 50

Candace, Gratien, 82, 84, 92, 110
Canivet, M. Charles, 43
C.A.O. *See* Committee of African Organisations
Caribbean (British, French, etc.), 16
Carlyle, Thomas, 19
Carmichael, Stokely, 3
Carol, W. Davidson, 96
Carter, John, 152
Cartwright, Dr. Margverite, 198
Casablanca Group, 212-13, 218
Chatellier, Marie Du, 65
Chicago (U.S.A.), 45, 98, 179
Chicago Congress on Africa, 45
Chicago Defender, 79
Chilembwe, John, 24
Christian, G. J., 52
Christian, J. H., 136
Churchill, Winston, 145-46, 156

Circles for the Liberation of Ethiopia, 119
Clark, Dr. G. S., 50
Clarke, John H., 50
Coka, Gilbert, 124
Colenso, Bishop, 50
Colenso, Dr. R. S., 50
Coleridge-Taylor, Samuel, 53, 67
Collet, Charles E., 136
Colonial Parliamentary Bulletin, 179, 185
Committee of African Organizations, 192-93, 223-24
Conakat, 210
Conakry, 201
Confederation des Associations Ethniques du Katanga. *See* Conakat
Constantine, Learie, 181
Creech Jones, Arthur, 124, 140, 149, 171, 181
The Crisis, 84
Crowther, Samuel Ajaji, 38
Crummell, Rev. Alexander, 25, 30, 45
Cudjoe, Dr. S. D., 4, 185-89
Cuffee, Paul, 9-10
Cullen, Susan, 14
Cunard, Nancy, 124, 152
Curtis, Helen, 83

Daily Negro Times, The, 73
Danquah, J. B., 96, 115-16, 184
Davies, Chief H. O., 162
Davies, John H., 77-78
Delaware (U.S.A.), 13
Deniga, Adeoye, 22
Deressa, Ato Yiema, 205
Deressa, T., 105
Diagne, Blaise, 80-81, 88-90, 110
Dingwell, Dr. H., 136
Dipcharima, Mallam Bukar, 181
Diop, Alioune, 2
Doherty, J. Akanni, 96
Douglass, Frederick, 15
Dube, J. L., 84
DuBois, W. E. B., 1, 3, 5, 45, 53, 65-66, 80-81, 84, 85, 9091, 114, 161, 162, 164, 199